THE ULTIMATE BOGART

THE ULTIMATE BOGART

Ernest W. Cunningham

RENAISSANCE BOOKS
Los Angeles

Permissions
Norman Rosten, "Nobody Dies Like Humphrey Bogart," from *Thrive Upon the Rock*,
Trident Press, New York, 1965. With permission of Patricia Rosten.

Library of Congress Cataloging-in-Publication Data
Cunningham, Ernest W.
     The ultimate Bogart / Ernest W. Cunningham.
        p. cm.
     Discography: p.
     Filmography: p.
     Includes bibliographical references and index.
     ISBN 1-58063-093-6 (alk. paper)
        1. Bogart, Humphrey, 1899–1957—Miscellanea. I. Title
     PN2287.B48 C86 1999
     791.43'028'092—dc21

                                                                          99-036166

10 9 8 7 6 5 4 3 2 1

Design by Jesus Arellano and Lisa-Theresa Lenthall

Published by Renaissance Books
Manufactured in the United States of America
Distributed by St. Martin's Press
First Edition

This book is for my sisters:
Shirley, Margaret, Linda, and Mildred

Contents

Acknowledgments

The Academy of Motion Picture Arts and Sciences: Margaret Herrick Library; Rudy Behlmer; Brand Public Library: Art and Music Center, John Cocchi, Lloyd Curry, Diane and George Fain, Howard Mandelbaum, George Marcelle, Jonathan Rosenthal, Patricia Rosten, Brenda Scott Royce, Allan Taylor. And thanks to my editor, Jim Parish.

Preface

Some forty years after his death in 1957, Humphrey Bogart is alive today as no other Hollywood movie figure is. Each new generation thinks it is rediscovering Bogart—rescuing him from the dusty film vaults—when in reality he's never been away. Today's viewers in particular may be the most avid of all Bogart fans—and they were not even around when his movies were first shown in theaters.

But what better alternate/antidote to the simpleminded heroics of our current big-screen action heroes and leading men? After all the special effects and colorful explosions and car chases, there's something reassuring about the bruised Bogart screen heroes who use their fists instead of high-flying karate kicks to subdue their opponents, who prefer a single gun to those ear-splitting explosions, and who know how to make effective use of sneers and quiet threats on-camera. With Bogart, you always know where his heroes are coming from, what they stand for, and just how far they can be pushed.

Humphrey Bogart is, no doubt, Hollywood's most durable personality because he continues to speak to each new age of movie watchers. No other star has ever appealed to so many different generations.

After nearly fifty years, everyone still comes to Rick's Café Americain. And the rest of the world is still three drinks behind Humphrey Bogart.

Is it "Bogie" or "Bogey"?

Bogart preferred "Bogie" but said, "Spell it any way you want."

Most seem to prefer "Bogey," but it is quoted both ways in this book to reflect the way different people originally used it.

Part I

The Legend

Chapter 1

Humphrey Bogart's Dead But He Won't Lie Down!

A Chronology of Humphrey Bogart's Life Since His Death

1957

January 14—Humphrey Bogart dies in his sleep at his home in Holmby Hills, adjacent to Beverly Hills, California. He had wanted to have his ashes sprinkled over the Pacific Ocean but it was not legal then, or fashionable. He is cremated and his ashes deposited in the Columbarium of Eternal Light, in the Gardens of Memory, in the Court of the Christus, in Forest Lawn Memorial Park in Glendale, a few miles east of Hollywood. It's a locked section off-limits to the tourists.

1960

January—The Brattle Theatre in Cambridge, Massachusetts, begins regular festival programs of Bogart films, in response to the cult that has been growing steadily since 1957. The cinema is frequented mainly by Harvard University students who wear trench coats and fedoras to the Bogart screenings, and recite the dialogue in unison with the screen actor. *Casablanca* (Warner Bros., 1942) is the favorite of the students.

◆   ◆   ◆

Jean-Luc Godard's *Breathless* (1960), a low-budget black-and-white French thriller shot on the streets of Paris, is the first movie to pay homage to the Bogart screen persona.

1965

Citadel Press (New York) publishes *Bogey: The Films of Humphrey Bogart* by Clifford McCarty, an illustrated account of all his movies, with cast, credits, and synopsis for each film. This is said to be the first such book in a *Films of...* series that is still in print.

◆   ◆   ◆

The first Bogart biography appears: *Bogey: The Man, the Actor, the Legend*, by Jonah Ruddy and Jonathan Hill (New York: Tower paperback.)

◆   ◆   ◆

Time magazine writer Ezra Goodman authors *Bogey: The Good-Bad Guy* (New York: Lyle Stuart), based on past interviews with the star. This becomes the source of many familiar quotes attributed to Bogart and his associates.

1966

Joe Hyams, a writer friend, publishes *Bogie* (New York: New American Library), a profile that becomes the basis for the 1980 television movie *Bogie*, which stars Kevin O'Connor.

1969

February 12—Woody Allen's comedy *Play It Again, Sam* opens on Broadway. Woody stars as a nebbishy film critic who idolizes Humphrey Bogart. Within the play, he falls in love with the wife (Diane Keaton) of his best friend (Tony Roberts). Jerry Lacy is seen as Bogie, a phantom drifting in and out of the story, offering advice and encouragement to the would-be hero. Woody exults in giving up the girl: "It's from *Casablanca*—I waited my whole life to say it!" The show is a hit, running for 453 performances.

◆   ◆   ◆

The movie *Easy Rider*, from Columbia pictures, opens in September and is extraordinarily successful. This virtually plotless account of two bikers on a cross-country trip becomes a watershed event in the history of the rebel-lious counterculture. In a scene where the film's stars Dennis Hopper and Peter Fonda roar down the highway on their motorcycles, we hear the song "Don't Bogart Me," asking that a marijuana joint not be hogged, and that, instead, it be passed around. The song was written and performed by the group known as Fraternity of Man.

1971

Czechoslovakian director Milos Forman makes his first American movie for Universal, *Taking Off*. It's a social comedy, with the parents of a teenage girl becoming aware of the mushrooming drug culture. There's a scene of a young man hogging a marijuana joint and being warned, "Don't bogart the roach!"

◆   ◆   ◆

Albert Finney appears in the movie *Gumshoe*, a British film about a man who has seen too many Bogart movies. His dreams of becoming a private eye get him involved in a murder case.

◆   ◆   ◆

The advertising for Pan-Am Airways promotes flights to Morocco using the familiar shot of Bogart at the end of *Casablanca*.

1972

May 4—From Paramount, the movie version of Woody Allen's *Play It Again, Sam* opens to favorable reviews. The film stars the cast of the orig-inal 1969 Broadway production: Woody Allen, Diane Keaton, Tony Roberts, and Jerry Lacy as Bogart.

◆   ◆   ◆

The London *Sunday Times* asks its readers which movies they would most like to see again, and the letters pour in. Four Bogart films are in the top twelve—a record no other actor comes anywhere near equaling. The film most hotly demanded is *The African Queen* (United Artists, 1951). In second place, a mere one vote behind, is *Casablanca*. *The Maltese Falcon* (Warner Bros., 1941) is sixth, and *The Treasure of the Sierra Madre* (Warner Bros., 1948), eleventh.

1974

Robert Sacchi, who physically resembles Bogart, puts together a one-man show, *Bogey's Back*. In it, the screen icon returns to check things out, reminisces, and acts out memorable scenes from his movies.

1977

The Man with Bogart's Face (Chicago: Contemporary Books), a novel by Andrew J. Fenady, is published. The book is successful, unlike the 1980 movie version made by Twentieth Century–Fox with Franco Nero, Michelle Phillips, and George Raft. The film stars Robert Sacchi as a man who has plastic surgery to look like the famous actor and gets involved with a homicide case similar to *The Maltese Falcon*.

1978

Bogart's widow and costar Lauren Bacall publishes her autobiography, *Lauren Bacall: By Myself* (New York: Knopf), which deals at length with her life with the star. The book becomes a best-seller.

1980

March 4—The CBS made-for-TV movie *Bogie* airs, starring Kevin O'Connor as Humphrey Bogart. Others in the cast are Kathryn Harrold (Lauren Bacall), Ann Wedgeworth (Mayo Methot), Richard Dysart (Jack L. Warner), and Stephen Keep (Leslie Howard). The teleplay is based on Joe Hyams's 1966 *Bogie* biography.

THE WORD "BOGART" ENTERS THE LANGUAGE

Oddly, sadly, the meanings are based on the early image of Bogart as gangster or tough-guy, not on the later, now classic Bogart of the 1940s in *The Maltese Falcon* and *Casablanca*: the rebellious hero, the loner with a strong sense of integrity. There are three meanings:

1. Holding on to a communal joint past the point of politeness: "Don't bogart that joint, my friend!"

2. Pushing someone around: "Don't try to bogart me, wise guy!"

3. An aggressive move in basketball: "Bogart that shot, man!"

(*The Dictionary of Contemporary Slang*, edited by Jonathon Green.
New York: Stein and Day, 1984)

1982

The image of Bogart and Bacall as ideal lovers inspires a best-selling song, "Key Largo," written and performed by Bertie Higgins: "We had it all, just like Bogie and Bacall. . . ."

•   •   •

Full-page magazine ads for CasaBlanca Fans re-create the airport farewell from *Casablanca* with Rick telling Ilsa, "Sorry, kid, but I just can't say good-bye to all my CasaBlanca Fans." Look-alike Robert Sacchi is identified in the advertisement as the model.

•   •   •

Verita Thompson, Bogie's mistress of fifteen years, publishes *Bogie and Me: A Love Story* (New York: St. Martin's Press).

1983

Maxell, manufacturer of blank videotapes, runs full-page magazine ads featuring an illustration of Humphrey Bogart saying, "Play it again, Sam," promoting the tape VHS users will appreciate more and more—"as time goes by."

1984

A retail shop named Humphrey Yogart opens in Sherman Oaks, California, an upscale suburb of the San Fernando Valley, fifteen miles northwest of Hollywood. The clever brainchild of Maria Baker, Humphrey Yogart blends yogurts into healthy, ice-creamlike concoctions. Apparently, there are no legal ramifications, as the name is just a catchy, fanciful spelling, and there are no visual references to the actor. Currently there are nine Humphrey Yogart stores: seven in California, one in Detroit, and another on the Pacific island of Guam.

1986

The Lufthansa airline features the airport farewell scene from *Casablanca* in its advertising.

•   •   •

The HBO cable network's *Tales from the Crypt* series boasts an appearance by Bogart, thanks to modern wizardry, in an episode directed by

Robert Zemeckis, who later used this technology in his movie *Forrest Gump* (1994).

1988

March 11—PBS-TV airs the documentary "Bacall on Bogart" as part of its *Great Performances* series. Lauren Bacall is host/narrator, joined by various costars, directors, and friends of her late husband. Says John Huston, who directed six of Bogart's best movies, "He's a bigger star today than when he was alive."

◆　　◆　　◆

The book *John Kobal Presents the Top 100 Movies* is published by New American Library (New York). The list is compiled from the choices of over eighty cinema professionals: directors, writers, critics, historians, et al. *Citizen Kane* (1941) is number one; the Bogart films: *Casablanca* (number 9), *The Maltese Falcon* (number 38), and *The African Queen* (number 85).

1992

The fiftieth anniversary of the release of *Casablanca* is celebrated with special film screenings, and a deluxe video edition which includes a new documentary on how the screen classic was made.

There are four excellent new books on *Casablanca*: Aljean Harmetz's *Round Up the Usual Suspects: The Making of Casablanca*; a Fiftieth Anniversary Edition of Howard Koch's *Casablanca: Script and Legend*; a deluxe *Casablanca: As Time Goes By*, by Frank Miller; and Jeff Siegel's *The Casablanca Companion: The Movie and More* [see Appendix 2: "The Annotated, Opinionated Bibliography of Humphrey Bogart" for details].

There is also the widely publicized *As Time Goes By*, a novel by Michael Walsh (New York: Warner), which picks up the romantic adventure story where the movie ended.

1993

August 13—*Entertainment Weekly* has a special issue featuring "The 30 Greatest Movie Stars Ever—the thirty stars who made the movies matter"—"not actors, not sex symbols, but stars, with all the charisma, appeal, and influence that the word brings with it."

Humphrey Bogart is number one: "With the possible exception of Bugs Bunny, nobody has ever physically dominated the screen the way he did."

The other twenty-nine are Katharine Hepburn, Cary Grant, Marilyn Monroe, Marlon Brando, Clark Gable, Charlie Chaplin, Bette Davis, James Stewart, Jack Nicholson, James Cagney, Greta Garbo, Gary Cooper, Ingrid Bergman, John Wayne, Fred Astaire, Elizabeth Taylor, Clint Eastwood, Laurence Olivier, Dustin Hoffman, Robert De Niro, Judy Garland, Paul Newman, Spencer Tracy, Sean Connery, James Dean, Shirley Temple, Henry Fonda, Jodie Foster, and Rudolph Valentino.

1995

Humphrey Bogart's son Stephen, who was eight years old when his father died in 1957, publishes *Bogart: In Search of My Father* (New York: Dutton).

◆　　◆　　◆

A popular crime movie—*The Usual Suspects*—borrows its title from *Casablanca*. Christopher McQuarrie's original screenplay for the Columbia/TriStar production wins an Academy Award, and its star Kevin Spacey is given an Oscar for Best Supporting Actor.

1996

Magazine ads for Sara Lee Layer Cake reproduce a familiar scene from *Casablanca*—with Bogie turning to his piano player, asking, "How could I forget her, Sam? She stuck me with the Pepperidge Farm. And she took off with the Sara Lee."

Through the magic of digitized computer technology, Humphrey Bogart appears with singer Paula Abdul in a television commercial for Diet Coke.

◆　　◆　　◆

November 6—The island of Guernsey, in the English Channel, issues a set of five postage stamps commemorating the detective-film genre. The stamps depict Basil Rathbone as Sherlock Holmes, Margaret Rutherford as Miss Marple, Warner Oland as Charlie Chan, Peter Sellers as Inspector Clouseau, and Humphrey Bogart as Philip Marlowe (of *The Big Sleep*, Warner Bros., 1946).

1997

January 5—Cable TV's Turner Classic Movies begins a weeklong tribute to Bogart, a fifty-two-film marathon running nonstop twenty-four hours a day. Highlights include *Bogart: The Untold Story*, a new documentary hosted by the star's son Stephen, and a compilation of preview trailers from many of Bogie's movies.

✦   ✦   ✦

Two major biographies are published: *Bogart*, by A. M. Sperber and Eric Lax (New York: William Morrow); and *Bogart, A Life in Hollywood*, by Jeffrey Meyers (Boston/New York: Houghton Mifflin). Both books are widely reviewed.

✦   ✦   ✦

July 31—The United States Postal Service unveils its newest commemorative stamp, honoring Humphrey Bogart, in a ceremony at Mann's Chinese Theatre in Hollywood. Lauren Bacall attends the ceremony with son Stephen and daughter Leslie. She tells reporters that Bogie would have been surprised but impressed by the honor.

The Bogart stamp is the third in the Legends of Hollywood series, following Elvis Presley and Marilyn Monroe. A total of 195 million Bogart stamps are printed.

✦   ✦   ✦

December—Rhino Records issues a new CD recording of the soundtrack of *Casablanca* which includes many of the film's oft-quoted dialogue passages. Some purists feel the dialogue gets in the way of Max Steiner's sweeping orchestral music; others love to hear the great lines played again.

1998

The British *Sight and Sound* magazine publishes a list of 360 classic films, as compiled by the National Film and Television Archive. Movies featuring Bogart are: *The Maltese Falcon* (1941), *Casablanca* (1942), *To Have and Have Not* (1944), *The Big Sleep* (1946), and *In a Lonely Place* (1950)—most of these are from his Warner Bros. years. Some fans might argue with the inclusion of Columbia's *In a Lonely Place*, but more will question the exclusion of *The Treasure of the Sierra Madre* (1948) and *The African Queen* (1951).

◆   ◆   ◆

June—A "Virtual Humans" conference is held in Los Angeles to discuss the technical and legal aspects of creating realistic computer-generated actors. To what end?—making money from dead celebrities. With "virtual human" technology, stars long dead could star in new films, or sell new products. A demonstration using Humphrey Bogart is on display.

◆   ◆   ◆

The American Film Institute issues its ranking of "The 100 Best American Movies." There is a TV special, a special Summer 1998 issue of *Newsweek* magazine, and much advertising tie-in with the studios that made the honored movies, and with retail stores selling them on video or the new DVD format.

Casablanca is number two on the list of the one hundred chosen entries, but *Citizen Kane* (1941), in first place, is seen by many fans as a cop-out, a token tribute to art and class—*Casablanca* is really America's favorite. Three other Bogart films figure prominently in the list: *The African Queen* (number 17), *The Maltese Falcon* (number 23), and *The Treasure of the Sierra Madre* (number 30).

For the record, William Holden, Marlon Brando, and Robert De Niro each have four movies represented in the list of the top one hundred; James Stewart has five.

◆   ◆   ◆

August 8—*TV Guide* responds to the AFI list with "the list that gets it right— the classic films that viewers watch again and again" on television or VCR. Its list of "The Fifty Greatest Movies" put *Casablanca* as number two, with *The Godfather Part 2* (1974) in first place. *The African Queen* is number 35.

◆   ◆   ◆

Exclusive Premiere produces limited-edition 9-inch collectible dolls of Humphrey Bogart as Rick Blaine, in trench coat, and Ingrid Bergman as Ilsa Lund. KB Toy Stores is the initial exclusive retail outlet.

1999

June 15—An American Film Institute ballot selects Humphrey Bogart as the number one male "American Screen Legend" of the century.

25

Katharine Hepburn is chosen number one female "American Screen Legend." The top fifty screen legends—chosen on the basis of star quality, craft, legacy, popularity, and historical context—are announced on a three-hour CBS-TV special.

Cary Grant is number two on the list, followed by James Stewart, Marlon Brando, Fred Astaire, Henry Fonda, Clark Gable, James Cagney, Spencer Tracy, and Charlie Chaplin. The voting was by 1,800 movie critics, historians, directors, producers, and screenwriters.

Lauren Bacall is number twenty on the list of female screen legends.

◆   ◆   ◆

December 25—The centennial birthday of Humphrey Bogart.

Chapter 2

To Debunk or Not to Debunk

The Stories about Humphrey Bogart that Just Won't Go Away

Public figures will always generate gossip.

Movie stars will forever provoke fantasies.

Heroes are often elevated into myths (but sometimes become bums).

So it becomes difficult, if not impossible, to separate the fantasies of starstruck fans from tabloid tidbits dreamed up by publicists and legends that have been created over time. No one wants to write about a movie star who puts in a day's work and goes home to his wife and children. It's easier—and lots more fun, and sells more tabloids, and gets higher ratings—to deal with boozers and adulterers and those of wavering sexuality.

The publicity department at Warner Bros. worked around the clock to create interest in their stars. The Burbank, California, film lot did not really care what the media said about their stars as long as they spelled the names right, and got in a plug for their newest movie.

Humphrey Bogart knew the value of publicity, and willingly cooperated. After "The Panda Incident" (see below), Bogie was asked if he was drunk at the time. "Isn't everyone at three A.M.?" he asked.

Hey, great line—who do you suppose wrote it?

Humphrey Bogart Was a Drunk

Bogie apparently spent much of his twenties and thirties in bars and cocktail parties. When he married actress Mayo Methot (1904–1951) in 1938, the two became the boozing "battling Bogarts." Lauren Bacall married and domesticated him in 1945, but he enjoyed his afternoon cocktail right up to the very end, in 1957. And his motto, "The world is two drinks behind," is still widely quoted. However, this image of the boozer may be just part of the tough-guy Bogart wanted to present to the world.

Writer-producer Nunnally Johnson described Bogart's "alcoholic thermostat," which enabled him to drink with pleasant and stimulating results, without ever slopping over: "Bogart just set his thermostat at noon, pumped in some scotch and stayed at a nice even glow all day, automatically redosing as necessary." But the star still liked to give people the impression he was a heavy drinker. Johnson also tells how Bogart would pick up a glass of liquor just to answer the front door.

He Once Chewed Glass to Show How Tough He Was

Bogart supposedly once met a man at a cocktail party who chewed glass in the circus. The movie star took the stranger's challenge, smashing a glass and chewing the pieces. However, when he couldn't swallow them, he coughed them up, resulting in bleeding mouth and lips. Jeffrey Meyers reports this story in *Bogart: A Life in Hollywood* (1977).

Biographer Terence Pettigrew says that Bogart stuffed the remains of a broken cocktail glass into his mouth and chewed it, to prove his toughness to a Frenchman who ate glass.

Another version is recounted in the biography by Jonah Ruddy and Jonathan Hill (*Bogey: The Man, the Actor, the Legend*, 1965). This time it's at a party given by veteran film director Lewis Milestone. The Frenchman is visiting writer Jeff Cassels, who challenges Bogey—"Do something tough!" Bogie dares him: "What do *you* do that's so tough?" The writer proceeds to chew up a champagne glass, but Bogart declines the offer to join him.

In yet another version, Bogie chews up a champagne glass *and* half a razor blade. Common sense should tell us that this is barroom blarney. Confronted with the story, Bogart smiles ruefully and says, "I may be a little nuts, but I don't think I'm that nuts!"

His Most Famous Line Is "Play It Again, Sam!"

The author of this line is Woody Allen, who wrote a popular play (1969) and a movie (1972) with this title, which is a misquote from *Casablanca*. What Rick Blaine (Bogart) actually says to Sam (Dooley Wilson) is, "You played it for her and you can play it for me. If she can stand it, I can. Play it!"

Bogart Was the Model for the Baby on the Gerber Baby-Food Label

Bogart's mother, Maud Humphrey Bogart (1866–1940) was a popular illustrator who may have sketched her child for baby-food advertisements—but that would have been back in the early 1900s. Gerber's line of baby food was first introduced in 1928, when Bogie was twenty-nine (and looked every day of it). The Gerber baby is actually Ann Turner Cook, now in her seventies, who was sketched by artist Dorothy Hope Smith. (Bogart as an infant was sketched by his mother for ads used by Mellin's baby food.)

Ronald Reagan and Ann Sheridan Were the Original Choices to Star in Casablanca

In Hollywood's heyday, studio publicity departments worked non-stop to keep their contract players' names fully in the public eye. Exotic births and childhoods were concocted. Romances were routinely fabricated and fed to an eager public. Every starlet was about to become a star. So, on January 5, 1942, the *Hollywood Reporter* noted that Ann Sheridan and Ronald Reagan, who had teamed together in *Angels Wash Their Faces* (1939), would costar in the upcoming *Casablanca* at Warner Bros. It was stated that Dennis Morgan would also be featured in the World War II drama/love story.

Bunk! Bogart was the first and only choice to play Rick. He had made more than his share of mediocre pictures for Warner Bros., and he had served on projects rejected by George Raft, a bigger but dumber Warner Bros. luminary. However, by the time *Casablanca* rolled around, Bogart was already a star. The movie was tailored to fit him. And keep in mind that no one expected *Casablanca* to be the most popular movie ever made: In 1942, it was just one of dozens of projects on the studio's busy production schedule.

As for Ronald Reagan (b. 1911): In her definitive history of the film, *Round Up the Usual Suspects: The Making of Casablanca* (New York: Hyperion, 1992), Aljean Harmetz writes, "There was never any chance of Ronald Reagan starring in *Casablanca*. The studio had been writing deferment letters for him for months, but with the war continuing, they knew he couldn't get deferment much longer."

CASABLANCA WAS MADE ON WARNER BROS.' BACK LOT IN BURBANK; BOGART NEVER SET FOOT IN NORTH AFRICA

The movie was made on the back lot, but Bogie paid a visit to the actual Casablanca in 1943, just after the movie was released, and just after the Allied Forces landed in Morocco.

BOGART HELPED STEAL JOHN BARRYMORE'S BODY FROM THE MORGUE AND PLACE IT IN ERROL FLYNN'S LIVING ROOM

Alcoholic actor John Barrymore (1882–1942) spent many hours drinking in the home of the equally inebriated actor Errol Flynn (1909–1959); the older man liked to think that he might be the father of the younger. When Barrymore died, a group of pranksters, perhaps led by director Raoul Walsh, bribed a morgue attendant to let them borrow Barrymore's corpse, which they propped up in the living room of Flynn's mansion in the Hollywood Hills, then hid to see his reaction—which you can imagine.

This story is in all the books on Errol Flynn, and has entered the hallowed halls of Hollywood mythology. The Jeffrey Meyers biography of Bogart recounts this dubious episode as being suggested by Peter Lorre to Bogart, Paul Henreid, and others.

A variation of this anecdote is adapted, in an updated version, into the story line of *S.O.B.* (1981), Blake Edwards's savage film satire on Hollywood.

BOGIE GOT THAT SCAR ON HIS LIP WHEN HIS SHIP WAS ATTACKED BY A GERMAN SUBMARINE

You pay your money on this one, and you can take your choice of the variations:

a. His father inflicted it during his childhood.

b. Bogart was hit by a flying splinter from an exploding shell when his ship was attacked by a U-boat during World War I.

c. Bogart was guarding a handcuffed prisoner at the Portsmouth (New Hampshire) Naval Station north of Boston, in early 1919, when the guy slammed him in the face and made a break for it. Bogart shot the running man in either his leg or his buttock. A Navy doctor botched the repair of the lip.

d. Louise Brooks (1906–1985), the actress with the pageboy bangs, said, "It was taken for granted that he got punched in the mouth at some speakeasy."

e. Bogie's mistress Verita Thompson recounts the tale of him being interviewed in the early 1950s by an obnoxious female journalist who asked about the scarred lip. "A big, bucktoothed broad bit me," he explained to her. "Looked a lot like you."

The one version here that can safely be eliminated is (b), which is the most frequently cited account of the scar; sorry, folks—Bogart had reported for active duty on the USS *Leviathan* troop carrier, on November 9, 1918 . . . and two days later the armistice was signed and the war was over. The only sea battles Humphrey Bogart saw were the ones staged at Warner Bros. in Burbank, California.

The Bogart biography by A. M. Sperber and Eric Lax (*Bogart*, 1997), which involved seven years of research, finds the Louise Brooks version (d) the most credible.

Bogart Was Not Born on Christmas Day

This story holds that those same busy Warner Bros. publicists concocted the story to help humanize him to moviegoers and that he was actually born on January 23, 1899.

Bunk. The *Ontario County Times*, New York, listed Bogart's Christmas Day birth, on December 25, 1899, in its issue of January 10, 1900. School records, Navy archives, and wedding licenses also confirm the December 25 date.

THAT RUNT TRUMAN CAPOTE ONCE BEAT BOGART AT ARM-WRESTLING

True, apparently. It happened in Italy, in 1954, during the filming of *Beat the Devil* (United Artists, 1954). Truman Capote (1924–1984), a short, effeminate writer who was receiving critical acclaim for his Southern Gothic stories, was hired to inject some life into the still-born script.

One night there was arm-wrestling. Director John Huston describes it in *An Open Book* (New York: Knopf, 1980): "Bogie and Truman were engaged, and it almost became a fight. It did, in fact, turn into a wrestling match. And Truman took Bogie! He pinned Bogart's shoulders to the floor and held him there. Truman's epicene comportment was downright deceptive; he was remarkably strong and had pit bulldog in him."

THOSE LEECHES IN THE AFRICAN QUEEN WERE REAL!

It's one of the ickiest scenes in screen history. Bogart, as grizzled Charlie Allnut, captain of the boat *The African Queen*, dives underwater to free obstructions from the boat's propeller. When he climbs back onboard, there are dark lumps on his body—leeches! Charlie, shivering in horror, urges Rosie (Katharine Hepburn) the missionary to pull the slimy things from his naked body.

Huston biographer William F. Nolan, and other sources, claim the leeches were real, that Bogart would not shiver like that if they hadn't been real. However, look at it again, folks; the footage does not match up that well. Ninety-five percent of *The African Queen* was shot on location in Africa, but the leech sequence was filmed in a tank in a London studio. The leeches were rubber.

BOGART WAS A FINK—HE CRITICIZED THE INVESTIGATION INTO HOLLYWOOD COMMUNISM . . . AND THEN BACKED DOWN, SAYING HE WAS "MISINFORMED"

In 1945, Congress established the House Un-American Activities Committee (HUAC) to root out Communism in America. In January of 1947, the Committee turned its attention to Hollywood, gleefully finding Commie sympathizers everywhere.

In late October of that year, a planeful of notables, the most famous being Humphrey Bogart and Lauren Bacall, went to Washington, D.C., to protest HUAC's bullying, heavy-handed tactics. The Committee ignored them. The HUAC hearings ended with ten uncooperative witnesses, the so-called Hollywood Ten, who were each sent to prison for a year.

The mood of the country soon changed, and the public began calling for censorship, demanding the entertainment industry clean itself of Communist sympathizers—people like Humphrey Bogart and all those others who went with him to Washington.

For obvious and personal reasons, such as likely unemployment, Humphrey Bogart recanted, saying his trek to Washington had been foolish, that he had been used by the Communists. Many understood Bogey's actions; many others attacked him, accusing him of betrayal.

Stephen Bogart today thinks his father was wrong: "Maybe he was just trying to save his career. Maybe he was a human being and was expressing the simple human desire for self-preservation" (*Bogart: In Search of My Father*, 1995).

Lauren Bacall still maintains that Bogie was used.

(See also chapter 5: Highlights of the Life, Loves, Career, and Other Exploits of Humphrey Bogart.)

During the Filming of Across the Pacific, Bogart Was Tied to a Chair with Guards Blocking Every Exit

This story began when Director John Huston was called away to report for World War II duty. It was said he left it to the thriller's new director, Vincent Sherman, to figure out how to get Bogart's screen character out of this tight jam at the film's climax.

John Huston himself is the one responsible for spreading this tale. The director liked a good joke, but he was also well known (at the least he was accused, or suspected) for elaborately embroidering the entertaining stories he told.

In truth, Huston sat down with replacement director Vincent Sherman to discuss how the screen thriller (Warner Bros., 1942) should be completed. And, of course, the scriptwriters had already solved all the story problems.

BOGART WILL NEVER LIVE DOWN THOSE EARLY BROADWAY PLAYS IN WHICH HE WOULD BOUND ONTO THE STAGE ASKING "TENNIS, ANYONE?"

For most of his undistinguished theatrical career, Humphrey Bogart played secondary, "juvenile" roles: mainly young men in comedies and romantic dramas of the upper class. "Tennis, anyone?" is an identifying phrase to label that type of character in that type of play—the way "Head 'em off at the pass!" became a catchphrase for westerns, and "Okay, you screws!" identifies a prison film.

It is not certain that Bogart even said those famous words. However, columnist Louella Parsons claims she heard the actor say, "Tennis, anyone?" in the 1925 play *Cradle Snatchers*. Drama critic Richard Watts Jr. also recalled hearing it but couldn't remember which play it was in.

Bogart denies ever saying the line; he insists it was, "It's forty-love outside—anyone care to watch?" He also said he'd spoken every bad line ever written except, "Give me the ball, Coach, and I'll get you a touchdown!"

NO FILM IN WHICH BOGART WEARS A MUSTACHE IS ANY DAMN GOOD

It's probably closer to the truth to say that Bogart with a mustache was no damn good. Look at *Isle of Fury* (Warner Bros., 1936), in which he's attacked by a silly rubber octopus; or *Virginia City* (Warner Bros., 1940), in which he plays a Mexican bandit who says, "It will be a cinch!"—which comes out "ceeench!" Perhaps, because Bogart looks so stupid in a mustache, viewers are predisposed to dislike the movie in question.

BOGART'S FIRST WIFE, HELEN MENKEN (1901–1966), WAS TEN YEARS HIS SENIOR

This was a story originated by Bogie, and was really mean of him. Helen Menken was actually two years younger than he was. The reason behind this calumny might have been Bogart's professional jealousy, as Helen was a major Broadway star, and he never came close until his stage work in *The Petrified Forest* (1935).

BOGART WAS ARRESTED FOR FIGHTING WITH A WOMAN IN A NIGHTCLUB OVER A GIANT STUFFED PANDA

On September 25, 1949, Bogie and a friend dropped into the El Morocco nightclub in New York for a nightcap. They were carrying two 20-pound stuffed pandas, which came to the attention of two young women who decided to take the pandas. There was some shoving, some breaking of plates, and the ladies wound up on the floor. Bogart was arrested for assault, but the judge threw it out, dismissing the incident as a publicity stunt.

Years later, Bogey described "the Panda Incident" to biographer Ezra Goodman: "Partly I was loaded and partly it was a frame. A little tart who wanted to get some money" (*Bogey: The Good-Bad Guy*, 1965).

HUMPHREY BOGART MIGHT NOT HAVE BEEN THE LEGEND HE IS TODAY IF IT HADN'T BEEN FOR GEORGE RAFT

Without a doubt, this is true.

George Raft (1895–1980) grew up on the streets of New York City, where he associated with gangsters. He became a prizefighter, a ballroom dancer, then a nightclub and Broadway star. He went to Hollywood in the late 1920s and became typecast as a gangster. While he was under contract at Warner Bros. (1939–42), Raft rejected a number of screen projects he'd been assigned, which then went to Humphrey Bogart, who was successful in most of them. (See the section on George Raft, page 206, in chapter 11: The Warner Bros. Cast of Characters for the incredible details.)

For whatever reasons, George Raft rejected all of the following Warner Bros. movie projects, at which point they went to Humphrey Bogart.

Dead End (1937)
It All Came True (1940)
High Sierra (1941)
The Wagons Roll at Night (1941)
The Maltese Falcon (1941)
All Through the Night (1942)
The Big Shot (1942)

WHEN BOGART MARRIED BACALL HE STARTED TAKING FERTILITY SHOTS—THIS CAUSED HIS HAIR TO FALL OUT

He may have needed the fertility shots, but the forty-five-year-old Bogart had needed a toupee many years before he married twenty-year-old Lauren Bacall in 1945. The Sperber/Lax biography says he was wearing a toupee at the time of *The Maltese Falcon* in 1941.

Biographer Ezra Goodman quotes Bogart: "I had lost all my hair. I wore a wig in *The Treasure of the Sierra Madre* and in *Dark Passage* [Warner Bros., 1947] I was covered by a bandage. Jack Warner was not aware of this and signed me to a fifteen year contract with no options. Then he saw me in the hall and damn near fainted!

"How did I lose my hair? A little too much drinking, not eating enough, wives, my third wife."

Bogart's tell-all mistress, Verita Thompson (*Bogie and Me: A Love Story*, 1982), says she began her lengthy backstreet affair with Bogart when she was called in to create a toupee for him in 1942, at the time he was married to Mayo Methot.

Say what you will, Verita furnished Bogart with the best-looking, most realistic toupee in the business: look at any photo. It's too bad Verita is not available now to help celebrities like Charlton Heston.

IN WHICH MOVIE DID BOGART SAY, "DROP THE GUN, LOUIE!"?

This misremembered line may have been snarled in any number of his indistinguishable gangster movies. However, Bogart claimed he never delivered that particular gem.

THAT'S NOT LAUREN BACALL SINGING IN TO HAVE AND HAVE NOT, THEY DUBBED IN THE VOICE OF ANDY WILLIAMS

The Sperber/Lax biography, which entailed years of serious research, examined the movie's production records (in the Warner Bros. archive at the University of Southern California, just south of downtown Los Angeles). The data on file there leaves no doubt that the voice you hear is Bacall's.

Bogart Stood on Blocks For His Scenes with Ingrid Bergman in Casablanca, to Hide the Height Difference

The wooden-blocks story can't be verified. It sounds like nonsense, but Bogie *did* wear lifts in his shoes, and shoes with built-in heels, to make him look taller. (George Raft, another Warner Bros. star in the late 1930s and early 1940s, also used lifts in his shoes.) Bogart openly discussed these lifts with reporters, referring to them as his "wedgies." You can see these shoes in various candid production shots of Bogart while he's relaxing with other cast members between scenes.

There's also a terrific photo taken on the set of *High Sierra* (Warner Bros., 1941) showing the actor with the little dog used to play Pard in the film: Bogie is snapping his fingers for the dog to jump over his outstretched leg. Bogie's high-heeled shoes are on view for the world to see. This picture is on page 63 of the Jonathan Coe biography (*Humphrey Bogart: Take It and Like It*, New York: Grove Weidenfield, 1991), and in other books.

But just how short *was* Humphrey Bogart? The general consensus puts him at five feet eight-and-one-half inches (the same height as wife Lauren Bacall.) His *Casablanca* co-lead, Ingrid Bergman, was five feet six inches. Ida Lupino, his *High Sierra* costar, was five feet four inches. No doubt these ladies would have worn heels, so naturally Bogey would want to compensate for the difference.

This male-female comparison overlooks the most obvious reason Bogart might have wanted to add to his height: He would have wanted to be as tall as the other *actors* in the film.

Chapter 3

Bogart Described, Explained, and Imitated

Just How Ugly Was He?

Few male stars have had their physical appearance analyzed at such length as Humphrey Bogart—this much emphasis on looks is usually reserved for the Greta Garbos and the Marilyn Monroes.

To begin with, he was of average height—probably five feet eight-and-a-half inches (accounts differ wildly)—and medium build. Some published photos show him wearing built-up shoes. He weighed around 160 pounds most of his life. Brown eyes. Brown hair—what he had of it. Many sources tell of him taking hormone shots when he married Lauren Bacall who was twenty-five years younger, to sire children, with his hair falling out as a result. A touching story . . . or maybe not. Verita Thompson, his hairdresser/mistress, claims he was losing his hair long before Bacall came along. Bogart himself told the tale of how Warner Bros. honcho Jack L. Warner once had passed the actor on the lot and did not recognize him without his toupee.

Okay, so a bald spot can be disguised—but what could be done with the mysterious scar on his upper lip (a mystery because there are so many different versions of its origin)? (See chapter 2: To Debunk or Not to Debunk for a discussion of this subject.) And what about the wet lower lip?—the lisp? Not a thing.

But the scar, and the grimace, and the wince, and the leer—pulling his lips back over his teeth—all made the man distinctive; made him easy to imitate. And helped turn him into the legend he is. His was the face that launched a thousand quips.

Add to this the mannerisms—the way he held a cigarette between thumb and forefinger, the way he tugged at an earlobe or rubbed his forehead, the way he hiked up his pants with both thumbs and forefingers—put them all together, they spell "Bogie."

Warner Bros. historian James R. Silke describes the studio's male-star lineup: "Except for Errol Flynn . . . they were an ugly bunch. James Cagney was made like a hammer, Edward G. Robinson's cigar was the best-looking part of him and Bogart had a face, even at thirty, that looked like it had been used to break rocks" (*Here's Looking at You, Kid*; Boston: Little, Brown, 1976).

Said Bogart's friend, director Jean Negulesco, "He stood in the doorway drawing you into his magnetic field. He had a face of romantic ugliness, the eyes riveting, the cigarette angled in his hand so that the fighting knuckles showed, the voice gravel scraping on a dry creek bed" (*Things I Did . . . and Things I Think I Did*; New York: Linden Press/Simon and Schuster, 1984).

Entertainment Weekly described Bogart's "basset-hound face, mashed upper lip, bad toupee, and scrawny, hunched physique," but called him "the greatest movie legend of all time" anyway. English film critic Terence Pettigrew saw Bogie's features as "wolverine," in *Bogart* (1977; revised 1981).

Biographer Ezra Goodman depicted the unique movie star this way: "Bogart looks his role on screen and off. Although nature gave him rather photogenic features to start with, he has, as a result of four marriages, innumerable bouts with the bottle and a paucity of food and sleep, developed a look of intelligent depravity that appears to be the product of one of the most monumental hangovers in saloon annals" (*Bogey: The Good-Bad Guy*, 1965).

Jeffrey Meyers, in his biography *Bogart: A Life in Hollywood* (1997) discusses the actor's looks at some length: "Bogart was one of the first male stars who was not handsome in the conventional way. His expressive, craggy face had great interest and character. His raspy, nasal voice, metallic, adder-like hiss, and snarling mannerisms—his wince, his leer, his diabolical grimace—were riveting and widely imitated."

The publicity writers for *Casablanca*—recognizing that Bogart was a star with unconventional looks—even capitalized on his imperfections, calling him "that man with the divine lisp!" (Decades later, in the 1960s, publicists would take the same approach to singer Barbra Streisand and her unavoidable nose).

Poking fun at his own screen image, Bogart described his familiar mannerisms in his look-alike gangster movies of the late 1930s: "I'd twisted the lower lip, spoken through the teeth, worn my hat over my eyes, pulled the coat collar up, put the right hand in the gun pocket, sneaked around corners, and climbed over roofs, until I was all out of sinister parts."

Why the Screen Character Works, and Why We Care

Despite and/or because of his looks, Humphrey Bogart became the most popular Hollywood star ever, and the movies' first real cult figure. How did he reach that distinguished status? What is it about Bogart that reviewers respond to?

Here are some theories:

Film critic Pauline Kael:

"In the role of the cynic redeemed by love, Bogart became the great adventurer-lover of the screen during the war years. There isn't an actor in American films today with anything like his assurance, his magnetism, or his style. In *Casablanca*, he established the figure of the rebellious hero—the lone wolf who hates and defies officialdom" (*Kiss Kiss Bang Bang*; Boston: Little, Brown, 1969).

◆　　◆　　◆

Bogart biographers A. M. Sperber and Eric Lax:

"It was a new kind of screen character [as Roy Earle in *High Sierra*]—an embattled man equally at odds with public morality and himself. He was a strange mix of ambiguity and integrity, someone who might be on both sides of the law, but whose true allegiance was to the man within, and whose world had neither ideals nor absolutes" (*Bogart*, 1997).

◆   ◆   ◆

Actor, costar, and Warner Bros. studio rival Edward G. Robinson:

"I think he was a good actor. He had great personality and great talent of his own. He had terrific restraint. It was sort of the great turmoil going on inside of him that made him very appealing to an audience" (Quoted in Goodman; *Bogey: The Good-Bad Guy*, 1965).

◆   ◆   ◆

Novelist Raymond Chandler, author of the 1939 novel *The Big Sleep*:

"Bogart can be tough without a gun. Also he has a sense of humor that contains that grating undertone of contempt. [Alan] Ladd is hard, bitter, and occasionally charming, but he is after all a small boy's idea of a tough-guy. Bogart is the genuine article. Like Edward G. Robinson when he was younger, all he had to do to dominate a scene is enter it" (*Selected Letters of Raymond Chandler*; New York: Columbia University Press, 1981).

◆   ◆   ◆

Again, biographers Sperber and Lax:

"Bogart created the character of the modern private detective with Sam Spade, in *The Maltese Falcon*, and as Philip Marlowe in *The Big Sleep*. The underlying appeal of Bogart as both Spade and Marlowe is not so much that he is tough (with or without a gun) as that he is romantic. He makes these characters desirable and remote, both too cynical and too honorable to be true anywhere but in the fantasies of his audience. These contradictory qualities already existed in the fictional characters, but Bogart enhances them by what is most special about him as an actor: his suggestiveness, his ability to project a sense of something going on beneath the surface. His characterizations advance the story as much as the plot does" (*Bogart*, 1997).

◆   ◆   ◆

English critic-essayist Kenneth Tynan:

"We trusted him because he was a wary loner who belonged to nobody, had personal honour . . . and would therefore survive. Compared with many of his Hollywood colleagues, he seemed an island of integrity, not perhaps very lovable but at least unbought" ("The Bogart Boom: The Man and the Myth," in *Playboy* magazine, June 1966).

♦   ♦   ♦

Film theorist/feminist Joan Mellen:

"He taught the young that self-confidence was a moral, rather than a material, quality and need have no connection with physical perfection" ("Humphrey Bogart: Moral Tough-guy," in *Close-Ups*, edited by Danny Peary; New York: Workman, 1978).

♦   ♦   ♦

Novelist Budd Schulberg:

"Bogey seems to personify the rare adult who doesn't lose his cool when the fuzz or the Nazis or the white supremacists come barreling down on us. Somehow he's that intrinsic link between the 'Play it again, Sam' of World War II and the Berkeley [college] kids who dig him for an uncompromising irreverence that testily conceals a heart that cares" (*New York Herald Tribune Book Week*, January 2, 1966).

♦   ♦   ♦

Political columnist Max Lerner:

"Bogart caught the imagination of the people . . . he caught and held our affection because he expressed something both in himself and in us that we needed to see expressed. . . . There was always an edge of bravado in both Bogarts—the movie tough-guy and the real-life tough-guy. It was a nose-thumbing, to-hell-with-it bravado. I think we liked him so much mainly because most of us, in our own actual lives, have so little chance to thumb our noses and consign the fakes, the stuffed men and the hollow men to hell" (*New York Post*, January 18, 1957).

♦   ♦   ♦

New York Times film critic Bosley Crowther:

"What is the powerful fascination of this old, gravel-voiced movie star? Let's begin by observing bluntly that the fervor is for a myth that has accumulated around a character that is part fictitious and part historical. The fictitious part is the fellow Bogart plays in his favored films—the disillusioned, disenchanted individual moving through what is generally an alien world. And the historical part is the image of Bogie as a Hollywood personality of great independence, coolness, candor and disdain for the brass and all the manifestations of smugness and hypocrisy that are shown by the establishment. This latter image emerged from his behavior in later years—behavior that naturally attracted attention and got a great deal of unplanned and unplanted publicity. And this accumulation of the fictitious and the historical have merged so it is hard to tell where the screen character leaves off and the historical character begins" (*Playboy* magazine, June 1966).

◆   ◆   ◆

Actress costar Mary Astor:

"There he is, right there on the screen, saying what everyone is trying to say today, saying it loud and clear. 'I hate hypocrisy. I don't believe in words and labels or much of anything else. I'm not a hero. I'm a human being. I'm not very pretty. Like me or don't like me!'" (*A Life on Film*; New York: Delacorte, 1971).

◆   ◆   ◆

Norman Rosten (1914–1995), once poet laureate of Brooklyn, captures the essence and appeal of Bogart in this poem, first published in 1965.

NOBODY DIES LIKE HUMPHREY BOGART

Casual at the wheel, blinding rainstorm,
The usual blonde doll alongside—only
This time our man knows she's talked,
The double-c, and by his cold eyes
We can tell it's the end of the line for her.

It's all in the corner of his mouth:
Baby if we're gonna go we'll both go
My way, and his foot deep on the gas
With the needle (close-up) leaping to eighty.
She's shaky but ready to call his bluff.

Rain and the wipers clearing the glass
And dead ahead the good old roadblock.
Quick shot moll—the scream forming.
Quick shot Bogey—that endearing look
Which was his alone, face and soul.

Any way we go, baby, one or the other,
You'll look a lot prettier than me
When we're laid out in the last scene,
You in pink or blue with the angels,
Me in the same scar I was born with.

Some Other Bogarts: Bogie Imitated, Idolized, Copied, Paid Tribute

From the beginnings of her film career in Hollywood, in 1943, twenty-year-old **Lauren Bacall** was usually described as a hard-boiled, wise-cracking, very independent woman—Humphrey Bogart in skirts. Director Howard Hawks, who guided her early career, apparently had just that image in mind when he brought her to the movie capital. Before her future costar and husband ever set eyes on her, Hawks told Bogart, "I'm going to try something. I'm going to try and make a girl as insolent as you are." And Bogart responded, "Fat chance of that." Was he ever wrong!

In the 1997 TNT cable documentary *Bogart: The Untold Story*, Bacall herself had this analysis of why their great real-life love story worked: "He wanted me to be the kind of woman he had always fantasized about, and dreamed of: a woman who behaved kind of like a man—who was as arrogant as a man, as tough as a man—and yet . . . was a woman."

Bacall and Bogart made four films together: *To Have and Have Not* (1944), *The Big Sleep* (1946), *Dark Passage* (1947), and *Key Largo* (1948), and appeared in cameo roles as themselves in the romantic comedy *Two Guys from Milwaukee* (1946)—all for Warner Bros.

She's played strong, independent women in a number of movies since, including a great nasty bitch in Warner Bros.' *Harper* (1966), but nothing with the impact of her first, great, surly entrance, asking, "Anybody got a match?"

From 1961 to 1969, Lauren Bacall was married to Jason Robards Jr. (b. 1922), an actor many consider a Bogart type, even a look-alike. Robards is best known for his Academy Award winning supporting roles in *All the President's Men* and *Julia* (1976 and 1977, respectively). Bacall has always said she does not see the resemblance—sure she doesn't.

◆ ◆ ◆

French actor **Jean-Paul Belmondo** (b. 1933) became a star overnight when he appeared in Jean-Luc Godard's film *Breathless* (1960), one of the very first features of the French low-budget "New Wave" which revolutionized moviemaking around the world.

Belmondo plays a small-time hood who kills a cop and is on the run (with American-born actress Jean Seberg) for much of the thriller. At one point, he stops in front of a theater showing Bogart's last film, *The Harder They Fall* (Columbia, 1956). The Belmondo character plays with his cigarette, draws his thumb across the upper lip, does a mean Bogart grimace, and then whispers, with reverence and awe, "Bogie!"

Breathless was the first film homage to Bogart—movie critic Pauline Kael described the character as "Bogart apotheosized"—and one of the first manifestations of the growing culthood.

Breathless was Americanized in a 1983 remake (Orion) with Richard Gere, who didn't remind *anyone* of Humphrey Bogart.

◆ ◆ ◆

The French philosopher-novelist **Albert Camus** (1913–1960) was active in the resistance movement during World War II, and was the editor of the underground paper *Combat*—a description which should immediately remind you of Humphrey Bogart in *Passage to Marseille* (Warner Bros., 1944), playing a fighting French journalist named Matrac.

Camus's philosophy was that we exist in a meaningless universe and that the only values are acceptance of life's absurdity, the inescapable solidarity with other human beings, and a responsibility for their freedom. The characters in his novels often remind readers of the characters Bogart played.

Camus was often photographed wearing a trench coat and with a cigarette drooping from the side of his mouth. He was said to be pleased when journalists compared him to Humphrey Bogart.

The Stranger (1942), a novel, is Camus's most important work. His philosophy is fully expressed in *The Myth of Sisyphus* (1942) and *The Rebel* (1951). He was killed in an automobile crash in 1960.

◆ ◆ ◆

Novelist **Raymond Chandler** (1888–1959) created the cynical but honorable detective Philip Marlowe in his first novel, *The Big Sleep* (1939).

Describing his hero, Chandler wrote, "But down these mean streets a man must go who is not himself mean, who is neither tarnished or afraid." This image became part of the myth of the private detective, and of the screen persona of Humphrey Bogart, when he starred in the first movie version of *The Big Sleep* in 1946.

Chandler's other detective novels include *Farewell, My Lovely* (1940), *The High Window* (1942), *The Lady in the Lake* (1943), and *The Long Goodbye* (1954), all of which were turned into Hollywood films.

Philip Marlowe was later played by Robert Mitchum in the Avco-Embassy 1975 film of *Farewell, My Lovely*, and in United Artists' 1978 remake of *The Big Sleep*.

Philip Marlowe has also been portrayed by George Sanders in *The Falcon Takes Over* (1942), adapted from the Chandler novel *Farewell, My Lovely*; also by Lloyd Nolan as a Marlowe type in *Time to Kill* (1942); Dick Powell in *Murder, My Sweet* (1944); Robert Montgomery in *The Lady in the Lake* (1946); George Montgomery in *The Brasher Doubloon* (1947); James Garner in *Marlowe* (1969); Elliott Gould in *The Long Goodbye* (1973); and James Caan in the cable TV movie *Poodle Springs* (1999)—all with varying degrees of success.

(For the record, Van Heflin and then Gerald Mohr played the detective on radio's *The Adventures of Philip Marlowe* [1947, 1948–51], while Philip Carey was the star of ABC-TV's *Philip Marlowe* [1959–60].)

•   •   •

The current actor who best embodies the Bogart screen persona is the Australian actor **Russell Crowe** (b. 1964), who came into his own in *L.A. Confidential* (1997). This acclaimed Warner Bros. adaptation of James Ellroy's 1990 novel of 1950s Los Angeles is centered around three cops suffering from varying degrees of corruption.

The law enforcer played by Crowe witnessed his mother being killed by his father when he was a boy, an experience that provokes him into violent rages when he sees a woman being mistreated. This man's seething anger will remind you of Bogie's tortured character in *In a Lonely Place* (Columbia, 1950). His passion for justice evokes the classic Bogart line, "When a man's partner is killed. . . ."

Crowe is better-looking than Bogie, but he does have that grizzled, "When did you last shave?" look.

47

Russell Crowe was born in New Zealand, moved to Australia at age four, and started working in TV at six. He came to international attention playing a homicidal skinhead in the Australian film *Romper Stomper* (1991). Sharon Stone brought him to America to play a gunslinger priest in her TriStar western *The Quick and the Dead* (1995), which, for most viewers, unfortunately, lived up to its title.

*   *   *

The one actor who came closest to the Bogart screen persona is French star **Jean Gabin** (1904–1976), who, in the mid twentieth century, enjoyed a worldwide popularity that was probably equal to Bogart's. Gabin was more of a loner, an outsider. He was the strong, silent, anti-hero of such classics as *Pepe le Moko* (1937); Jean Renoir's *La Grande Illusion* (1937), which often heads lists of the "world's greatest films"; and *Quai des Brumes* (1938), released in America as *Port of Shadows*.

Gabin found refuge in Hollywood during the German occupation of France during World War II, and starred in two American movies: *Moontide* (1942), costarring Ida Lupino (Humphrey Bogart was in the *Lux Radio Theatre* adaptation on April 30, 1945, with Virginia Bruce), and *The Impostor* (1944), a war film with a cast of dozens.

When Bogart was fighting with Warner Bros. and refusing to make *Conflict* (1945), the studio threatened that he would not get the lead in *Passage to Marseille*—that they would give it to Jean Gabin instead.

After the war, Gabin regained his star status in Europe, often appearing as men of great success and confidence. *Au-dela des Grilles* (*The Walls of Malapaga*) won an honorary Academy Award as the most outstanding foreign-language film of 1951. Gabin also danced in Jean Renoir's *French Can-Can* (aka *Only the French Can!*, 1955) and tangled with Brigitte Bardot in *Love Is My Profession* (1958).

*   *   *

Life led **Jerry Lacy** (b. 1936) on a long and circuitous route before he got around to playing Humphrey Bogart for public consumption.

Born in Iowa, Lacy grew up in a series of Midwestern towns. After serving as a Marine in Korea in the early 1950s, he settled in Los Angeles and became a truck driver to pay for acting classes. When someone remarked that he looked like Bogart, he studied the actor's voice and mannerisms and started doing his version of Bogart at local parties. His breakthrough came in 1968 when he impersonated Bogie in a magazine ad, and then in various television commercials. In 1969, Woody Allen spotted Lacy and hired him to portray the late actor in his new Broadway play *Play It Again, Sam*. Lacy repeated the role in Paramount's movie version (1972), and then decided to hang up his Bogart impersonation.

While doing the Woody Allen play, Jerry Lacy also continued his long-running role (three years!) as Reverend Trask on the ABC-TV Gothic soap opera *Dark Shadows*.

✦   ✦   ✦

Western star **Lash LaRue** (1917–1996) claimed he'd made a screen test at Warner Bros. but was rejected because he looked too much like Humphrey Bogart. This didn't stop Lash from capitalizing on the Bogart resemblance, or from copying the all-black outfit Bogart wore in *The Oklahoma Kid* (Warner Bros., 1939). And Lash also rode a black horse.

Lash LaRue went on to crack his whip in low-budget westerns like *The Caravan Trail* (1946), *Law of the Lash* (1946), *Border Feud* (1947), and *Mark of the Lash* (1948). Aficionados of the genre claim *King of the Bullwhip* (1951) as his best.

The man in Bogart black was even more colorful when he left the movies and fell on hard times, traveling with carnivals and Wild West shows. He resurfaced in the 1960s as an evangelist-cowboy, preaching reincarnation and astrology while he did gun and whip tricks at the Hollywood Western Revue for the Lord, in (where else?) Florida.

✦   ✦   ✦

Impressionist **Rich Little** (b. 1938) has shown his funny and affectionate Bogart on television variety shows and in commercials and advertisements. Rich Little has appeared on dozens of TV shows, and was a regular on the series *Love on a Rooftop* (1966–71), *The ABC Comedy Hour* (1972), his own *The Rich Little Show* (1976), and *The New You Asked For It* (1981).

Little was born in Ottoway, Ontario, Canada.

✦   ✦   ✦

Kevin O'Connor (1938–1991) starred as Humphrey Bogart in the 1980 made-for-TV movie *Bogie* (CBS/Chuck Fries Productions.) The *New York*

Times trashed the movie but had praise for O'Connor's performance, saying that he deserved a better script. O'Connor was a good choice for the part; he was stockier than Bogart but had the same tough, cynical attitude.

O'Connor was a New York–based stage actor who appeared in a few films: *Let's Scare Jessica to Death* (1971), *The Brink's Job* (1978), and *Special Effects* (1984).

* * *

Lauren Bacall married actor **Jason Robards Jr.** (b. 1922) in Mexico, on July 4, 1961. Their relationship was not idyllic: Bacall was seen as trying to re-create the spirit of her relationship with Bogie, when the only thing the two actors had in common was a fondness for scotch. A son, Sam, was born to the Robardses in November 1961. They divorced in 1969.

Many entertainment writers insist that Robards is a Bogart type, even physically resembling him, but Robards is too much of a chameleon, becoming each character he plays. The "real" Robards is not identifiable, which means he's convincing in a wider range of parts—from tortured dreamer, to vanishing cowboy, to romantic leading man.

Like Bogart, Robards's breakthrough was on the New York stage; in Robards's case, it was in the dramas of Eugene O'Neill. He's also been active in TV, and appeared in a number of European films. He's one of our best actors, but he's never been a "star" in the sense Bogart is.

Jason Robards won the Best Supporting Actor Oscars for *All the President's Men* (1976), for his role as newspaper editor Ben Bradlee, and for *Julia* (1977), as novelist Dashiell Hammett. He was also nominated for *Melvin and Howard* (1980), playing a grizzled, eccentric Howard Hughes.

Robards appeared in the *Casablanca* clone *Caboblanco* (1981), as the Nazi general, with Charles Bronson in the Bogart-like screen role.

* * *

The resemblance of **Robert Sacchi** (b. 1941) to Humphrey Bogart was pointed out to him as early as high school in the Bronx, New York. Sacchi was not flattered, as he thought himself better-looking than that.

He went into acting at New York University, did summer stock, and, when the Bogart cult started mushrooming in the mid-1960s, Sacchi was suddenly in demand. His first commercial was for London Fog raincoats.

He appeared in some twenty feature films, including *Pulp* (1972), with Michael Caine and Lizabeth Scott; *Across 110ᵗʰ Street* (1972), with Anthony Quinn; and *Crazy Joe* (1974), with Peter Boyle.

Sacchi was living in Europe when Woody Allen cast look-alike Jerry Lacy as Humphrey Bogart in his Broadway play *Play It Again, Sam* (1969). Sacchi returned to New York in time to be cast in the national touring company of the Allen comedy, in which he played Bogey for over a thousand performances on the road. In 1974, he put together a one-man show, *Bogey's Back*, and toured the country with it for five years.

In 1980, Sacchi had the starring role in Twentieth Century–Fox's *The Man with Bogart's Face*, as a private eye who undergoes plastic surgery to look like his idol, and becomes involved in a *Maltese Falcon*–type case. The plot is taken from a best-selling novel by Andrew J. Fenady, who wrote and produced the film. After an unspectacular opening, the film's title was changed to *Sam Marlowe, Private Eye*; it did not help the box-office flop.

◆   ◆   ◆

Reviewing the HBO cable network's 1998 movie *The Rat Pack*, *Entertainment Weekly* gave thumbs-down to much of the acting, saying Ray Liotta's "rabbity middle-aged **Frank Sinatra**" looks like "an exhibit from the Hollywood Wax Museum." The other actors bore even less resemblance to their real-life counterparts.

The Rat Pack production was also accused of playing around with the facts, pointing out that the original group was a Bogart-Bacall lark, but "when Bogie died, Sinatra climbed into the driver's seat. As always, his genius lay not in imagination but interpretation. He had already adapted Bogart's on-screen-outlaw status. Now he took on Bogart's circle of friends—and even courted his widow."

Frank Sinatra (1915–1998) played tough-guy roles, as a detective or a cop, in *Tony Rome* (1967), *The Detective* (1968), *Lady in Cement* (1968), *Contract on Cherry Street* (1977), and *The First Deadly Sin* (1980).

(Sinatra is also discussed in chapter 6: The Main Players in the Life of Humphrey Bogart.)

Chapter 4

The Ultimate Bogart Trivia Quiz

Part One

1. Bogie in his trench coat is one of the most familiar images in popular culture—you must have seen it a hundred times! But do you remember whether Bogart wore his coat belted . . . or tied?

2. In which movie does the Bogart character make a remarkable recovery from death?

3. What role do Bogart, Paul Newman, and Mickey Rourke have in common?

4. Which one of Bogie's four wives was arrested for "indecency"?

5. Name a film in which Bogart smokes a cigarette—no, no, just kidding! Name a movie in which Bogart *does not* smoke a cigarette, but instead puffs on a *cigar*.

6. What was Bogart's first color feature film?

7. One of the following was *not* a member of the original "Holmby Hills Rat Pack," Bogie's informal group of fun-loving pals (later

taken over by singer Frank Sinatra). Which one of these Bogart associates does not belong on the list: singer Frank Sinatra, director Howard Hawks, singer Judy Garland, restaurateur Mike Romanoff, or writer-actor Noël Coward?

8. In *Casablanca* (Warner Bros., 1942), Rick says to Sam, "If she can stand it, I can. Play it!" Sound vaguely familiar? Okay, name the picture in which Bogart says, "Go ahead. If he can stand it, I can."

9. Who is "the man with Bogart's face"?

10. Why is it called a "trench coat"?

11. Moviegoers first saw *Casablanca* (Warner Bros.) in November 1942 . . . but when they started handing out Oscars, it won Best Picture of 1943. What's going on?

12. What is the first movie with Bogart as the romantic hero who gets the leading lady by the fade-out?

13. In which screen entry does romantic hero Bogart give up the leading lady?

14. In which feature does Bogart send the leading lady to prison?

15. If Bogart's screen characters had filed tax returns, many of them might have listed their profession as "gangster." What would have been the second-most-frequently-cited profession?

16. Of the nine top-billed stars in *Casablanca*, how many were American-born?

17. What was so special about Bogart's last ten feature films (*not* cameo roles) that the first sixty-five did not have?

18. Name the film in which Harrison Ford (b. 1942) is much better in the remake than Humphrey Bogart was in the original big-screen version.

19. Humphrey Bogart was born and raised in a wealthy section of New York City's Upper West Side. Do you remember what his parents did to pay the rent?

20. Does Captain Queeg of *The Caine Mutiny* (Columbia, 1954) have a first name?

21. What screen part originally intended for Bogart was taken by actor Kirk Douglas?

22. What are the two movies in which the Bogart character is called "Duke"?

23. What was the name of Bogart's independent film production company?

24. Who went to the electric chair on-screen for killing Bogart's character?

25. Here's the trickiest question in this book: You'll remember that Bogie wore a mustache in two movies: the silly melodrama *Isle of Fury* (Warner Bros., 1936) and the western *Virginia City* (Warner Bros., 1940), and looked foolish each time—he just didn't have the face for a mustache! But there's a third title, in which the Bogart *character* wears a mustache. Can you figure it out?

Answers on page 265

Part II

The Man

Chapter 5

Highlights of the Life, Loves, Career, and Other Exploits of Humphrey Bogart

1899

December 25—Humphrey DeForest Bogart is born in Sloane's Hospital, at Fifty-ninth Street and Ninth Avenue, in New York City. His father, Belmont DeForest Bogart, age thirty-three, is a successful doctor, and a direct descendant of the Dutch immigrants who settled in New York in the 1600s. Bogart's mother is Maud Humphrey, age thirty-one, a descendent of successful businessmen with roots in England. In spite of her entrepreneurial background, she opted to study art in Paris with the great James McNeill Whistler and later became a popular illustrator. (Humphrey Bogart was a distant relation of Winston Churchill and the late Princess Diana.) The family home—with the doctor's office and the mother's studio—is in a town house at 245 West 103rd Street (between fashionable West End Avenue and Broadway.)

Soon after his birth, Humphrey Bogart becomes a celebrity, as "the original Maud Humphrey baby," sketched by his mother for Mellin's baby-food advertising.

1901

A sister, Frances (but called Pat) is born.

1903

A second sister is born: Catherine (called Catty and, later, Kay). The three Bogart children are mainly the responsibility of the maids. Humphrey Bogart later describes his parents as "too busy to be intimate." Of his mother, he admits, "I can't say truthfully that I loved her."

1905

Five-year-old Humphrey enters Delancey School, a private institution on Manhattan's Upper West Side.

1908

The eight-year-old transfers to the Trinity School, a private boys' school on New York City's Ninety-first Street, where "Humphrey" is considered a sissy name.

Summer—Childhood vacations are spent on Canandaigua Lake, one of the Finger Lakes near Rochester, in western New York State. The boy takes to the water and becomes a good sailor.

1914

Fourteen-year-old Humphrey, now more assertive, becomes leader of Lake Canandaigua's Seneca Point Gang. They have water fights, play soldiers, and stage theatrical productions. As his father had done before him, the teenager becomes a skilled yachtsman. He grows up hating pretense.

Back in New York City, Humphrey becomes friends with William A. Brady Jr., son of the famous Broadway producer, who is a neighbor and a patient of Dr. Bogart's. The two boys often go to matinees of plays and musicals, or to the new movie palaces.

1916

The last summer at Lake Canandaigua; next year the family will summer on Fire Island, off the south shore of Long Island, so Maud can be nearer to a high-paying staff job in New York City.

1917

Humphrey is set to graduate from the Trinity School in June, but his grades are not good enough to gain him admission to college.

Dr. Bogart had always planned for his son to attend his own prep-school alma mater, Phillips Academy, at Andover, Massachusetts (an hour from Boston). Now he has to ask for favors from administrative friends at the school to get his son admitted for a year of pre-college studies.

September—Seventeen-year-old Humphrey enters Phillips Academy. He shows little interest in formal education.

1918

February—Phillips Academy puts the indifferent student on probation.

May 24—Phillips Academy expels him.

May 28—Four days later, Humphrey Bogart enlists in the U.S. Naval Reserve. He's eighteen years old and does not require his parents' permission; he would not have asked for it, anyway.

Medical records give Bogart's vital statistics at that time:

Height: five feet eight-and-a-half inches
Weight: 136 pounds
Eyes: brown
Hair: light brown
Complexion: fair

June 19—He's called for active service , but World War I is nearly over.

November 27—He is assigned to the USS *Leviathan* troop carrier.

November 29—The armistice is signed, and the Great War has ended. Bogart spends the next six months on the *Leviathan* transporting American soldiers home from France.

1919

February 15—Bogart is transferred to the USS *Santa Olivia* . . . which sails from New York to Europe without him. He accidentally misses the boat and is declared a deserter. The Navy accepts his explanation and he's sentenced to three days in solitary. Ten days later he goes home with an honorable discharge.

Over the next year or so, Bogart works for the Pennsylvania Tug and Lighterage Company in New York City, "mostly tracing lost shipments and doing reports on damage to tugs and barges." He later works for the Wall Street investment company of S. W. Strauss and Co., as assistant to the purchasing agent. He does not like the drudgery, and in particular, he does not appreciate getting up early in the morning.

He spends much of his time going to the theater with friend Bill Brady Jr., taking riding lessons from Stuart Rose (who would later marry his sister Frances)—and drinking at parties and speakeasies.

1920

Someone suggests that William Brady find employment for Bogart; thus, Bogart works as an office boy for the producer for two weeks, then asks for something more important to do.

Brady pays him fifty dollars a week to be the production manager of Brady's movie studio in Fort Lee, New Jersey. Bogart works on the movie *Life*, based on a play Brady had produced on the New York stage and starring Nita Naldi and Arlene Pretty.

Grace George, Brady's actress wife, has Bogart hired as stage manager for the tour of her new play, *The Ruined Lady*. He's paid a weekly salary of fifty dollars.

1922

January—Bogart, twenty-two years old, makes his Broadway debut in the melodrama *Drifting*, at the Playhouse Theatre, which stars Alice Brady. He appears briefly as a Japanese butler with a tray of cocktails . . . and drops the tray. (Some versions have this incident happening at a pre-Broadway tryout in Brooklyn.)

June—Humphrey Bogart takes over a small role in another William Brady production, *Up the Ladder*, at the Playhouse Theatre in New York City.

October 16—He has the second male lead in *Swifty*, starring Frances Howard and Neil Hamilton. *New York Herald* critic Alexander Woollcott writes, memorably, that Bogart was "what is usually and mercifully described as inadequate."

1923

November 27—The comedy *Meet the Wife*, starring Mary Boland and Clifton Webb, opens at the Klaw Theatre in New York City. It receives excellent reviews, including this one: "Humphrey Bogart is a handsome and nicely mannered reporter, which is refreshing" (*New York World*). The show runs for thirty weeks.

1924

September—The war drama *Nerves* debuts on Broadway, with Bogart listed fourth, and pretty newcomer Mary Philips (sometimes listed as Mary Phillips) in fifth billing. Bogart gets good notices, but the play does not, and it closes after sixteen performances.

Bogart goes back to being a stage manager, for the touring company of *Drifting*. The noted actress Helen Menken (b. 1901) takes over for Alice Brady. Within a few weeks, Bogart and Menken are talking of marriage.

1925

January—Bogart is featured in the comedy *Hell's Bells*, at New York City's Wallack's Theatre, with Shirley Booth. It runs for fifteen weeks.

September—The farce *Cradle Snatchers* premieres on Broadway, starring Mary Boland and Edna May Oliver, with Bogart as a member of the cast. A critic from Chicago compares Bogart's looks to those of movie star Rudolph Valentino. The play lasts for forty-two weeks, the longest run of the season.

1926

May 20—Uncertain, even reluctant, Bogart marries Helen Menken in a ceremony held in her East Side apartment . . . which is simultaneously translated into sign language for the benefit of her deaf parents. There is no honeymoon trip. From the very beginning, the lovers fight.

1927

Early in the year—Bogart replaces an actor in the play *Saturday's Children*, at the Actors Theatre.

June 9—The disgraced silent-movie comic Roscoe "Fatty" Arbuckle, who was the victim of a huge scandal involving the death of a starlet at a wild party in San Francisco, attempts a comeback in the farce *Baby Mine*. Bogart is in the cast, along with actress Lee Patrick (who will be featured in future Bogart films), in the production at the Forty-sixth Street Theatre. The show lasts for only twelve performances.

Bogart immediately accepts a role in the Chicago production of *Saturday's Children*. Helen Menken won't join him in the Windy City . . . and the marriage is more or less over. Years later, she admits that her career always came first.

November 18—Helen Menken is granted a divorce from Humphrey Bogart, after eighteen months of marriage.

Autumn—Bogart begins dating actress Mary Philips (b. 1903).

1928

April—Twenty-eight-year-old Humphrey Bogart and twenty-five-year-old Mary Philips are married at her mother's home in Hartford, Connecticut. Bogart insists it is "the most wonderful thing that could happen" to him.

1929

January 11—Bogart and wife Mary play a married couple in the Broadway production of the comedy-drama *The Skyrocket*, which doesn't.

Alice Brady offers Bogart a role in her current hit, *A Most Immoral Lady*, at the Cort Theatre, which, in contrast, plays 160 performances.

August 5—Bogart has a small role in *It's a Wise Child*, a comedy that becomes a big success at the Belasco Theatre. He's noticed by a talent scout from Fox Pictures.

October—The New York Stock Market crashes. Theater attendance plummets.

1930

Bogart appears in *Broadway's Like That*, a ten-minute sound short made in New York City by Vitaphone, featuring Ruth Etting and Joan Blondell. The film was rediscovered in 1963, but the soundtrack is still missing.

Bogart is screen-tested in New York City by the Fox Film Corporation; he is liked, and is signed. He departs for Los Angeles, but Mary refuses to go—her New York stage career is more crucial . . . as it had been with first wife Helen Menken.

In Los Angeles, Bogart is cast in the Fox movies *A Devil with Women*, starring Victor McLaglen, and in *Up the River*, directed by John Ford and starring Spencer Tracy. He and Tracy become lifelong friends. Tracy calls his friend "Bogie."

1931

Bogart is in the Fox war film *Body and Soul* (1931), starring Charles Farrell. Bogart is loaned out for a small part in *Bad Sister* (Universal, 1931), with Bette Davis; films *Women of All Nations* (Fox, 1931), again cast with

Victor McLaglen . . . and does a George O'Brien western, *Holy Terror* (Fox, 1931), wearing elevator shoes.

Then, the disillusioned would-be movie star Humphrey Bogart boards a train back to New York.

December 3—Bogart opens on Broadway at the Booth Theatre, in the play *After All*, a British comedy. This time he's spotted by a scout from Columbia Pictures, who signs him to a six-month contract.

1932

Early in the year—Bogart returns to Hollywood. He has the second lead, after Dorothy Mackaill, in Columbia's romantic comedy, *Love Affair* (1932). But then he's loaned to Warner Bros., where he's given a small part in *Big City Blues* (1932), with Joan Blondell. Director Mervyn LeRoy likes him and offers him sixth billing in *Three on a Match* (Warner Bros., 1932), as "The Mug," a kidnapper.

Bogart appears in a Los Angeles tryout of the play *The Mad Hopes*, starring Billie Burke, at the Belasco Theatre. And then he gets back on the train to New York!

Bogart lands parts in four Broadway plays in succession:

I Loved You Wednesday (opening October 11, 1932) in which he and Frances Fuller costar as lovers. Henry Fonda appears briefly, in a wordless part. At the Harris Theatre, it plays for sixty-three performances.

Chrysalis (opening November 15, 1932) is blessed with a cast now seen as extraordinary: Margaret Sullavan, Osgood Perkins, Bogart, Elisha Cook Jr., June Walker, Elia Kazan, and Mary Orr (future author of *All About Eve*, the short story that became the classic 1950 movie). *Chrysalis* opened at the Martin Beck Theatre for twenty-three performances.

Our Wife (opening March 2, 1933) a romantic comedy starring Rose Hobart and Bogart, has the misfortune of opening on a bank holiday. It bows at the Booth Theatre for only twenty performances.

The Mask and the Face (opening May 8, 1933), an Italian comedy starring Stanley Ridges and Shirley Booth, has Bogart in a supporting part. It is performed at the Guild Theatre for forty performances.

1934

Early in the year—Bogart plays a small part as a gangster in the movie *Midnight* (Universal, 1934), filmed in New York City.

May—He is picked for the part of an aristocrat named Horatio Channing in the Broadway play *Invitation to a Murder*. In the audience is the important theater producer-director Arthur Hopkins, who is impressed by Bogart, and remembers him when casting the upcoming Broadway production of *The Petrified Forest*.

Early September—Bogart's father lies dying in a New York City hospital, at age sixty-six. It is only at this moment that Bogart realizes he loves his dad. "I love you, Father," he tells him. The old man smiles, and dies in his son's arms.

1935

January 7—Robert E. Sherwood's drama *The Petrified Forest* opens at the Broadhurst Theatre in New York City. The drama, and Bogart—as the escaped killer Duke Mantee—are immediate hits. "The Mantee role seemed to have a Jekyll-and-Hyde effect on his personality. Mantee put hair on his chest, professionally and personally" (Jonah Ruddy and Jonathan Hill: *Bogey*, 1965). When Warner Bros. buys the property, *The Petrified Forest*'s star, Leslie Howard, lets it be known that he wants Bogart to appear with him in the movie version.

Summer—Bogart appears in three summer-stock productions in Skowhegan, Maine, in supporting roles.

At age thirty-five, Bogart once again embarks by train to Hollywood. Wife Mary Philips again refuses to go with him. This time Bogart has a round-trip ticket.

October 26, a Saturday—Bogart reports for work on *The Petrified Forest* (1936) at the Warner Bros. studio in Burbank, over the hill from Hollywood.

Nine days after the end of production, Bogart is signed to a new contract at the studio, and added to the Warners Bros. assembly line of filmmaking. Over the next year, he appears as a mobster named Bugs in *Bullets or Ballots* (1936); he's a radio manager programming trash in *Two Against the World* (1936); a daredevil pilot in *China Clipper* (1936); and he wrestles a rubber octopus in *Isle of Fury* (1936). He has a strong scene in *The Great O'Malley* (1937), as a veteran trying to pawn his wartime medals.

1936

February—The film version of *The Petrified Forest* opens to enthusiastic reviews.

Spring—Mary Philips flies to Hollywood to be with her husband—perhaps she's heard the stories about his affair with the flamboyant blonde actress Mayo Methot (b. 1904).

Early July—Bogart and Mary Philips move into a small house on North Horn Avenue above Sunset Boulevard, in West Hollywood.

October—The FBI releases its report on Communist influence within the fledgling Screen Actors Guild. Bogart is one of twenty-one members listed as having "strong Communist Party leanings." (There is no basis for this charge.)

December—Work begins on *Marked Woman* (1937), a Bette Davis drama project at Warner Bros., with Bogart in a supporting role and Mayo Methot in a character part that will become her best-known movie appearance.

1937

January 30—The hard-hitting drama *Black Legion* opens. This attack on the Ku Klux Klan and the white-supremacy movement is favorably reviewed in the movie section, and discussed in the editorial pages. Bogart earns his best reviews since *The Petrified Forest*, and many proclaim screen stardom for him . . . but it doesn't happen—yet.

Early 1937—Bogart has third billing, after Edward G. Robinson and Bette Davis, in the boxing entry *Kid Galahad*. Next, he's the convict brother of Ann Sheridan in *San Quentin*.

February—Mayo Methot gets her life in order to marry Bogart, by filing for divorce from her restaurateur husband.

Summer—Bogart does Shakespeare, live on radio, for the CBS *Shakespeare Theater*. He is heard with Walter Huston and Brian Aherne in *Henry IV, Part One*.

Bogart is loaned out, a one-shot deal, to United Artists and veteran producer Samuel Goldwyn, for the part of Baby Face Martin in the prestigious film of the Broadway hit *Dead End*.

Bogart's alcoholic sister Kay dies in New York City, of peritonitis from a ruptured appendix, at the age of thirty-five. Around this time, Bogart also takes financial responsibility for his other sister, Frances, who has become manic-depressive. He brings her to Los Angeles to look after her.

Summer—Bogart is borrowed by independent producer Walter Wanger for *Stand-In* (United Artists, 1937). Then the actor goes home to

Warner Bros. for the hillbilly musical *Swing Your Lady* (1938), and *Crime School* (1938) in which he plays a crusading youth worker.

Fall—Mary Philips divorces Humphrey Bogart.

December—Bogart signs a four-year contract with Warner Bros., guaranteeing him forty weeks' work per year at $1,100 per week—but then the studio puts him into the depressingly bad *Men Are Such Fools* (1938).

1938

Early in the year—During the production of *The Amazing Dr. Clitterhouse* (Warner Bros., 1938), Humphrey Bogart and writer (and future director) John Huston meet and become friends. Theirs will be one of the most productive actor-director teams in Hollywood film history.

Bogart is a mobster in the routine *Racket Busters* (Warner Bros., 1938). Next he's a crooked lawyer shot by James Cagney in *Angels with Dirty Faces* (Warner Bros., 1938).

August 30—Bogart marries Mayo Methot at the Bel Air home of his agent, Mary Baker. The day ends with a drunken fight, the newlyweds spend their wedding night apart—and the legend of "the battling Bogarts" is officially launched. The couple lives at 8787 Shoreham Drive in West Hollywood for the first three years; then in January 1942, they move to 1210 North Horn Avenue, called "Sluggy Hollow" (also in West Hollywood, near to where Bogart lived with his previous wife, Mary Philips).

Late in the year—Bogart's mother, Maud, comes for a visit, and decides to stay in Los Angeles. Bogart finds her a small apartment nearby, on Sunset Boulevard in West Hollywood. Mayo gets along with her better than her son does.

1939

March—Bogart is cast in an important role in the period drama *The Old Maid*, as the romantic hero who dies an early death but continues to haunt the women—played by Bette Davis and Miriam Hopkins—who love him. After only a few days of shooting, Warner production head Hal B. Wallis realizes he's made a mistake, and Bogart is replaced by George Brent. Bogie is hurt, and angry.

Late in the year—Bogart buys a small powerboat which he names *Sluggy*. He and Mayo often sail to Santa Catalina Island, twenty-one miles west of Los Angeles.

Humphrey Bogart goes from one film to another at Warner Bros., with seven features released this year. He's a gangster in *King of the Underworld*, *You Can't Get Away with Murder*, *The Roaring Twenties*, and *Invisible Stripes*; a cowboy bandit in black in *The Oklahoma Kid*; and a mad scientist who comes back from the dead in *The Return of Dr. X*. He has a small but important role in the Bette Davis vehicle, *Dark Victory*, as a horse trainer secretly in love with the heroine.

December 1—Warner Bros. records show the following per-week salaries of its current male stars (only Paul Muni, its leading star, is missing from this list):

James Cagney	$12,500
Edward G. Robinson	$8,500
Claude Rains	$6,000
George Raft	$5,500
Errol Flynn	$5,000
Pat O'Brien	$4,000
George Brent	$2,000
Frank McHugh	$1,600
Donald Crisp	$1,500
John Garfield	$1,500
Humphrey Bogart	$1,250

December 25—Bogart is forty years old, a frustrated actor who gets good roles in small films and small parts in big pictures. He's made twenty-five movies for Warner Bros., most of them routine and familiar, and often hard to tell apart.

1940

Bogart's performance in *Dark Victory* (1939) attracts attention from other studios—Universal even asks to borrow him for *My Little Chickadee* (1940), with Mae West and W. C. Fields, but Warner Bros. refuses. Instead Bogart is cast in the gangster comedy *It All Came True* and the western *Virginia City* (both 1940), which are shot at the same time. Then, he's a gangster yet again in *Brother Orchid* (1940), with Edward G. Robinson in the starring role.

March 13—Warner Bros. acquires the screen rights to W. R. Burnett's new crime novel *High Sierra*, as a project for Paul Muni, the studio's most distinguished male star (he won the Best Actor Oscar for the 1936 film *The Story of Louis Pasteur*).

July 17—Angry that the studio refuses to star him in a promised screen biography project of the German composer Ludwig van Beethoven, Muni, age forty-five, tears up his contract, and severs relations with Warner Bros. Since they're in the star-making business, word goes out that Humphrey Bogart is going to be made a star, to replace the miffed Muni.

Summer—The Special Committee on Un-American Activities of the House of Representatives, starving for publicity, comes to rid Hollywood of its Communists.

August 5—Filming begins on *High Sierra* (1941), which will become one of Warner Bros.' top-grossing films, and will be the first quality production in which Humphrey Bogart has top billing.

August 16—Bogart testifies under oath that he is not and has never been a member of the Communist Party.

September—*They Drive by Night* is released, and co-lead Ida Lupino receives starmaking critical reviews. Warner Bros. decides to give her top billing over Bogart in *High Sierra* . . . but is it because of her rave reviews, or because Bogart has been called a Communist?

November 23—Maud Humphrey dies at age seventy-two. She is buried in Forest Lawn cemetery, where her son will later be. Bogart says of his mother, "She died as she had lived. With guts."

1941

January—*High Sierra* opens to rave reviews. "Mr. Bogart plays the leading role with a perfection of hard-boiled vitality," says the *New York Times*.

Early in the year—Public opinion in the United States about the war in Europe is shifting from a position of neutrality to that of inevitable involvement. The Navy calls for civilian crafts to help patrol the California coastline, with its defense plants, and Bogart turns up every weekend in his powerboat *Sluggy*.

Early February—Bogart and George Raft are cast in *Manpower*, to play opposite Marlene Dietrich. Right off, there are problems between the two men. At Raft's insistence, Bogart is replaced (by Edward G. Robinson).

A week later, a newly rebellious Bogart refuses to report for work on *Bad Men of Missouri*. He's immediately put on suspension, and Dennis Morgan is cast in this grade-B western.

May—Both audiences and critics hoot at Bogart's new film *The Wagons Roll at Night,* in which he plays an obsessed carnival owner.

Warner Bros. allows screenwriter John Huston his first chance to direct, and he asks for Dashiell Hammett's novel *The Maltese Falcon.* Huston is secretly delighted when George Raft refuses the screen project and Bogart is cast in the lead as private investigator Sam Spade.

June 5—Production begins on *The Maltese Falcon.*

October 4—*The Maltese Falcon* opens. It is an immediate hit, and Bogart is now seen as a new kind of rugged screen sex symbol.

In turn, George Raft is now seen by the industry as a jerk. He will make only one more movie for Warner Bros.

December 7—The Japanese bomb Pearl Harbor, and America enters the war. The studios quickly lose stars and personnel—who rush to enlist—but Warner Bros., with its stable of older leading men, including Bogart, is able to continue production without major problems.

December 11—West Coast story editor Irene Lee sends Warner Bros. production head Hal B. Wallis a copy of the never-produced play *Everybody Comes to Rick's* with her recommendation to translate it to the screen. Wallis likes it. Remembering the success of the romantic, exotic-sounding *Algiers* (1938), Wallis changes the project's title to *Casablanca.*

1942

January—Bogart's new movie, *All Through the Night,* is released. It's a routine comedy of gangsters vs. Nazis, but, at the time, it is more successful than *The Maltese Falcon.*

Bogart negotiates a new contract with Warner Bros. He gets a straight seven-year deal, at $2,750 a week. The problem of role approval is not resolved in his new pact.

Then George Raft rejects Warner Bros.' *The Big Shot* (1942), another aging-gangster clinker and, inexplicably, Humphrey Bogart is assigned to the project.

February—Production begins on *Across the Pacific* (1942), which is seen as a recycling of *The Maltese Falcon,* with Mary Astor and Sydney Greenstreet cast in familiar roles.

Bogart comes home from work one night and an angry Mayo Methot goes after him with a butcher knife, sticking him in the middle of his back. (Lauren Bacall will later verify the scar.)

May 25—Filming begins on *Casablanca* (1942), although the script is not completed, and major cast members are not yet signed.

Summer—A month after finishing *Casablanca*, Bogart begins *Action in the North Atlantic* (1943).

November 8—*Casablanca* is being previewed and readied for release . . . when American and British troops invade North Africa, landing in Algiers and Casablanca—turning the movie into a news event, creating enormous interest and record-breaking box office for the picture.

At some point during this year, there's a wrap party on a Warner Bros. soundstage. Ann Sheridan introduces Bogart to young Verita Thompson, who will become his personal hairdresser and mistress.

1943

January—Bogart is loaned to Columbia Pictures for *Sahara* (1943), a "World War II in the desert" action picture, filmed in the desert of California.

March—The cover of this month's issue of *Harper's Bazaar* fashion magazine features Betty Bacal (misspelled Bacall), an eighteen-year-old blonde New Yorker with a knowing, sexy smolder. There are inquiries from Columbia Pictures, David O. Selznick, Howard Hughes—and Warners Bros. director Howard Hawks, who offers to put her under personal contract. She accepts Hawks's screen deal.

Early April—Betty Bacall arrives in Hollywood.

Bogart's agent Mary Baker negotiates a new contact with Warners which gives the actor $3,500 a week.

Production is to begin in May on *Passage to Marseille* (1944), reuniting many of the cast and crew of *Casablanca* . . . but then Warner Bros. demands that Bogart first make *Conflict* (1945), a potboiler about a man who kills his wife. The studio threatens to replace him on *Marseille*, with French actor Jean Gabin, a refugee from occupied France now working in Hollywood. (Note: "Marseilles" was misspelled—"Marseille"—in the film's title.)

June 2—Actor Leslie Howard, whom Bogart idolized, is killed when his commercial flight from Lisbon, Portugal, to England is shot down by German fighter planes, reportedly under the impression that Winston Churchill is aboard.

A depressed Bogart agrees to the demands from Warner Bros. He makes *Conflict*, which is not released until 1945, to mixed reviews, and then *Passage to Marseille*, which does not remind *anyone* of *Casablanca*.

October—Howard Hawks takes Betty Bacall to the set of *Passage to Marseille* and introduces her to Humphrey Bogart.

November—Bogart and Mayo spend ten weeks on a USO tour of Africa and Italy, entertaining the American troops and visiting hospitals.

There is an unconfirmed account of a drunken Bogart pulling a gun on a two-star general in Italy. He is put under arrest and removed from the sector. This story was related by Warner Bros. press agent Bill Blowitz, who'd worked with Bogart for years, to biographer Ezra Goodman (*Bogey: The Good-Bad Guy*, 1965).

1944

Early February—Bogart is officially introduced to Lauren Bacall, as his costar in *To Have and Have Not*. "We'll have a lot of fun together," he promises her.

February 29 (a leap year)—Start of production on *To Have and Have Not* (1944). Lauren Bacall is nineteen; Humphrey Bogart is forty-four years old. Slowly, so slowly no one really notices, the two fall in love.

March 2—The Sixteenth Annual Academy Awards ceremony is held at Grauman's Chinese Theatre in Hollywood. *Casablanca* wins for Best Director (Michael Curtiz), Best Screenplay (Julius J. and Philip G. Epstein, and Howard Koch), and Best Supporting Actor (Claude Rains). The Oscar for Best Actor that should have gone to Bogart is instead awarded to sentimental favorite Paul Lukas, for *Watch on the Rhine* (1943).

Early May—Shooting wraps on *To Have and Have Not*. The studio immediately casts Bogart in *God Is My Co-Pilot* (1945), a war film, which he refuses—he's tired of clichéd combat dramas, and he needs a vacation. Once more, he's put on suspension.

October 10—Shooting begins on *The Big Sleep*, costarring Bogart and Bacall. Soon after, Bogart leaves the self-destructive Mayo Methot. The studio announces the separation . . . but then a reconciliation is announced two weeks later.

One morning at three A.M. during this period, Lauren Bacall, staying with her mother in Hollywood, answers the phone and it's Mayo Methot yelling at her: "Listen, you Jewish bitch—who's going to wash his socks? Are *you*? Are *you* going to take care of him?!" It's further proof, as if it were needed, that the Bogart-Methot marriage is dead.

November 6—The Hollywood Democratic Committee sponsors an all-star rally, with Bogart as the anchor, in support of Franklin D. Roosevelt's reelection as president and Harry S. Truman, his teammate, as vice president. It airs on all major radio networks.

December 4—Bogart again leaves his raging wife Mayo. He looks for solace in alcohol, and begins to show up at the studio late for work, and then not at all.

1945

January—"The battling Bogarts" call a truce. *The Big Sleep* wraps production, a month behind schedule. Thinking to separate the lovers, the studio sends Bacall to New York . . . but Bogart follows.

January 29—Bogart tells columnist Earl Wilson that he and Bacall will marry.

February—The *Saturday Evening Post* publishes a three-page article by Bogart, "I Stuck My Neck Out," in which he states his political views. He defends the right of actors and artists to speak out on social and political issues. Give us time, and Hollywood will produce a president, he brashly claims.

April—The busy actor begins the turgid drama *The Two Mrs. Carrolls* (1947), costarring Barbara Stanwyck.

May 10—Bogart and Mayo are divorced. Bogart is said to be very generous in his settlement, giving her two-thirds of his cash assets and his shares in two Safeway supermarkets.

May 21—Bogie and Bacall are married in Lucas, Ohio, at writer friend Louis Bromfield's Malabar Farm. Only a small group of family and friends are in attendance . . . with an army of photographers and reporters waiting outside.

The Bogarts spend a one-week honeymoon on the *Sluggy*, cruising up and down the California coast.

August 15—World War II is over. The Cold War begins, and a wave of conservatism begins to sweep the country.

November 10—*Confidential Agent* (Warner Bros., 1945), teaming Charles Boyer and Lauren Bacall, opens to reviews that attack the young actress as being inept, saying she's being pushed into screen stardom too fast. Some blame her unsatisfactory screen performance on the dictatorial and arbitrary director Herman Shumlin; others say the studio was not protecting its investment. Many agree that the movie's anti-fascist message is already outdated.

1946

January—In light of the failure of *Confidential Agent*, Warner Bros. calls for rethinking and retakes on the already completed *The Big Sleep*. New scenes are written for Bogart and Bacall that play off their sexual chemistry and their insinuating banter. The movie will not be released until August in the United States.

The Bogarts buy Hedy Lamarr's isolated house and swimming pool, called Hedgerow Farm, at 2707 Benedict Canyon Road in Beverly Hills. After a few years it proves to be too remote for them and they look for a new home.

August—*The Big Sleep* is released to enthusiastic reviews. Bacall is seen as having redeemed herself after *Confidential Agent*.

Summer—Bogart leaves his hand- and footprints in the wet cement at Grauman's Chinese Theatre. He writes, "Sid [Grauman]—May You Never Die Till I Kill You."

October—The Bogarts shoot a cameo appearance for the Warner Bros. comedy *Two Guys from Milwaukee* (1946). They are heard on the prestigious *Lux Radio Theatre* in an adaptation of *To Have and Have Not*.

Winter—Bogart pays actor Dick Powell $50,000 for the yawl *Santana*, a fifty-five foot championship racer. Actors George Brent and then Ray Milland had previously owned it.

The Bogarts film location scenes in San Francisco for their costarring vehicle *Dark Passage* (1947), a film noir thriller.

Bogart signs a remarkable new contract with Warner Bros. It's for fifteen years. The terms include one studio project per year at a fee of $200,000 each; script and director approval; as well as permission to do one outside project annually.

Bogart's salary for 1946 is $467,000, making him the highest-paid actor in the world.

1947

Early in the year—Mark Hellinger, who had produced the hit *The Killers* (1946), from the Hemingway short story, forms a production company with Bogart to film other Hemingway short stories.

January—The House Un-American Activities Committee (HUAC) initiates an investigation of Communist influence in Hollywood.

May—Studio head Jack L. Warner testifies before HUAC. He identifies "un-American" screenwriters, among them the Epstein twins, who had won an Academy Award for their *Casablanca* screenplay.

October 20—HUAC hearings begin in Washington, D.C. Studio head Walt Disney testifies that Communists tried to take over his company. Popular character actor Adolphe Menjou urges Americans to arm themselves against the Communists.

October 26—A gung-ho group of Hollywood notables, the most prominent being Humphrey Bogart and Lauren Bacall, charter a plane to Washington, D.C., to protest the outrageous actions of HUAC. The group includes actors Danny Kaye, June Havoc, Evelyn Keyes, Paul Henreid, Gene Kelly, Richard Conte, and Marsha Hunt.

October 27—At the HUAC hearing, the presence of the Hollywood stars is largely ignored by the Committee.

October 29—The HUAC hearings are suspended without explanation. The number of unfriendly witnesses is reduced to ten—"the Hollywood Ten"—mainly screenwriters, each of whom is sentenced to a year in prison.

Public opinion turns against the group of actors that went to Washington. Newspapers demand that the Hollywood studios fire all Communists, and call for movie censorship. Box-office receipts for *Dark Passage* are dismal, and the film is quickly pulled from many locations— but are moviegoers refuting Bogart, or a bad Bogart movie?

November 24—Studio executives issue "the Waldorf declaration" promising to dismiss all Communists on their payrolls.

December 2—With the threat of unemployment hanging over his head, Humphrey Bogart holds a news conference and recants. He says that the trip to Washington the month before was "ill-advised, even foolish," that his behavior was "foolish and impetuous."

Hollywood liberals are shocked by Bogart's very public recantation. Business picks up for *Dark Passage* across the country. (Bogart later insisted that he'd been "used" by the Communists. Lauren Bacall continues to use that word in documentaries and other interviews.)

December 15—Bogart and John Huston begin work on *Key Largo* (Warner Bros., 1948) with costars Lauren Bacall, Lionel Barrymore, and Edward G. Robinson.

December 20—Producer Mark Hellinger dies in West Hollywood, ending the plans for he and Bogie to co-produce movies starring Bogart.

1948

This is the year that the Supreme Court issues its Consent Decree, ruling that the movie studios cannot also be distributors or exhibitors—they are forced to sell off their theater chains, cutting off a guaranteed source of income.

This is also the year that television starts its rapid consumer growth, offering free in-home entertainment. Theater attendance begins its decline.

April 7—Bogart forms his own independent film production company, the first actor in Hollywood to do so. It's called Santana, after his boat.

Late spring—Lauren Bacall tells Bogey that they're going to be parents.

Mid-year—Bogart stars as a lawyer in the Santana Production of *Knock on Any Door* (Columbia, 1949), one of the first films directed by Nicholas Ray.

1949

January 6—At the age of forty-nine Humphrey Bogart becomes a father, when Lauren Bacall gives birth, at Cedars of Lebanon hospital in Hollywood, to a six-pound, six-ounce boy, Stephen, called Steve, the name of the Bogart character in *To Have and Have Not*, in tribute to the movie that brought them together.

Mid-year—Bacall goes back to work at Warner Bros., filming *Young Man with a Horn* (1950), opposite Kirk Douglas. Bogart begins *Chain Lightning* (1950) with Eleanor Parker as his co-lead at Warner Bros.

September 25—Bogart and a friend end a night of drinking by stopping for a drink at New York's El Morocco nightclub, in the company of two twenty-pound stuffed pandas they'd bought earlier. Two young women apparently try to take the pandas from them, and wind up on the floor, bruising their reputations. Did they fall, or were they pushed?

Bogart is accused of assault. The magistrate in Mid-Manhattan Court throws the case out, saying that it's all a publicity stunt. El Morocco bans Bogart for life, and a society of 250 restaurants and nightspots declare they'll put up with no nonsense from Bogart *or* Errol Flynn (who also has a reputation for hot-tempered partying). Bogart calls himself the Boris

Karloff of the supper clubs (referring to that actor's identification with the Frankenstein monster).

"The Panda Incident" is cited as the source of Bogie's famous retort, when asked if he was drunk at the time: "Isn't everybody at three A.M.?"

1950

Late winter—Bogart reluctantly appears in Warner Bros.' *Murder, Inc.* (later changed to *The Enforcer*, 1951), because he feels it's too old-fashioned.

May—*In a Lonely Place* (Columbia, 1950) is praised as one of Bogie's best efforts. Warner Bros. had refused to loan out Lauren Bacall for the film, and she begins to rebel just as Bogie (and Bette Davis and James Cagney and others) had done, against the studio's dictatorial policies.

July 12—Bacall is released from her Warner Bros. contract. She begins to star in projects at Twentieth Century–Fox and other studios.

1951

Early spring—The Bogarts appear in their own syndicated radio series, *Bold Venture*, utilizing the setting and the characters from *To Have and Have Not*. Thirty-six half-hour episodes are aired.

Late spring—Production begins in a remote area of the African Congo on *The African Queen* (United Artists), an adventure film starring Bogart and Katharine Hepburn, and set during World War I. Bogie points out that Bacall is going with him because his other marriages failed when the partners were separated by work.

Mid-June—News arrives that Bogart's third wife Mayo Methot—she of "the battling Bogarts"—is dead at age forty-seven of complications following surgery.

Late July—The Bogarts and Katharine Hepburn fly to London to shoot the remaining scenes for *The African Queen* (including the famous leeches sequence).

1952

January—Bogart is eager to play the male lead in Paramount's movie of the Broadway hit *Come Back, Little Sheba*. However, he owes Warner Bros. a film and they refuse to release him. The project they do offer him is an insult—about a football coach whose winning team saves a small college. Bogie refuses. *Come Back, Little Sheba* (1952) is filmed with Burt Lancaster, who is praised for his sensitive performance.

March 20—Humphrey Bogart wins his first and only Academy Award, as Best Actor for *The African Queen*, in a ceremony held at the Pantages Theatre in Hollywood. He wins over Marlon Brando (*A Streetcar Named Desire*), Montgomery Clift (*A Place in the Sun*), Fredric March (*Death of a Salesman*), and Arthur Kennedy (*Bright Victory*). Bogart thanks John Huston nine times (or maybe it just seems like it).

Bogart signs to make M.A.S.H. 66, later changed to *Battle Circus* (MGM, 1953), a name change which doesn't help the resultant film a bit.

The Bogarts move from Benedict Canyon to a brick colonial mansion in Holmby Hills, one of the wealthier Los Angeles suburbs adjacent to Beverly Hills. Their neighbors are Judy Garland, Hoagy Carmichael, Lana Turner, producer Walter Wanger and actress wife Joan Bennett, and songwriter Sammy Cahn.

August 23—Lauren Bacall gives birth, again at Cedars of Lebanon hospital, to a six-pound, five-ounce daughter, named Leslie Howard Bogart in appreciation for the late actor who insisted Bogie appear in the movie of *The Petrified Forest*.

October 27—The Bogarts, with many other celebrities, appear at a rally for Adlai Stevenson, Democratic candidate for president, in Madison Square Garden. Bogart chooses not to wear his toupee.

1953

January—Bogie leaves for Italy to star in *Beat the Devil* (United Artists, 1954), which will be his final screen collaboration with John Huston. Lauren Bacall stays behind to appear in *How to Marry a Millionaire* (1953), a comedy with Betty Grable and Marilyn Monroe at Twentieth Century–Fox.

May 21—The Bogarts celebrate their eighth wedding anniversary in London.

June—Shooting starts on *The Caine Mutiny* (1954) at Columbia Pictures, with Bogart as loony Captain Queeg.

Early September—Bogart begins filming *Sabrina* (1954) for Paramount . . . in the screen role written for Cary Grant. There is much animosity on the set between Bogart and costar William Holden, and between Bogart and director Billy Wilder.

September 22—After an eighteen-year relationship, Bogart and Warner Bros. go their separate ways, with no obligation to the other on either part.

Free at last, free at last!

1954

January—Bogart flies to Rome for *The Barefoot Contessa* (United Artists, 1954). He does not get along with costar Ava Gardner, perhaps because she has recently separated from husband Frank Sinatra, a friend of Bogie's.

Bogart is developing a persistent cough that's beginning to interfere with his work. Coughing spells leave him gasping for air.

March—*Beat the Devil* opens to baffled audiences, some of whom demand their money back. Ironically, or perversely, some critics like the film. *Time* magazine calls it a "screwball classic."

Mid-year—Filming begins on the hostage drama *The Desperate Hours* (Paramount, 1955).

September 3—The Bogarts appear on the popular CBS-TV show *Person to Person*, interviewed from New York by host Edward R. Murrow. The loving husband lets his young wife take the spotlight.

December—Columbia Pictures mogul Harry Cohn buys Bogart's production company, Santana, for a million dollars.

1955

February—Bogart goes directly from *The Desperate Hours* into *The Left Hand of God* (Twentieth Century–Fox, 1955), in which he appears with Gene Tierney; and when that has finished, he makes *We're No Angels* (1955) for Paramount, costarring with Peter Ustinov and Aldo Ray.

Spring—The Holmby Hills Rat Pack is born when Lauren Bacall surveys the ruins of a four-day party in Las Vegas and tells her friends and neighbors, "You look like a goddamn rat pack!"

Memorial Day—Bogart plays Duke Mantee for the third time (after the play and the movie) in a live television production of *The Petrified Forest* on NBC. Henry Fonda and Lauren Bacall costar.

On Bogart's filmmaking schedule is the boxing drama *The Harder They Fall* (Columbia, 1956) and *Melville Goodwin, U.S.A.*—a romantic comedy (from the novel by John P. Marquand) which will reunite Bogart and Bacall on-camera for the first time since *Key Largo* (1948). Also, Columbia wants Bogart to star in a film of *The Good Shepherd*, from the novel by C. S. Forester, author of *The African Queen*.

September—Bogart forms another production company: Mapleton Pictures. The first project is to be *Underworld, U.S.A.*, which will costar Bacall.

Work begins on *The Harder They Fall*.

1956

January—Bogart and Bacall report to Warner Bros. to do wardrobe tests for *Melville Goodwin, U.S.A.*

A week before production begins, Bogart, a heavy smoker all his life, is diagnosed as having cancer of the esophagus (the tubular canal from the throat to the stomach). Symptoms of this cancer do not appear until it has spread through the whole body.

February 29—Bogart is operated on at Good Samaritan Hospital in Los Angeles, and his esophagus removed. The prognosis is poor.

Bogart spends most of the rest of his life in his upstairs bedroom. Each afternoon at five o'clock, the cocktail hour, he is brought downstairs to receive a steady stream of friends and well-wishers. When he can no longer walk, he is brought downstairs in a dumbwaiter.

September 16—Bogart is to join a birthday celebration for Lauren Bacall in Las Vegas, to hear Frank Sinatra sing. Instead, he takes seven-year-old son Stephen out on the *Santana*.

Bogart is upset by frequent rumors in the press of his imminent death. Sardonic to the end, he gives this statement to his columnist friend Joe Hyams: "I'm down to my last martini. The only thing I'm fighting is to keep my head above the press."

November 26—Bogart enters St. John's Hospital in Santa Monica for further cancer treatment, which is not successful. He's returned to his home.

Christmas Day—Bogart's fifty-seventh birthday. The doctors tells Bacall that her husband has little time left.

1957

January 13—Bogie drifts into a coma.

January 14—Humphrey Bogart dies at 2:25 A.M., attended by two nurses.

Bogart had not wanted a funeral, but asked to have his ashes scattered at sea (which was illegal at the time). Bacall arranges for cremation, a memorial service, and a repository for his ashes in the Gardens of Memory section of Forest Lawn Memorial Park, in Glendale, California.

The actor's will is probated in February. He leaves an estate of more than a million dollars, approximately half of which goes to Lauren Bacall. There are trust funds for his two children, plus small bequests for his secretary and for the family cook. Lauren Bacall gives the *Santana*'s crewmembers the tackle and gear, and then sells the yacht.

January 18—At the same time Bogie is being cremated, a memorial service is held at All Saints Church on Santa Monica Boulevard in Beverly Hills. Dozens of Hollywood notables attend, along with Bogey's sailing buddies.

The Reverend Kermet Costellano speaks a few words, then reads the Ten Commandments and Tennyson's poem, "Crossing the Bar."

Director friend John Huston delivers the eulogy, in which he concludes, "He got all that he asked for out of life and more. We have no reason to feel any sorrow for him—only for ourselves for having lost him." (Huston's complete eulogy is in the autobiographies of both Lauren Bacall and Stephen Bogart.)

Where the coffin would have been is placed a glass case containing a small-scale model of the *Santana*. (See also chapter 1: Humphrey Bogart's Dead But He Won't Lie Down!, page 17.)

Chapter 6

The Main Players in the Life of Humphrey Bogart

Four Wives and One Mistress

"He cried at every one of his own weddings. And with good reason."

—fourth wife Lauren Bacall

Humphrey Bogart met his first wife, Broadway actress **Helen Menken** (1901–1966) when she replaced Alice Brady in the touring production of *Drifting* in 1922.

Helen, a fiery redhead, had been born poor, and had little education, but became an acclaimed actress—her career lasted from 1906 until 1961— and a woman of great sophistication. As a child actress she had supported her deaf-mute parents and sent a brother to college. Her breakthrough role was in Austin Strong's 1922 play *Seventh Heaven*. Menken also created the role of Charlotte Lovell, in *The Old Maid* (1934). In 1926, Menken appeared in another play that made her a sensation, the French drama *The Captive*, by Edouard Bourdet, in which she portrayed a defiant lesbian.

Bogart and Menken announced their engagement in 1922, and even got the license, but did not marry until May 20, 1926. ("I have been so frightfully busy, you know," said Helen. "I just haven't found time to marry.") The wedding was held in her apartment in the Gramercy Park

Hotel, attended by many of Helen's theatrical friends. The ceremony was translated into sign language for the benefit of her deaf-mute parents.

Bogart was infatuated with Helen, but she was a star and he a bit player, which was an uncomfortable situation for both of them. Also, perhaps, he was disappointed that marriage to her had not given his acting career a needed boost. Ungallantly and untruthfully, he told friends that she was ten years older than he was. They formally separated ten months after their wedding and were officially divorced on November 18, 1927. In her suit for divorce, Menken charged that her spouse beat her, striking her in the face and body. Bogart had no comment. She waived alimony payments.

But—would you believe it?—they remained friends. In the early 1940s, when his marriage to Mayo Methot (wife number three) had become a living hell, Bogart is said to have made secret visits to Helen when he was in New York City. For old times' sake.

Helen Menken's only movie credit is *Stage Door Canteen* (1943) in which she appears in a cameo, along with dozens of other film and theater notables.

◆   ◆   ◆

In April 1928 Humphrey Bogart married **Mary Philips** (1901–1975) also an actress, at her mother's home in Hartford, Connecticut. Mary was never a star but was highly regarded in her profession. The two had earlier appeared in the Broadway play *Nerves* (1924), and were man and wife in the 1929 play *The Skyrocket*. When Bogart went to Hollywood for the first time, in 1930, Mary was appearing in a play and refused to go with him. After his success in the film of *The Petrified Forest*, Mary did join him in Hollywood, but it was probably because she'd heard the rumors of her husband's affair with the flamboyant actress Mayo Methot.

Helen and Humphrey were formally separated in January of 1937; the divorce was final in June. She married a friend of his from New York, actor Kenneth MacKenna, a week before Bogie married Mayo Methot. Little else is known about Mary Philips, for she remained in the background and was seen as a sensible and stabilizing influence on him. In later years Bogart would say nothing about her. The photo of Mary in the Jeffrey Meyers biography (*Bogart: A Life in Hollywood*, 1997) shows an attractive woman with a strong resemblance to actress Suzanne Pleshette.

Mary Philips had small parts in various Hollywood movies: *As Good As Married* (1937), billed ninth; *That Certain Woman* (1937) starring Bette Davis; *Mannequin* (1938) with Joan Crawford; *Incendiary Blonde* (1945) with Betty Hutton; and *Captain Eddie* (1945) with Fred MacMurray. One source also puts her in *Broadway's Like That*, the 1930 Vitaphone short with Ruth Etting, Bogart, and Joan Blondell.

Apparently, Mary preferred using "Phillips" as her professional name, instead of "Philips," by which she was most commonly known.

◆　　◆　　◆

Third wife **Mayo Methot** was born in Portland, Oregon, on March 3, 1904, and died there on June 9, 1951. Her father was a sea captain on the Orient run.

Mayo was a child actress, playing with the Baker Stock Company in Portland. She went to New York in 1922, and became a Broadway star with *The Song and Dance Man* (1923), written, produced by, and starring George M. Cohan. Mayo appeared in three plays in 1929: *Great Day, All the King's Men,* and *Half Gods.* Her appearance in *Torch Song* (1930) prompted New York theater critic Brooks Atkinson to write, "Mayo Methot gives a splendid performance—vivid in composition, sincere in feeling."

The New York newspapers described Mayo as a "little blonde beauty." She developed into a sensual blonde with prominent cheekbones; but then, as she aged and began drinking heavily, she became the sullen, overweight, blowsy blonde of *Marked Woman* (Warner Bros., 1937), her best-known feature film. Bogart biographer Terence Pettigrew calls her "a cut-price Mae West." Filmmaker John Huston described her as looking and acting "like a bull terrier. Though not quite as pretty."

Mayo's first husband was film cameraman John M. Lamond; her second was Hollywood restaurateur Percy Tredgar Morgan.

Cult film actress Louise Brooks had an interesting take on the Bogart-Methot relationship. In her collection of Hollywood profiles, *Lulu in Hollywood* (New York: Alfred A. Knopf, 1982), Brooks says Bogie met Mayo when he had lost his spirit, and that she "set fire to him. Those passions—envy, hatred, and violence, which were essential to the Bogie character, which had been simmering beneath his failure for so many years—she brought to a boil, blowing the lid off all his inhibitions forever."

Though still married to others at the time, Mayo Methot and Bogart began an open affair in 1936. After their respective divorces, they wed on August 20, 1938, at the Bel Air home of his agent Mary Baker. They began fighting before the day was over, launching the intriguing legend of "the battling Bogarts," who matched each other drink for drink, blow for blow. They fought in public places and in the streets of Hollywood, and in the homes of friends. Some saw the fighting as foreplay to sex, as they seemed to share a genuine intimacy. "She's an actress without work," Bogart once explained, "and it's necessary for her to make scenes. So I give her the cue."

When sultry nineteen-year-old Lauren Bacall came on the scene in early 1944, Mayo must have sensed (correctly) that her days as Mrs. Bogart were numbered. After months of wrangling, Mayo finally agreed to a separation; the divorce was granted on May 10, 1945.

Humphrey Bogart and Mayo Methot were known as the "Battling Bogarts" during their 1938–45 marriage. In ten memorable rounds, here's a look at some of the hot-tempered behavior that earned them that nickname. Let the countdown begin!

Round 1. The first documented sign of, shall we say, *tension* between Bogey and Mayo occurs on their wedding day, on August 20, 1938. The ceremony takes place at the Bel Air, California, home of Bogart's talent agent Mary Baker.

No one remembers exactly what set it off, but a monumental fight develops between the new bride and groom at the nuptial celebration. Bogart and his best man, host Mel Baker, drive off to Tijuana, while Mayo staggers away to sleep it off in Mary Baker's bedroom. Bogart reappears the next day to claim his unblushing bride, and later sends a rubber plant to Mary Baker as a limp apology.

Round 2. In March 1939, Warner Bros. sends a celebrity-packed train from Los Angeles to Kansas for the world premiere of Errol Flynn's new western movie, *Dodge City*. There are fourteen sleeping cars, two dining cars, an observation car . . . and a saloon car.

Along the way, Mayo accuses Bogie of paying too much attention to the lovely Lane sisters, Priscilla and Rosemary, with whom he has costarred on-screen. Two photojournalists come upon the drunken Bogarts in the vestibule of a train car. Mayo is waving an empty Coke bottle, which she dramatically smashes against the wall (where'd she get a dumb idea like that—from the movies?) and lunges at Bogie with the broken half. The photographers intervene, one of them even hitting her to slow her down, while she struggles to get loose, screaming, "I'll kill the son of a bitch!"

Kansas never knew what it missed.

Round 3. In August 1940, Mayo accompanies her husband to Lone Pine, in eastern California, for location filming on *High Sierra*, where they continue their running battle. Bogie's stuntman, Buster Wiles, is quoted as suggesting that the couple should put on a pugilistic show at Madison Square Garden.

One day a wreath is delivered to Bogart on the set. It has condoms hanging from the leaves, so everyone assumes it's from Mayo. Perhaps it's her way of criticizing the "friendship" between her husband and attractive, feisty costar Ida Lupino.

Round 4. One of the main problems with the Bogarts is that while he is becoming a star, in the late 1930s and early 1940s, Mayo is devolving into a has-been—the more she drinks, the more dissipated she becomes, and the less chance there is of her being hired for a major film.

One observer describes them as being like firecrackers together, and always on a short fuse.

Gossip hound Jaik Rosenstein recalls an occasion when he came out of a fashionable restaurant on the Sunset Strip in West Hollywood and encountered Mayo astride Bogart determinedly banging his head on the sidewalk.

Round 5. One of the many benefits of being a movie star in Hollywood's Golden Age was that your studio had the power and wherewithal to cover up, or hush up, your indiscretions. Like the time Mayo set their West Hollywood house on fire. Bogie calls faithful agent Mary Baker, who calls Blayney Matthews, head of the Warner Bros. studio police force. Matthews helps Bogart extinguish the fire, and the incident never makes the gossip columns. Baker also finds a doctor when Mayo stabs Bogie (see round 10).

Round 6. Mayo is diagnosed as alcoholic (hey, good guess!), paranoid, and schizophrenic, but she defiantly refuses to seek treatment.

A Warner Bros. publicist recounts the story of an evening with the Bogarts in their home in West Hollywood. The more alcohol they consume, the louder and uglier they become. In a blind fury, Mayo stumbles, falls backward, becomes lodged behind the sofa, but continues to scream away. Bogart strikes out at her, in anger and frustration, yelling, "You bitch! You filthy bitch!"

Round 7. Actress Gloria Stuart (later rediscovered for 1997's *Titanic*) is a guest at another memorable evening with the Bogarts, a dinner party at their home in West Hollywood, where Stuart protests the "games" the two hosts are playing. It seems Mayo has a gun, and has locked herself in the bedroom. Bogie insists she's just kidding. However, when he, Stuart, and the other guests check on Mayo, she threatens to shoot them through the door. Also around this time, Mayo apparently tries to slash her wrists.

Round 8. In the fall of 1943, Bogart and Mayo spend ten weeks in Africa and Italy entertaining the American troops.

Actor friend Peter Lorre would remember, "The day before Bogie and Mayo were leaving Hollywood for their USO Camp Show foreign tour, they met me in Hollywood's famous Cock 'n Bull bar. I told them the boys at the front would soon be seeing some real fighting when those two arrived." Lorre told Mayo, "As for you, you'll come back with a Purple Heart and a black eye."

Even before they stepped aboard the plane to fly to North Africa they had a preliminary bout in the airport itself. They had a stand-up fight in the lounge.

Round 9. The Bogarts invite a few friends in for Thanksgiving festivities. A lot of drinking is done before dinner, so when the turkey is wheeled in there is a sudden argument over who's going to carve the bird.

"Okay, Bogie, the hell with it!" yells the unpredictable Mayo. "No one's going to carve the ——— turkey!" She grabs the silver platter, swings it around, and throws the turkey through the window.

Round 10. Mayo's drinking and instability steadily escalate in relationship to Bogart's growing screen success. As his fame increases with *Casablanca*, so does Mayo's fury. She's becoming more prone to physical violence, but at least she usually gives warning: she begins humming "Embraceable You."

Bogart would often go to the Finlandia Baths on Sunset Boulevard in Hollywood to relax, sweat out the alcohol, and to get away from Mayo, who was convinced that the establishment was a whorehouse. Bogart comes home from the Finlandia one night to find Mayo waiting for him, her eyes glazed and swollen. And she's humming "Embraceable You." She lunges at him with a butcher knife. He ducks and tries to run for the door. Somehow she stabs him in the small of his back. By luck, the blade does not penetrate deeply. The studio police are called, a discreet doctor stitches up Bogart, and regular law enforcers are never notified.

Lauren Bacall confirms this story, noting the scar Bogey had on his back.

Mayo Methot returns home to Portland, where she lives with her mother. She was not heard of again until 1951, when news comes of her death in Holladay Park Hospital. Her mother states that Mayo's final illness began as influenza, and was followed by complications leading to surgery, the exact nature of which is not revealed.

Verita Thompson, Bogie's longtime mistress (roughly 1942–56), writes about Mayo at length (*Bogie and Me: A Love Story*, 1982), repeating what she'd heard from Bogart. She describes Mayo as a two-fisted drinker and partygoer, a fun-loving, sharp-tongued wit: "a woman after Bogie's own heart." It was only after several years of marriage to Bogart that Mayo's crazy streak and penchant for physical violence gradually began to emerge: "Bogie was trapped in her crazy web before he even realized it was developing."

Gaye Dawn, the alcoholic girlfriend played by Claire Trevor in *Key Largo* (Warner Bros., 1948), is probably suggested by Mayo Methot (the character is not in the original play). Edward G. Robinson, as the gangster Rocco, describes the early Gaye Dawn: "A regular hellion. She even stuck a knife in me once."

In the movies, Mayo Methot appeared in bit parts and character roles. She was usually seen as toughened, wisecracking types: kept women, "hostesses," prison inmates. Her films include *The Corsair* (1931), *The Night Club Lady* (1932), *Counsellor-at-Law* (1933), *Jimmy the Gent* (1934), *Dr. Socrates* (1935), *Mr. Deeds Goes to Town* (1936), *Marked Woman* (1937) [Note: Humphrey Bogart and Bette Davis star in this urban melodrama of gangsters forcing women into white slavery. This is probably Mayo's most important screen role, as the aging Estelle, one of the nightclub B-girls being shoved around by the underworld bosses], *Women in Prison* (1938), *The Sisters* (1938), *Unexpected Father* (1939), *Brother Rat and a Baby* (1940).

The fourth Mrs. Bogart, **Lauren Bacall**, was married to Humphrey Bogart from May 1945 until his death in January 1957. They made four feature films and two children together. She later wed actor Jason Robards Jr. (b. 1922), a man described by many as a Bogart type.

She is born Betty Joan Perske on September 16, 1924 in the New York City borough of the Bronx. Her father is Polish, her mother Romanian. The family name is Weinstein-Bacal. She studies acting as a teenager and appears in tiny roles on Broadway in the early 1940s without attracting much attention. When she turns to modeling she attracts a lot of attention.

At age eighteen, Lauren Bacall is thin, weighs 120 pounds, has sandy-blonde hair, and is a tall, five feet eight and a half inches. A striking photo of Bacall as a blood donor appears on the cover of the March 1943 *Harper's Bazaar* magazine. Movie producer David O. Selznick sends inquiries as to her interest or availability for movies, as does millionaire movie producer Howard Hughes, and then Warner Bros. director Howard Hawks—who is the only one to mention the magic word "money." He pays for her to come West for a screen test.

Hawks puts the newcomer under personal contract, and works with her to prepare her for a screen test. She sees him as tailoring her, inventing her, perhaps creating her in the pattern of his stylish wife Slim. Hawks thinks of pairing her on-screen with Cary Grant or Humphrey Bogart. She thinks, "Cary Grant—terrific! Humphrey Bogart—yuck!" Hawks takes her to meet Bogart on the set of *Passage to Marseille* at Warner Bros., and she finds him physically slighter than she'd imagined.

Hawks directs Bacall in a screen test, the "whistle" scene from *To Have and Have Not,* as the girl called Slim, appearing with actor John Ridgely. Later she bumps into Bogart, who's just seen her test. "We'll have a lot of fun together," he tells her. (Which means whatever you want it to mean.)

Shooting begins on *To Have and Have Not*. Gradually Bogart and Bacall fall in love. When they start sneaking off to see each other, Bacall becomes "the cast": when Bogart's angry wife Mayo Methot calls, she's told that he's out with the cast. Mayo won't go quietly, but money and cajoling and pleading finally get her to Las Vegas for a divorce, on May 10, 1945.

No one appreciates Lauren Bacall as an actress more than movie critic James Agee (who would later collaborate on the screenplay of *The African Queen*). In *Time* magazine for October 23, 1944, Agee writes: "She has a javelin-like vitality, a born dancer's eloquence in movement, a fierce female shrewdness and a special sweet-sourness."

For his other reviewing job, at *The Nation,* Agee writes, "A leisurely series of mating duels between Humphrey Bogart at his most proficient and the very entertaining, nervy, adolescent new blonde, Lauren Bacall. I can hardly look at her, much less listen to her—she has a voice like a chorus by Kid Ory [the prizefighter]—without getting caught in a dilemma between a low whistle and a belly laugh" (November 4, 1944).

Bogie and Bacall are married on May 21, 1945, at writer friend Louis Bromfield's Malabar Farm in Lucas, Ohio. In her 1978 autobiography *Lauren Bacall: By Myself* the actress mentions more than once that she entered marriage an innocent, but utters nary a word about when or how that situation changed.

They have two children: Stephen, born January 6, 1949, named after Bogie's character in *To Have and Have Not*; and Leslie, a girl, born August 23, 1952, named after Bogie's late actor pal Leslie Howard. Bogart happily allows Bacall to domesticate him. In June 1952 they buy a house in affluent Holmby Hills (between Beverly Hills and Bel Air), they give parties, they have open house. They organize a group of friends into "a rat pack." Frank Sinatra is elected president of the fun-loving group.

In January 1956 doctors find the actor has cancer of the esophagus. He's operated on in February, but doesn't get better. After a well-documented year of a valiant fight, Bogart dies the following January, at age fifty-seven.

In *Lauren Bacall: By Myself*, Bacall writes of the Bogarts' friendship with Frank Sinatra, noting that Bogie was "somewhat jealous of Frank—partly because he knew I loved being with him, partly because he thought Frank was in love with me . . . yet he was also crazy about Frank—loved having him feel that our home was his home." After Bogie's death, she found solace in the friendship of Sinatra—and then a romantic relationship. She confides that she expected to become a permanent part of his life. Frank asked her to marry him. But then agent friend Irving "Swifty" Lazar spilled the beans to columnist Louella Parsons, who told the world. Sinatra called to tell Bacall they had to cool it for a while . . . and she didn't see him again for six years.

Looking back ten years later, Bacall feels Sinatra did her a favor, saving her from the disaster their marriage would have been. "But the truth also is that he behaved like a complete shit."

However, there are other versions of the Bacall-Sinatra affair which suggest it began *before* Bogart's death.

Bogart biographer Ezra Goodman (*Bogey: The Good-Bad Guy*, 1965) remembers Lauren Bacall when she first arrived at Warner Bros. "She was a tall, skinny, aggressive broad.

"Miss Bacall, or Mrs. Bogart, did not seem to take . . . matters too seriously. For instance, she was palsy-walsy, if that was the word, with Frank Sinatra. Bogart didn't seem to care—but there was no doubt he knew about it, too.

"Sinatra was a character. Frankie boy liked to pal around with the wives of some of his cronies.

"Bogey didn't seem to care. Maybe he knew he was in bad shape and maybe even dying.

"He was philosophical about it all."

Actor William Campbell (b. 1926) developed a warm relationship with Bogart when they worked together in *Battle Circus* (MGM, 1953). Bogart talked with Campbell about what would later become known as the Rat Pack. Bogart was getting impatient with the whole thing, with the hangers-on who came to his house to drink and kill time, and—to

Campbell's surprise—with Frank Sinatra, whom he seemed to dislike. "He was not too . . . enamored. At least that's the way I picked it up. He didn't tell me this, but there is a case for his feeling about Sinatra based upon Bacall. Because there was some relationship there, more on her part than his. And I think Bogart was aware of it."

Sinatra biographer Kitty Kelley quotes playwright Ketti Frings, who visited Bogart during his last illness in 1956: "Everybody knew about Betty and Frank. We just hoped Bogie wouldn't find out. That would have been more killing than the cancer" (*His Way: The Unauthorized Biography of Frank Sinatra*; New York: Bantam, 1986).

Lauren Bacall appeared with Humphrey Bogart in *To Have and Have Not* (1944), *The Big Sleep* (1946), *Dark Passage* (1947), and *Key Largo* (1948), and the two make a cameo appearance in *Two Guys from Milwaukee* (1946)—all for Warner Bros.

Her other films include *Confidential Agent* (1945), *Young Man with a Horn* (1950), *Bright Leaf* (1950), *How to Marry a Millionaire* (1953), *Woman's World* (1954), *The Cobweb* (1955), *Blood Alley* (1955), *Written on the Wind* (1957), *Designing Woman* (1957), *The Gift of Love* (1958), *Flame Over India*, aka *Northwest Frontier* (UK, 1959), *Shock Treatment* (1964), *Sex and the Single Girl* (1965), *Harper* (1966), *Murder on the Orient Express* (1974), *The Shootist* (1976), the made-for-television *Perfect Gentlemen* (1978), *Health*, aka *H.E.A.L.T.H.* (1979), *The Fan* (1981), *Appointment with Death* (1988), *Mr. North* (1988), the made-for-television *Dinner at Eight* (1989), *Innocent Victim*, aka *Tree of Hands* (1989), *Misery* (1990), *All I Want for Christmas* (1991), the made for television *The Portrait* (1993), *A Foreign Field* (1993), *Ready to Wear*, aka *Prêt-à-Porter* (1994), the made-for-television *From the Mixed-up Files of Mrs. Basil E. Frankweiler* (1995), *My Fellow Americans* (1996), *The Mirror Has Two Faces* (1996), and the TV miniseries *Too Rich: The Secret Life of Doris Duke* (1999).

In *Bogart*, (1997) A. M. Sperber and Eric Lax discuss the other "flirtations" that Bacall mentions in her book *Lauren Bacall: By Myself*— including her undeniable sexual attraction to Adlai Stevenson, the 1952

Democratic candidate for president. Other flirtations/attractions include actor Richard Burton and composer-conductor Leonard Bernstein—indulged, Bacall said, by an understanding older husband.

Later Lauren Bacall meets Jason Robards, Jr. the actor many think resembles Bogart, though Bacall claims she does not see it at all. They marry in 1961, have a son they name Sam, and divorce in 1969.

Bacall has a wonderful second career, in the Broadway theater, appearing first in the comedy *Cactus Flower*, in 1965. She wins a Tony Award in 1970 for her performance in *Applause!* Bacall triumphs again in 1981 in another musical, *Woman of the Year*, based on the 1942 MGM comedy of the same name, which starred Bogart's pals Katharine Hepburn and Spencer Tracy.

More recently, in 1996, Lauren Bacall portrayed the mother in Barbra Streisand's vanity production *The Mirror Has Two Faces*. She was the sentimental favorite to win the Oscar for Best Supporting Actress, but somehow missed out.

Verita Thompson (birth date unknown) says she wrote her memoir, *Bogie and Me* (1982), to set the record straight, to keep from becoming "a sleazy footnote in Bogie's history" and to keep the star's image from becoming distorted by their affair.

According to her own book, Verita had been brought to Hollywood by Republic Pictures after she won an Arizona beauty contest. Her first and last film was a western: when she fell off her horse and broke an arm, Republic canceled her contract. While recuperating she met a French wig- and toupee-maker and became his Hollywood representative.

Verita claims that she and Bogart became lovers in 1942, and that her services (as a hairstylist) were written into all his contracts. After his divorce from Mayo Methot on May 10, 1945, Bogart proposed to Verita but she refused, feeling that he chose wives the way a fighter chooses sparring partners. Three months after he married Lauren Bacall on May 21, 1945, Bogart called Verita "to pick up when we left off," and Verita said yes.

Verita describes Bacall as cool, suspicious, condescending. "I had always considered her an opportunistic interloper, and when I got to know her better, I amended my opinion. I considered her a pretentious, opportunistic interloper."

The Sperber/Lax biography (*Bogart*, 1997) questions the Verita-Bogie relationship, having found only one reference to her in the Warner Bros. archives at the University of Southern California . . . yet they do quote her. Verita lends credence to her book by including eight photos of her with Bogart—and Lauren Bacall is also in three of them. Memorabilia collectors might be alarmed by Verita's claim that, during the period they were intimate, Bogart's autographed photos were signed by her.

Sailing Buddies on the Santana

In the climax of the 1948 hostage drama *Key Largo*, set in hurricane-torn Florida, the Bogart character (Frank McCloud) and the five gangsters are in a boat on the open sea. Then Frank begins to kill them off. Many books on Bogart will point to the lettering on the boat—SANTANA—and explain that this was Bogey's own boat. Wrong! That dinky little putt-putt boat is not the real *Santana*. The real *Santana* was a majestic yacht.

In 1946 Bogart fulfilled his lifelong ambition to own a racing yacht and bought the *Santana* for $55,000. Named after the Native American "devil wind,"—the hot desert winds that blow onto the Pacific—the yawl was fifty-five feet long, weighed sixteen tons, and had an eighty-five-horsepower engine. The cabin was made of Honduran mahogany, the decks of teak. Built in 1935 from an Olin-Stephens design by the Union Oil executive William Stewart, it had won several important races. In 1939 it was owned by a series of movie actors: it was sold first to George Brent, who transferred ownership to Ray Milland, who in turn sold it to Dick Powell, from whom Bogart bought it.

The *Santana* was tied up at Newport Beach, a yachtsmen's harbor some fifty-five miles southeast of Hollywood (and south of Long Beach on the coast). Bogie would drive down from Los Angeles after work on Friday night, with family and/or friends, sleep on the boat overnight, then spend the weekend on the water, often sailing over to Santa Catalina Island. When he had more time, he would circle Catalina for days, spending the nights in different coves, or go down the coast of Baja California.

Bogart had learned to sail as a teenager, on the lake at the family's upstate New York summer home. Bogart was passionate about it. Sailing represented freedom to him. As skipper of the *Santana* in a fair wind, he was in his element. Bogie frequently used the boat as a testing ground: If he didn't like someone, he would take him on the boat for a day's sail to find out why. His theory was that in the confinement of the *Santana*, a person's true character would become apparent, just as it would when a person was drunk.

Bogie's third wife, Mayo Methot, enjoyed sailing, but his fourth wife, Lauren Bacall, didn't really like it. Bogart spent forty-five weekends a year on the boat. He preferred the laid-back geniality on the *Santana* and the easy pleasures of boating life to the glamour of the film business. His relationships with his sailing comrades were affectionate and lasting.

According to director Richard Brooks, "He wanted to go away to his boat all the time. He loved that boat. He loved sailing and he got away from the gossip. You never talked about movies on his boat."

◆   ◆   ◆

Carl "Pete" Peterson was the *Santana*'s full-time caretaker and a highly regarded skipper. A retired fireman, he lived on the boat, and made sure its bar was always well-stocked. Bogart affectionately called him "Dumb-Bum" or "Squarehead."

◆   ◆   ◆

The only members of the Hollywood film crowd who went on the *Santana* regularly were actor **David Niven** (1909–1983) and his Swedish-born second wife Hjordis, who loved sailing as much as her husband did.

Niven was born in Scotland. He entered films as an extra, but his tremendous charm and appeal quickly brought him second leads and then starring roles. He won the 1958 Academy Award for Best Actor for his work in *Separate Tables*.

Bogart and Niven never worked together professionally. (At one point in the late 1940s, Warner Bros. owned the rights to *The African Queen* and intended to film it with Bette Davis and Niven.)

◆   ◆   ◆

Newspaper columnist **Joe Hyams** (b. 1923) and his son Jay, who was the same age as Bogart's son Stephen, occasionally went sailing with Bogie. Reported Hyams, "It was tacitly understood that since I was useless as a deckhand, my function was that of babysitter." When the Holmby Hills Rat

Pack was formally organized, in the spring of 1955, Bogie gave the details exclusively to Hyams, who announced it to the world in his syndicated column. Hyams published a quickie paperback bio, *Bogie*, in 1966, and then attempted a major work in *Bogart and Bacall: A Love Story* in 1975.

◆　　◆　　◆

George Roosevelt, nephew of the late president Franklin Delano Roosevelt, was a constant sailing companion. Bogart and the crew gave up a weekend of sailing to attend Roosevelt's wedding. They presented the groom with a life preserver from the *Santana*, signed by Bogart and the other shipmates, and inscribed, "Love and kisses to Mr. and Mrs. Roosevelt. Thanks for fucking up the weekend."

Hollywood Friends and Neighbors

Holmby Hills is a wealthy suburb of Los Angeles, set between Beverly Hills and Bel Air. The Bogarts bought a home there at 232 South Mapleton Drive in 1952. It was a large whitened-brick house of French colonial design, two stories, with fourteen rooms; there was a long tree-lined drive, and an acre of land behind it, with a four-car garage and two tennis courts.

Their neighbors were singer Judy Garland and her manager husband Sid Luft, actress Lana Turner and spouse Bob Topping, *Amos and Andy* actor Charles Correll, producer Walter Wanger and his actress wife Joan Bennett, songwriter Sammy Cahn, songwriter/performer Hoagy Carmichael, and TV host Art Linkletter. (And where do *you* live?)

Most of the Bogarts' circle were his old friends, people who had known him during his marriage (1938–45) to Mayo Methot. As he was twenty-five years older than Betty (as Lauren Bacall was known to her intimates) and had been in Hollywood for so many more years, it was only natural that she should acquire his friends as hers.

Among the Bogarts' closest friends in the film colony were Mel and Mary Baker (his agent), actor Raymond Massey and his wife Dorothy, Betty and John Reinhardt, and Patrick O'Moore and his wife Zelda O'Neil.

By and large, Bogie's best friends were writers like Louis Bromfield, Nunnally Johnson, Harry Kurnitz, Robert and Nathaniel Benchley, Noël Coward, Mark Hellinger, and John Huston.

The Bogarts had a kind of endless open home. There was a light above the front door of the home on South Mapleton Drive visible from the street. When it was switched on, it meant they were staying up, drinking, and not averse to having friends join them. Sometimes, for five nights in a row, they'd have a crowd in.

Humphrey Bogart's favorite bars were the Cock 'n Bull pub on Sunset Boulevard in West Hollywood; the Château Marmont Hotel, also on Sunset in West Hollywood; the restaurant of Dave Chasen on Beverly Boulevard in Beverly Hills; and the fancy dining establishment of Mike Romanoff on Rodeo Drive in Beverly Hills. Romanoff's became Bogart's main hangout: the second booth from the left corner as you entered the restaurant—that was Bogie's; no one else could sit there.

One of Hollywood's more colorful characters, **"Prince" Mike Romanoff** (1890–1972) claimed to be of Russian aristocracy, but was actually born in Lithuania and grew up in Brooklyn orphanages. He became an American citizen in 1958. Said Bogart, "I always had a genuine fondness for Romanoff. In a community of phonies, he was probably the biggest, and certainly the most honest, phony of them all. This was a definite mark of distinction."

Romanoff came up with one of the most-quoted summations of Bogart: "He's a first-class person with an obsessive compulsion to behave like a second-class person."

When not working, Bogart would go regularly to Romanoff's for lunch, usually ham and eggs, and then play a game of chess with Mike. (The restaurant at the beginning of In a Lonely Place is based on Romanoff's, with the owner appearing as himself.) Mike Romanoff was a pallbearer at Bogart's funeral in 1957.

There's an in-joke in Battle Circus, in the mess tent set up for the mobile-hospital unit in Korea. Bogart pauses in front of a sign that reads, "This Mess Recommended by Romanoff."

◆   ◆   ◆

Superstar **Frank Sinatra** (1915–1998) had many careers, lived many lives. Born in Hoboken, New Jersey, he first came to national prominence in the late 1930s and early 1940s as "The Voice," the skinny idol of screaming bobby-soxers. He made bright, candy-colored musicals for MGM (among them Anchors Aweigh, 1945; Take Me Out to the Ball Game, 1949; On the Town, 1949). His records sold in the millions.

After his career stalled in the early 1950s, he begged to be cast in the film of *From Here to Eternity* (1953), and won the Oscar for Best Supporting Actor for his role as Maggio. He was on top from then on out.

Bogart and Sinatra probably first met in 1947, when Hollywood stars were organizing to protest the witch-hunting tactics of the House Un-American Activities Committee. When Bogart first became a father, in 1949, to son Stephen, Frank Sinatra was master of ceremonies at the celebration party at Chasen's restaurant.

Sinatra became a regular at the Bogarts' parties. Bogie supposedly was flattered that the younger man idolized him, but also perhaps was suspicious of Sinatra's close attention to Lauren Bacall. When Bogart died, Sinatra took over his Rat Pack, and his wife. Bacall says she sought comfort in Sinatra after Bogie's death, and the friendship developed into a romance. Bacall and Sinatra might have married, but he stopped seeing her after Hollywood gossip columns got wind of the affair.

Humphrey Bogart described Frank Sinatra for Ezra Goodman as "a kind of Don Quixote, tilting at windmills, fighting people who don't wanna fight. He's a cop hater. If he doesn't know who you are and you ask him a question, he thinks you're a cop. Sinatra is terribly funny. He's just amusing, because he's a skinny little bastard and his bones kind of rattle together" (*The Fifty-Year Decline and Fall of Hollywood*; New York: Simon and Schuster, 1961).

•   •   •

Spencer Tracy (1900–1967) was acting on Broadway in the 1920s, the same time Bogart was, and both actors were summoned by Hollywood in 1930. Tracy's first film was *Up the River* (Fox, 1930), which was Bogart's second. They were friends from this time on. It was Spencer Tracy who coined the nickname "Bogie."

Bogart and Spencer Tracy had other similarities. Both were heavy drinkers. Both were studio troublemakers with their demands for better pay, better roles. Both actors had also been trapped in unhappy marriages: Bogart with his battling third wife, Mayo Methot, from 1938 to 1945, when she finally agreed to a divorce and the actor married Lauren Bacall. Tracy, on the other hand, was a devout Catholic: he married former stage actress Louise Treadwell in 1923 and never divorced her, although they lived apart for many years. Tracy had a scandalous affair in the early 1930s with actress Loretta Young, and began a relationship with costar Katharine Hepburn in the early 1940s that lasted until his death.

Tracy was the first actor to win back-to-back Oscars: for *Captains Courageous* (1937) and *Boys Town* (1938). He also received Oscar nominations for seven other films.

The two friends never acted together again, but came close in 1955, when William Wyler was prepping *The Desperate Hours* for Paramount Pictures. The director wanted Bogart for the villain, and Spencer Tracy for the father of the family held hostage. Both actors agreed . . . but the teaming never happened, as neither would take second billing; each said, "My name always goes first." A plan was proposed whereby half of the film's advertising would feature Bogart first, and the other half would list Tracy first. But there was no compromise. Fredric March eventually played the father.

Through Tracy, Bogart met and became friends with actress Katharine Hepburn, who later costarred with him in *The African Queen*. When Bogart won his Best Actor Oscar for that film, he said it never would have happened if he hadn't had the great Katharine to act with.

During Bogart's last days, in 1956, there was a steady stream of friends and well-wishers. Spencer Tracy and Katharine Hepburn came after the others had left, and stayed longer. On Saturday evening, January 12, the visitors got up to leave, saying good night, when Bogie put his hand over his friend's and said, "Good-bye, Spence." On Sunday morning, Humphrey Bogart went into a coma, and died on Monday morning.

Lauren Bacall asked Spencer Tracy to deliver the eulogy at Bogie's funeral, but his old friend was too distraught.

◆   ◆   ◆

Bogart met **Clifton Webb** (1891–1966) when they appeared in the 1923 Broadway play *Meet the Wife*. Webb starred, and Bogart had a brief part, but they immediately liked each other, and socialized over a lifetime. A major star on the New York and London stages, Webb had appeared in a few silent films but began a new career after returning to the screen in the 1944 film *Laura*, for which he won an Academy Award nomination for Best Supporting Actor. He also starred in a series of films as the pompous babysitter Mr. Belvedere: *Sitting Pretty* (1948), *Mr. Belvedere Goes to College* (1949), and *Mr. Belvedere Rings the Bell* (1951)—all for Twentieth Century–Fox.

Ephraim Katz's handy reference, *The Film Encyclopedia* (New York: HarperCollins; third edition, 1998), has a wonderful lineup of euphemisms for Clifton Webb: "fastidious and elegant," "waspish, acidulous, pedantic"— but *we* know what they mean, don't we?

Bogart and Clifton Webb were known to liven up parties by suddenly attacking each other, rolling around on the floor, knocking over furniture, shocking guests who weren't in on the joke—that the two men were mocking society's stereotypes of tough-guys and faggots.

In 1955 *Life* magazine published a photo of Humphrey Bogart dancing with Clifton Webb and Marilyn Monroe, à trois, at Romanoff's.

◆   ◆   ◆

Other regulars at the Bogarts' included director Nicholas Ray (1911–1979) and his actress wife Gloria Grahame (1924–1981); lyricist Ira Gershwin (1896–1983), whose wife Lee had been a teenage girlfriend of Bogart's; and actress Joan Bennett (1910–1990) and her producer husband Walter Wanger (1894–1968) for whom Bogart had made *Stand-In* (United Artists, 1937). Joan Bennett and Walter Wanger starred in a notorious off-screen scandal in 1951, when Wanger shot his wife's lover, agent Jennings Lang, in the groin. Wanger was jailed for several months, but Joan Bennett was blackballed by the movie industry. When Bogart contracted to star in Paramount's *We're No Angels*, he refused to make the film without Joan Bennett. The studio relented. Said Lauren Bacall: "Our house was a happy one and friends were always glad to be in it."

The Holmby Hills Rat Pack

Biographer Ezra Goodman described Humphrey Bogart's Holmby Hills Rat Pack as "an aggregation of fun-loving profiles with Dead End Kid inclinations. When things got a little dull in Hollywood, the Holmby Hills Rat Pack could be counted upon to provide some local color" (*Bogey*, 1965).

"The Rat Pack" began in the spring of 1955 when a group of friends, neighbors, and drinking buddies chartered a plane to Las Vegas for Noël Coward's club opening at the Desert Inn. This was the gang: Bogie and Betty, restaurateur Mike Romanoff and wife Gloria, actor David Niven and wife Hjordis, agent Irving "Swifty" Lazar and actress Martha Hyer, songwriter Jimmy Van Heusen and actress Angie Dickinson, agent Charles K. Feldman and model Capucine, writer George Axelrod and wife, screenwriter Charles Lederer, singer Judy Garland and husband Sid Luft.

At one point, after four days of serious partying, Lauren Bacall looked around at the group of debauched revelers and remarked, historically, "You look like a goddamn rat pack!"

The name stuck. At a dinner back in Beverly Hills, the group unofficially elected officials for the group. Frank Sinatra was named president of the rats. Judy Garland was vice president. Bacall was den mother. Bogart was the rat in charge of public relations. Swifty Lazar was the group's treasurer. Bogie gave newspaper columnist friend Joe Hyams permission to write it up, and soon everyone knew about the most exclusive club in the world, and would have killed to be part of it.

Bogart explained it to Ezra Goodman: "What is a rat? We have no constitution, charter or by-laws yet, but we know a rat when we see one. There are very few rats in this town. David Niven is a rat. Jimmy Van Heusen is a rat. Mike Romanoff is a rat—a Russian rat.

"Rats are extremely well behaved. We elected Noël Coward an honorary rat. He's our representative in Jamaica.

"You might say that rats are for staying up late and drinking lots of booze. We're against squares and being bored and for lots of fun and being real rats, which very few people are, but if you're a real rat, boy!

"A coat of arms was drawn up for the Rat Pack. There's a lamp representing late nights and a bottle and glass representing convivial imbibing. In one corner there's a dagger in a hand and in another a woman's breast floating on a cloud. There's a slogan underneath: 'Never rat on a rat.' We're also going to make up a pin showing an angry rat with a human arm in its mouth.

"One of our first principles is that we don't care who likes us as long as we like each other. We like each other very much."

On Bogart's death in early 1957, the Rat Pack was reborn into something *very* different. It was whittled down to just five members: Frank Sinatra, singer Dean Martin, too-much performer Sammy Davis Jr., actor Peter Lawford, and comic Joey Bishop, and sometimes actress Shirley MacLaine hung out with them. Perhaps it was such a small gathering because no one else could keep up with the manic energy of this group.

Las Vegas become the base of operations, with the group appearing in a high-spirited club act. The fun spilled over into movies, with projects such as *Ocean's Eleven* (1960), *Sergeants Three* (1962), *4 for Texas* (1963) (with the *real* Three Stooges thrown in for good measure), and *Robin and the Seven Hoods* (1964). All of these entries were apparently chosen to showcase as many of the group and their friends as possible, and to keep the party going on someone else's funds.

In August 1998, there was an HBO movie, *The Rat Pack*, with Ray Liotta playing Sinatra, Joe Mantegna as Dean Martin, Don Cheadle as Sammy Davis Jr., Angus Macfadyen as Peter Lawford, and Bobby Slayton as Joey Bishop. Critical opinion was, shall we say, mixed.

Then, the Rat Pack got the A&E cable channel's full *Biography* treatment in 1999, with a four-hour presentation that threw in gangsters and politicians and the kitchen sink. The narration claimed that the "Rat Pack" label had been coined by the media, and then, five minutes later, said that it had been coined by movie-studio heads angry with the stars' demands.

One gets the feeling that Humphrey Bogart would not have approved of what happened to his little Rat Pack.

Chapter 7

"Did You Hear What Bogie Said?"

A major contributing factor to the Bogart legend is that he always liked to hang out with writers—playwrights, novelists, screenwriters, journalists—who could be counted on to make note of what he said. And Bogart was always good for a quote, a comment, an opinion.

ON BEING HARD-BOILED:

"Physically, I'm not tough. I may think tough. I would say I'm kinda tough and calloused inside. I could use a foot more in height and fifty more pounds and fifteen years off my age and then God help all you bastards."

ON CHIVALRY:

"I'd never hit a lady—they're too dangerous."

ON LATE-NIGHT DRINKING:

Asked if he was drunk, after a nightclub brawl: "Isn't everybody at three A.M.?"

ON SOBRIETY:

Reporter: "Have you ever been on the wagon?"

Bogie: "Just once—and it was the most miserable afternoon of my life."

ON WORKING WITH "METHOD" ACTORS:

"Don't ever play an eating scene with them, because they spit all over you."

ON VISITING SALT LAKE CITY:

"The whole city is sober—the whole state, even. Can you imagine that? Surrounded by sober!"

ON SUCCESS:

"The only reason to have enough money is to tell any s.o.b. in the world to go f*** himself."

(Some sources quote this as, "to go to hell.")

ON HIS LOOKS:

"I'm not good-looking. I used to be, but not anymore. Not like Robert Taylor. What I have got is I have character in my face. It's taken an awful lot of late nights and drinking to put it there. When I go to work in a picture, I say: 'Don't take the lines out of my face. Leave them there.'"

ON MARRIAGE:

"I sometimes wonder if the fucking you get is worth the fucking you *get*."

(Note: This profound and wonderful line has also been attributed to actress Constance Bennett, as said to movie mogul Darryl F. Zanuck in reference to her boyfriend actor Gilbert Roland.)

ON WORKING AS A STAGE MANAGER:

"It is a stage manager's job to bring up the curtain, see that the shows goes on schedule, and throw lines to actors afflicted with loss of memory. A good stage manager must be at the theater all the time. There are a few good ones. I was pretty good. I was there at most performances and threw lines to actors like a man throws fish to seals. Once I threw the entire script at an actor and he resented it."

ON BALDNESS:

"It's not the hair on your head. It's the hair on your chest that counts."

ON HOW TO SUCCEED IN HOLLYWOOD:

"Whatever it is, be against it."

ON HIS EARLY CAREER AS A VILLAIN:

"I played more scenes writhing around on the floor than I did standing up!"

and:

"Do you realize you're looking at an actor who's made more lousy pictures than any other in history?"

ON THE YOUNG ACTORS OF THE 1950S:

"I defend my right to cut a caper if I feel like it—a man has the right to get rotten drunk and raise some trouble. The trouble with these young male stars today is that they have no color, no imagination."

ON UGLY ACTORS:

"You know, I think I owe my career to Clark Gable. He was the pioneer. Once it was found that women raved over him—big ears and all—the way was cleared for all us ugly mugs, like [James] Cagney and [Spencer] Tracy, and Edward G. [Robinson] to pour in and start a new fashion."

TO HEAVYWEIGHT COMIC JACKIE GLEASON:

"You look like the man who came to dinner and ate the guests."

On Religion (to Son Stephen):

"Listen, kid, there are twelve commandments. . . ."

On Raising Children:

"What do you do with a kid? They don't drink."

On Being Sexy:

"Of course I did nothing in *Casablanca* that I hadn't done in twenty movies before that, and suddenly they discover I'm sexy. Anytime that Ingrid Bergman looks at a man, he has sex appeal."

On the Secret of Life:

"The whole world is about three drinks behind."

On Awards for Acting:

"The only true test would be to have every actor play Hamlet and decide who is best."

On Natural Charm (After Being Barred from New York's Classy Stork Club for Brawling):

"I can probably get barred from Central Park and Ebbets Field. As a matter of fact, the only places I'm really socially acceptable at are '21' [nightclub] and Grand Central [train station]. Put it down to natural charm. I'm loaded with it. And experience, too. It takes a long time to develop a repulsive character like mine. You don't get to be the Boris Karloff of the supper clubs overnight. You've got to work at it."

On Women and Marriage:

"I'm not at ease with women, really. I must obviously like certain women. I've certainly married enough of them. But I don't like collective women with a mission or a purpose. I feel a little like [humorist James] Thurber does about women: we've lost the war, they've got us. I feel we never should have set them free. They should still be in chains and fettered to the home where they belong."

On Sailing:

"Unless you really understand the water, and understand the reason for being on it . . . and understand the love of sailing, and the feeling of quietness and solitude . . . you don't really belong on a boat anyway. I think Hemingway said one time that the sea is the last free place on earth."

On Acting:

"I was born to be indolent and this was the softest of rackets."

and:

"I would have liked to be anything but an actor. It's such a stupid thing to be."

On Acting, Being a Heavy [the Bad Guy]:

"When the heavy, full of crime and bitterness, grabs his wounds and talks about death, the audience is his and his alone."

On Typecasting:

"It makes stars out of people."

On Becoming a Star:

"Before I became a star, Charlie Einfeld [then head of Warner Bros.' publicity and advertising] said to me: 'I think you have sex appeal. We will make you a star. We will run lots of pictures of you in the press locally,' and [studio head] Jack Warner will say: 'Bogart is getting lots of publicity' and forget that the publicity department is doing it and say, 'We will do something about it.' And that's how it happened that I became a star."

ON HAPPINESS:

"I expected a lot more from me. And I'm never going to get it."

ON ACTING NUTTY IN THE 1954 MOVIE THE CAINE MUTINY:

"It was easy. I'm nuts, you know."

ON ACTING ON LIVE TELEVISION:

"Suppose I had laryngitis, suppose I just wasn't feeling up to par. I turn in a bad job and the critics rap me. I just don't like the idea of a one-shot. As for a regular weekly series, I'd sooner dig ditches."

ON HIS SCREEN VICTIMS:

"My best shot was Leslie Howard in *The Petrified Forest*. I got him with one bullet, and he died quick. The others have been slow bleeders and most of the time they lived long enough to kill me."

ON PLAYING FRED C. DOBBS IN THE TREASURE OF THE SIERRA MADRE:

"Wait till you see me in my next picture—I play the worst shit you ever saw!"

ON THE PROBLEM WITH FRIENDS:

"They're always dropping in."

Chapter 8

The Ultimate Bogart Trivia Quiz

Part Two

26. If you're "bogarting" a marijuana joint, you should
    a. be arrested.
    b. be more considerate.
    c. spend more time in the sun.

27. Bogart didn't become a father in real life until 1949, at age forty-nine. He had children on-screen much earlier. Can you name the pictures in which Bogart plays a father?

28. Bogart's screen character escapes from Devil's Island in *Passage to Marseille* (Warner Bros., 1944) and *We're No Angels* (Paramount, 1955). Which movie ends with him *headed* for Devil's Island?

29. Bogart plays a character loosely based on billionaire aviator Howard Hughes (1905–1976) in which film?

30. "Live fast, die young, and leave a good-looking corpse!" became one of the popular bylaws/philosophies of the 1950s. Which Bogart movie is it from?

31. Lauren Bacall once gave her husband a gold memento for a Christmas present . . . and slipped it into his pocket before he was cremated, in 1957. What was this item, and what was the inscription on it?

32. Name two Bogart movies with characters based on or inspired by infamous gangster Lucky Luciano (1897–1962).

33. Name this early Bogart film: Bogie is a kidnapper who gets caught because his address is written in lipstick on the nightgown of a dead woman.

34. Which actress appeared in the most Bogart pictures?

35. Okay, but most of those Bette Davis and Ann Sheridan pictures with Bogart weren't really for costarring roles. What actress appeared in the most costarring roles?

36. Humphrey Bogart and Spencer Tracy were best of friends . . . but both refused to costar in *The Desperate Hours* (Paramount, 1955). Why?

37. Lena Horne was considered for what part in which Bogart screen venture?

38. Much of the action of *Casablanca* (Warner Bros., 1942) takes place in Rick's Café Americain. Which Bogie movie was set in the Black Mesa Bar-B-Q?

39. What is the name of the popular 1951–52 radio series in which Bogie and Bacall appeared?

40. What two actors played the role of Humphrey Bogart in Woody Allen's comedy *Play It Again, Sam*?

41. Off-camera, Bogie wore a gold ring with two rubies and a diamond. Where did it come from?

42. A certain Hollywood movie project was planned to star Boris Karloff, but his work schedule was too crowded. At that point, Bela Lugosi was offered the part, but he too was unavailable. So they gave it to . . . Humphrey Bogart! What's the flick?

43. Bogart was married four times, each time to an actress. Which wedding ceremony was performed in sign language?

44. What contribution did Herman Hupfeld make to the mythology of Humphrey Bogart?

45. In his long movie career, Humphrey Bogart came up against many tough-guys . . . and a number of tough women characters! Can you identify these lethal ladies, and the actresses who portrayed them?
    a. Lana Carlsen
    b. Brigid O'Shaughnessy
    c. Coral Chandler
    d. Madge Rapf

46. Bogart should have won the Academy Award for Best Actor of 1943, for *Casablanca*, don't you agree? Who did win?

47. Bogart, the symbol of rugged American individualism and heroism, played foreigners in which films?

48. The image of death seen as a parachute drifting into a black void is from which Bogart movie?

49. Which western star of the 1940s reportedly copied his all-black screen outfit from the one worn by Bogart in *The Oklahoma Kid* (Warner Bros., 1939)?

50. Name the actress who appeared opposite Bogie in one of his most important movies—then refused to work with him again.

Answers on page 267

Part III

The Actor

Chapter 9

Humphrey Bogart in the Theater

With the major exception of *The Petrified Forest* (1935), the last play in which he ever appeared on Broadway, Humphrey Bogart made little impact as a stage actor. Much of his theatrical career was lumped under the umbrella grouping of, "Others in the cast were . . ."

He went into the theater, and he became an actor—by default.

When Humphrey was growing up, William A. Brady Jr. (1863–1950) was a famous neighbor of the Bogart family and a patient of Dr. Bogart's. Brady was one of the most successful producers on Broadway. He also had his own film studio in Fort Lee, New Jersey, and both wife Grace George and daughter Alice Brady were prominent actresses. Bogart and Brady Jr. hung out together, going to movies and plays.

On his discharge from the U.S. Navy, in 1919, young Humphrey drifted from one job to another, before becoming William A. Brady's office boy in New York City. Later, in 1920, Bogart was promoted to production manager for Brady's film studio in New Jersey. Shortly thereafter, he was hired as road-company manager for the touring production of Grace George's new hit, *The Ruined Lady*.

On the road for six months, Bogart kept the show on schedule, prompted the actors, tracked down lost luggage, collected tickets, and monitored the ticket receipts. Supposedly, he made disparaging remarks about the easy life of actors and was challenged to try it for himself. When it came time for Bogart to deliver his one line before an audience, he either froze or wet his pants, depending on who's telling the story.

But the die was cast: Humphrey Bogart became an actor. "I was born to be indolent," he said, "and this was the softest of rackets." He worked rather steadily during the next fourteen years (1922–35), mainly playing upper-class young men in largely frivolous comedies. During this time span, he was spotted by a Hollywood scout, taken to California where he made a handful of insignificant movies for Fox Pictures in the early 1930s, and then returned to New York City and employment on the stage. Then he did it again a few years later—he was spotted by another Hollywood scout, made a handful of mediocre movies at Warner Bros., and then returned again to Broadway.

Bogart was recommended for the Broadway role of the football jock in *The Petrified Forest* (1935), but producer Arthur Hopkins had a hunch he'd be better as the ruthless gangster Duke Mantee. He was not just better, he was sensational: audiences gasped at Bogart's stage entrance. This was *not* the Humphrey Bogart they remembered.

The actor went to Hollywood for a third time, for the filming of *The Petrified Forest* (Warner Bros., 1936), and this time he stayed for good.

Here is Humphrey Bogart's career on the stage.

The Ruined Lady, by Frances Nordstrom. Touring production, 1920.

Cast: Grace George (Mrs. William A. Brady).

A comedy about a woman who allows her engagement to the man she adores to run on from year to year until he begins to call her "old girl" and she realizes it's time to get married. The play opened on Broadway in January 1920, then toured for six months. Humphrey Bogart was stage manager for the tour, and may have stepped in once when the juvenile lead became ill.

> "I played lots of juveniles on the stage. A juvenile is simply a young man who is about to marry the ingenue. The juvenile was probably used sometimes by the playwright to take up a little time onstage while the leading players changed costumes or the scene was shifted."
>
> —as told to Ezra Goodman

Drifting, a melodrama by John Colton and Daisy H. Andrews. Playhouse Theatre, New York City. Producer, William A. Brady. Director, John Cromwell.

Opened January 2, 1922; 63 performances.

Cast: Alice Brady, H. Mortimer White, Robert Warwick, Lumsden Hare, Humphrey Bogart (listed as H. D. Bogart, as *Ernie Crockett*.)

A stern father kicks his daughter out for a schoolgirl prank. She becomes the glamorous Cassie Cook of the Yellow Seas. She meets a fellow drifter and they have many romantic adventures.

Bogart had a walk-on as a Japanese butler offering a tray of cocktails. At the tryout in Brooklyn, he is said to have dropped the tray. Bogart remembered it as happening on opening night.

Drifting was filmed by Universal as *Shanghai Lady* (1929), starring Mary Boland and James Murray.

Swifty, a comedy-drama by John Peter Toohey and Walter C. Percival. Playhouse Theatre, New York City. Producer, William A. Brady. Director, John Cromwell.

Opened October 16, 1922, and "closed soon after it opened."

Cast: Hale Hamilton, Frances Howard, Humphrey Bogart (*Tom Proctor*), William Holden, Robert Ayrton, Margaret Mosier.

Bogart plays an aristocrat who seduces an innocent country girl and refuses to marry her. The girl's brother retaliates by running off with Proctor's girlfriend.

Years later, Bogart still loved to quote from theater critic Alexander Woollcott's review in the *New York Herald* (October 17, 1922): "The young man . . . was what is usually and mercifully described as inadequate."

Meet the Wife, a comedy by Lynn Starling. Klaw Theatre, New York City. Producers, Rosalie Stewart and Bert French. Staged by Bert French.

Opened November 26, 1923; 232 performances.

Cast: Mary Boland, Clifton Webb, Ernest Lawford, Charles Dalton, Eleanor Griffith, Humphrey Bogart (*Gregory Brown*), Patricia Calvert, Charles Bloomer.

This drawing-room frivolity concerns a busybody woman who wins the honor of entertaining a great English novelist in her home . . . and he turns out to be her absconding first husband.

The play was a showcase for the popular Mary Boland, who was well received. Bogart did get mentioned: The *New York World* (November 27, 1923) described his role as "a handsome and nicely mannered reporter, which is refreshing."

Nerves, a war drama by John Farrar and Stephen Vincent Benet. Comedy Theatre, New York City. Producer, William A. Brady. Director, William A. Brady Jr.

Opened September 1, 1924; 16 performances.

Cast: Winifred Lenihan, Kenneth MacKenna, Paul Kelly, Humphrey Bogart (*Bob Thatch*), Mary Phillips, Walter Baldwin.

The story of three young men who meet by chance, go off to the war in France, then meet again and realize how the war has changed their lives. *Nerves* had the misfortune to open the night after *What Price Glory?*—a new play by Maxwell Anderson and Laurence Stallings, which garnered all the attention at that time and is hailed as a classic.

In his review, critic Alexander Woollcott made reference to his earlier condemnation of Bogart, in *Swifty* (1922), and said he'd now changed his mind, praising the actor's performance.

(Note: This was the first time Bogart and his future second wife, Mary Philips, were in a production together. They had met backstage during the run of *Meet the Wife*. Also, Mary's last name was spelled with two 'l's, both in the credits and the reviews, a choice she frequently used when performing onstage and in film.)

Hell's Bells!, a comedy by Barry Conners. Wallack's Theatre, New York City. Producer, Herman Gantvoort. Director, John Hayden.

Opened January 26, 1925; 120 performances.

Cast: Tom H. Walsh, Eddie Garvey, Shirley Booth, Olive May, Humphrey Bogart (*Jimmy Todhunter*), Camilla Crume, Virginia Howell, Violet Dunn.

Two lovable middle-aged adventurers pretend to be wealthy, and the plot evolves on how this charade changes the townspeople.

The reviews of the play were mixed, but Bogart garnered one kind word from Alan Dale of the *American*, when the critic stated that Bogart's part was "gorgeously acted."

Cradle Snatchers, a comedy by Russell Medcraft and Norma Mitchell. Music Box Theatre, New York City. Producer, Sam H. Harris. Director, Sam Forrest.

Opened September 7, 1925; 332 performances.

Cast: Mary Boland, Edna May Oliver, Margaret Dale, Humphrey Bogart (*Jose Vallejo*), Raymond Guion (who later became Gene Raymond), William Barton, Cecil Owen, Stanley Jessup.

This was a comedy of three middle-aged women who hire three college boys to pose as their lovers, to provoke their husbands' jealousy.

The *New York Times* (September 8, 1825) review grouped Humphrey Bogart with several other actors giving "pleasing performances." *Time* magazine saw the opening and was more impressed, saying "The three boys, especially Humphrey Bogart, contributed highly entertaining performances." And leading Chicago critic Amy Leslie really flipped: "Humphrey Bogart created a furor as one of the hired lovers. He is young and as handsome as Valentino, as dexterous and elegant in comedy as E. H. Sothern, and as graceful as any of our best romantic actors."

Cradle Snatchers was filmed in 1927 by Fox, with Louise Fazenda, Ethel Wales, and Dorothy Phillips as the ladies on a lark. Fox remade it two years later as a "musical-talkie" and renamed it *Why Leave Home?* It starred Sue Carol, Nick Stuart, Dixie Lee, Richard Keene, Jean Bary, Walter Catlett, and Ilka Chase.

In 1941, siblings Herbert and Dorothy Fields wrote the libretto for a musical adaptation of *Cradle Snatchers*, with music and lyrics by Cole Porter. It was a big hit on Broadway as *Let's Face It* with Danny Kaye and Eve Arden. Paramount Pictures bought the rights for a 1943 movie version, teaming their top comics, Bob Hope and Betty Hutton, with Eve Arden, ZaSu Pitts, and Phyllis Povah as the three neglected wives.

In 1954, *The Colgate Comedy Hour* televised a one-hour version of *Let's Face It,* with Bert Lahr (in drag), Vivian Blaine, Gene Nelson, Betty Furness, Robert Strauss, Gloria Jean, Pat Horne, James Gleason, and Virginia Gibson.

Saturday's Children, a comedy by Maxwell Anderson. Booth Theatre, New York City. Produced by the Actors Theatre, Inc. Director, Guthrie McClintic.

Opened January 26, 1927; 310 performances.

Cast: Ruth Hammond, Richard Barbee, Ruth Gordon, Humphrey Bogart (as *Rims O'Neil*, replacing the ailing actor Roger Pryor), Frederick Perry.

In this coy, sentimental entry, a woman traps a man into marriage, and the plot line concerns how the two finally mature into a happily married couple.

Saturday's Children was filmed by First National in 1929, starring Corinne Griffith and Grant Withers. In 1934, First National remade the story as *Maybe It's Love*, with Gloria Stuart and Ross Alexander. Warner Bros. remade it yet again, under its original title, in 1940, this time with Anne Shirley and John Garfield.

There were three television adaptations of *Saturday's Children*: *Lux Video Theatre* (October 2, 1950) with Joan Caulfield and John Ericson; *Celanese Theatre* (March 10, 1952) with Shirley Standlee and Mickey Rooney; and *Breck Golden Showcase* (February 25, 1962) with Inger Stevens and Cliff Robertson.

Baby Mine, comedy by Margaret Mayo. 46th Street Theater, New York City. Producer, John Turek. Staged by Bert French.

Opened June 9, 1927; 12 performances.

Cast: Roscoe "Fatty" Arbuckle, Lee Patrick, Humphrey Bogart (*Alfred Hardy*), W. J. Paul, W. J. Brady.

A revival of a 1910 farce, in which a woman pretends to be pregnant, then must "borrow" a baby. This was one of many futile attempts by silent-movie comic Fatty Arbuckle to get back into the public's good graces after being acquitted of manslaughter charges.

"He [Humphrey Bogart] played throughout with what appeared to be obvious reserve and showed a tendency to act not a few of his scenes as if he were facing a motion picture camera—but on the whole his may be set down as a fairly satisfactory performance. And that is considerably more than can be said for some of the other participants" (*New York Times*, June 10, 1927).

(Note: Lee Patrick would play Effie, secretary to private investigator Sam Spade [Humphrey Bogart] in the 1941 Warner Bros. movie *The Maltese Falcon*. Lee Patrick also appears in the 1975 feature *The Black Bird*, a limp takeoff of *The Maltese Falcon*. In it, George Segal played Sam Spade Jr.)

The Skyrocket, a comedy by Mark Reed. Lyceum Theatre, New York City. Producers, Gilbert Miller and Guthrie McClintic. Director, Guthrie McClintic.

Opened January 11, 1929; 11 performances.

Cast: Mary Phillips, Humphrey Bogart (*Vic Ewing*), J. C. Nugent, Howard Freeman, Ian Wolfe, Dorothie Bigelow, Clara Blandick.

Bogart and real-life wife Phillips are husband and wife in this comedy-drama, about a poor but happy couple who become miserable when they strike it rich. In the end they lose their wealth but find each other.

"Humphrey Bogart continues both to convince you and make you like him . . . and Mary Phillips gives a straightforward, attractive performance" (*New York Times*, January 12, 1929).

It's a Wise Child, a comedy by Laurence E. Johnson. Belasco Theatre, New York City. Producer and director, David Belasco.

Opened August 6, 1929; 378 performances.

Cast: Mildred McCoy, Humphrey Bogart (*Roger Baldwin*), Harlan Briggs, Minor Watson, Helen Lowell, Sidney Toler, Porter Hall, Olga Krolow.

A young woman talks her way out of an unwelcome engagement by pretending to be pregnant, and then must face the complications that follow. Bogart was a transitional beau, "a foolish kid afraid of losing his job."

It's a Wise Child was bought by MGM in 1931; the movie starred Marion Davies, Sidney Blackmer, James Gleason, and Lester Vail.

After All, a comedy by John Van Druten. Booth Theatre, New York City. Producer, Dwight Deere Wiman. Director, Auriol Lee.

Opened December 3, 1931; 20 performances.

Cast: Edmund George, Margaret Perry, Helen Haye [a British actress, not to be confused with our own Helen Hayes], Walter Kingsford, Humphrey Bogart (*Duff Wilson*).

An English couple spend their declining years worrying about the happiness of their children, who seem to be blundering into unhappy relationships. The son, played by Bogart, is an architect married to an invalid, and is having a secret affair.

After All was filmed by MGM as *New Morals for Old* (1932), with Robert Young, Myrna Loy, and Margaret Perry.

The Mad Hopes, by Romney Brent. Belasco Theatre, Los Angeles, California.

Opened May 28, 1932; 12 performances.

Cast: Billie Burke, Rex O'Malley, Peg Entwistle, Humphrey Bogart.

A comedy of giddy goings-on. In a role written for her, Billie Burke stars as a vague, charming, and irresponsible mother. Despite her ineptitude, she manages to solve all her problems and those of her children. Bogart is the suitor of the woman's daughter.

"Considerable work will be done on the piece before its New York premiere," reported the *New York Times* (May 29, 1932).

Billie Burke gives up on the play, which later opens on Broadway with Violet Kemble Cooper starring. It lasts for twelve performances.

I Loved You Wednesday, a comedy-drama by Molly Ricardel and William Du Bois. Harris Theatre, New York City. Producer, Crosby Gaige. Director, Worthington Miner.

Opened October 11, 1932; 63 performances.

Cast: Frances Fuller, Humphrey Bogart (*Randall Williams*), Rose Hobart, Jane Seymour, Henry O'Neill, Henry Bergman.

This rueful romance has Fuller and Bogart as a couple who have an affair in Paris, then marry others and go their separate ways. Years later, they plan a Paris reunion. Will they go through with it?

The *New York Times* (October 12, 1932) finds the play "surprisingly unimportant."

Stars-of-tomorrow Henry Fonda and Arlene Francis are among the extras, sitting in a bar.

Chrysalis, a melodrama by Rose Albert Porter. Martin Beck Theatre, New York City. Producers, Martin Beck, Lawrence Langner, and Theresa Helburn. Director, Theresa Helburn.

Opened November 15, 1932; 23 performances.

Cast: Margaret Sullavan, Osgood Perkins, Lily Cahill, Humphrey Bogart (*Don Ellis*), Elisha Cook Jr., June Walker, Elia Kazan, Mary Orr.

In *The Encyclopedia of the American Theatre 1900–1975* (Metuchen, NJ: A. S. Barnes, 1980), author Edwin J. Bronner dismisses *Chrysalis* as a "murky, ridiculously plotted melodrama . . . of a pampered debutante and her devil-may-care lover who learn the meaning of devotion from a small-time criminal and his adoring gun moll." Brooks Atkinson, of the *New York Times*, finds it "astonishingly insignificant . . . Mr. Bogart plays the wastrel in his usual style."

Elia Kazan, who would become a major stage and film director, is also the assistant stage manager. He later describes Bogart's character as a "patent-leather parlor sheik" (*Elia Kazan: A Life*; New York: Knopf, 1988). *Chrysalis* was turned by Paramount into the film *All of Me* (1934), with Fredric March, Miriam Hopkins, George Raft, and Helen Mack.

Our Wife, a comedy by Lyon Mearson and Lillian Day. Booth Theatre, New York City. Producers, Thomas J. R. Brotherton and Abe H. Halle. Director, Edward Clarke Lilley.

Opened March 2, 1933; 20 performances.

Cast: Rose Hobart, Humphrey Bogart (*Jerry Marvin*), June Walker, Edward Raquello.

This romantic comedy of runaway lovers has Hobart and Bogart living in Paris. His wife arrives from America in a final effort to recapture her husband.

The *New York Times* (March 3, 1933) likes the writing: "Especially when Humphrey Bogart speaks them, the flippant retorts bounce gaily over the footlights."

However: "Although it is not a vigorous plot . . . an animated performance might lift it into an evening's entertainment . . . [but] it is tamely acted and meagerly directed."

The Mask and the Face (*La Maschera e il Volto*), a satirical comedy by Luigi Chiarelli, adapted from the Italian by W. Somerset Maugham. Guild Theatre, New York City. Producers, The Theatre Guild. Director, Philip Moeller.

Opened May 8, 1933; 40 performances.

Cast: Stanley Ridges, Shirley Booth, Humphrey Bogart (*Luciano Spina*), Judith Anderson, Leo G. Carroll, Ernest Cossart.

Jealous Italians chase each other around a country estate on Lake Como in this popular comedy. A count claims he would kill his wife if she were unfaithful. She is, of course, and so he must do something about it. He secretly sends her away, then confesses to her murder—and is arrested. He's acquitted, but then a body identified as his wife's is found in the lake.

Invitation to a Murder, a murder mystery by Rufus King. Masque Theatre, New York City. Producer, Ben Stein. Director, A. H. Van Buren.

Opened May 17, 1934; 52 performances.

Cast: Gale Sondergaard, Walter Abel, Humphrey Bogart (*Horatio Channing*), Jane Seymour.

This melodrama of murder and mayhem among a rich, demonic family has the matriarch buried alive. And when she gets out—watch out! In the *New York Times* (May 18, 1934), Brooks Atkinson calls it "Overwrought . . . theatrically transparent . . . unskillfully written." Bogart was included in a list of actors who walked nervously through the playwright's valley of death.

This is Humphrey Bogart's first role as a villain. He later described it as "a gruesome little mishap." Bogart had no qualms about belittling many of his acting roles in hindsight.

Looking past the play's bad writing, Broadway producer Arthur Hopkins is impressed by Bogart's characterization; that he's able to project deep despair and anguish. Hopkins remembers this later when he is casting Robert E. Sherwood's new play, *The Petrified Forest*.

Invitation to a Murder was made into a Warner Bros. movie, *The Hidden Hand* (1942), and featured Craig Stevens, Julie Bishop, Cecil Cunningham, and Ruth Ford.

The Petrified Forest, a drama by Robert E. Sherwood. Broadhurst Theater, New York City. Producers, Gilbert Miller, Arthur Hopkins, and Leslie Howard. Director, Arthur Hopkins.

Opened January 7, 1935; 181 performances.

Cast: Leslie Howard, Peggy Conklin, Charles Dow Clarke, Frank Milan, Blanche Sweet, Humphrey Bogart (*Duke Mantee*), Walter Vonnegut, Tom Fadden, Ross Hertz, Robert Hudson, John Alexander.

A confrontation in a cafe at the edge of the desert between a disillusioned poet, a young girl with dreams, and a killer on the run, leads inevitably to tragedy.

An instant success, the *New York Times* (January 8, 1935) critic Brooks Atkinson calls it "a roaring Western melodrama," "an exuberant tale of poetic vagabonds and machine gun desperadoes," and "good, gusty excitement." "Humphrey Bogart does the best work of his career as the motorized guerrilla."

The Sperber/Lax biography (*Bogart*, 1997) says that playwright Sherwood suggested to producer Hopkins that Bogart would be good for the part of the football player. The Joe Hyams biography (*Bogart and Bacall*, 1975) has it that Sherwood wrote the part of the football player with Bogart in mind, to help the actor get his mind off his problems. Both versions agree that producer Hopkins felt Bogart would be better as Duke Mantee.

The Petrified Forest was first filmed by Warner Bros. in 1936, with Leslie Howard and Humphrey Bogart repeating their original stage roles. Warner Bros. remade it in 1945, with Nazis substituting for gangsters, as *Escape in the Desert*. Then there were television productions on the *Lucky Strike Theatre* (1950), *Celanese Theatre* (1952), and the *Producers' Showcase* (1955). (See chapter 10: The Films of Humphrey Bogart for further details.)

Before going to Hollywood (for the third time) for the filming of *The Petrified Forest*, Bogart spends the summer of 1935 appearing in a trio of stock productions at the Lakewood Theatre in Skowhegan, Maine.

Despite his widely hailed success on Broadway in *The Petrified Forest*, his roles in these three Skowhegan productions are insignificant supporting parts.

The Stag at Bay, by Beverly Nichols. Director, Melville Burke.

Cast: Moffat Johnston, Joanna Roos, Frank Green, Humphrey Bogart, Keenan Wynn.

A melodrama about the theft of a formula for poison gas and the pursuit of the thief from Detroit to Paris.

Ceiling Zero, by Frank Wead.

The advertising claims this to be the first play ever produced with life around a commercial airport as its theme. The leading roles are three war veterans. It was first produced on Broadway in 1935, with Osgood Perkins, John Litel, Nedda Harrigan, and Margaret Perry.

The author is a World War I naval aviator, whose life story later was dramatized in MGM's film, *The Wings of Eagles* (1957), with John Wayne as Wead.

Ceiling Zero was filmed by Warner Bros. in 1936, with James Cagney and Pat O'Brien; and then again in 1941, retitled *International Squadron* and starring Ronald Reagan.

Rain, by W. Somerset Maugham. Director, A. H. Van Buren.

Cast: Sally Rand, Raymond Bramley, Rose Winter, Frank Wilcox, Grant Mills, Humphrey Bogart.

Fan dancer Sally Rand "proved that her ambition to be a legitimate actress is not a mistaken one; that she has inherent dramatic ability," said the *New York Times* (August 27, 1935), which also mentioned Bogart in the supporting cast list.

Rain, the story of Sadie Thompson, was first seen on Broadway in 1922, with the legendary Jeanne Eagels scoring a remarkable success. Other players who have portrayed hard-boiled Sadie include Tallulah Bankhead (the 1935 Broadway revival), Gloria Swanson in United Artists' first film attempt (1928), and then Joan Crawford for United Artists' second go at the Maugham property (1932). For Columbia, Rita Hayworth took on the role (as *Miss Sadie Thompson*, 1953), and then June Havoc starred in the 1944 Broadway musical, *Sadie Thompson*.

As an actor on the Broadway stage, one critic said Bogart was "mercifuly described as inadequate." Another called him "handsome as Valentino."

COURTESY OF THE MUSEUM OF THE CITY OF NEW YORK/ARCHIVE PHOTOS

A late 1930s portrait of a stylish, smooth-shaven Bogart, barely hinting at the rumpled cynic that would later emerge. Compare this with the portrait on page 134.

COURTESY OF ARCHIVE PHOTOS

When forty-four-year-old Humphrey Bogart met nineteen-year-old Lauren Bacall, his costar in *To Have and Have Not* (1944), he promised, "We'll have a lot of fun together."

When Rick tells Ilsa, "We'll always have Paris," he's referring to this happier time in a flashback in *Casablanca* (1942), everyone's favorite movie.

Bogie in *King of the Underworld* (1939), in a pose to remind viewers of his breakthrough role in *The Petrified Forest*—in which he was sitting down for most of the movie.

"Oh, I'd kissed him, but I didn't know him," said Ingrid Bergman of her costar in *Casablanca* (1942). Until they actually shot the ending, no one was really sure who Ingrid was going to get on the plane with.

Bogie in his trademark uniform, ready for action: trench coat with collar up and sash always tied, never belted; hand in gun pocket; fedora with turned-down brim; and cigarette—always a cigarette.

Bogart and third wife Mayo Methot on their wedding day (August 30, 1938), which ended in a drunken fight. The "Battling Bogarts" did not spend their wedding night together.

COURTESY OF ARCHIVE PHOTOS

Bogart was usually described as short, wife/costar Lauren Bacall was often described as "towering" or "statuesque," but they were virtually the same height: five feet, eight-and-one-half inches.

COURTESY OF GLOBE PHOTOS

Bogie always said he was a leg man, which didn't stop him from looking at other feminine assets. This photo was taken at the premiere of *How to Marry a Millionaire* (1953), with the film's stars Lauren Bacall and Marilyn Monroe.

COURTESY OF DARLENE HAMMOND/ARCHIVE PHOTOS

Bogart and Bacall lead the protest against the House Committee on Un-American Activities witchhunt in Washington, D.C., in October 1947. Also in the group: June Havoc, Danny Kaye, Gene Kelly, Paul Henreid, Marsha Hunt, Richard Conte, Evelyn Keyes, and Geraldine Brooks.

COURTESY OF POPPERFOTO/ARCHIVE PHOTOS

In late 1955, near the end of his life, a domesticated Humphrey Bogart poses for a family portrait. He never wore his toupee off-screen.

Courtesy of Archive Photos

Bogart with writer/director John Huston: theirs is one of the most notable collaborations in film history. Bogie won the Best Actor Academy Award for Huston's *The African Queen* (1951).

Actor George Raft, who rejected the movie projects that made a star of Humphrey Bogart: *Dead End* (1937), *High Sierra* (1941), *The Maltese Falcon* (1941). There's speculation that Raft may have turned down the scripts because he didn't know how to read.

The children Bogie never lived to see grow up: Leslie (born 1952) and Stephen (born 1949), with mother, Lauren Bacall, at the July 31, 1997, dedication ceremony for the postage stamp honoring Humphrey Bogart.

Chapter 10

The Films of
Humphrey Bogart

(including the films he didn't make, the remakes and the sequels, foreign leading ladies, a quick quiz on nicknames, and other trivia and digressions)

An Annotated Directory to the Feature Films

Note: All films are black-and-white unless noted. Bogart did not make a color feature film until *The African Queen* (1951), only six years before his death.

A Devil with Women (Fox, 1930) 76 minutes.

Director, Irving Cummings; associate producer, George Middleton; screenplay, Dudley Nichols and Henry M. Johnson (based on the Clements Ripley novel *Dust and Sun*).

Cast: Victor McLaglen (*Jerry Maxton*); Mona Maris (*Rosita Fernandez*); Humphrey Bogart (*Tom Standish*); Luana Alcaniz (*Dolores*); Michael Vavitch (*Morloff*); Soledad Jiminez (*Jiminez*).

Tom Standish is a rich American playboy who tags along with tough soldier-of-fortune Jerry Maxton as they track down a notorious bandit in a Central American banana republic.

"Humphrey Bogart . . . makes his debut in talking pictures and gives an ingratiating performance. Mr. Bogart is both good-looking and intelligent" (*New York Times*, October 20, 1930).

Up the River (Fox, 1930) 92 minutes.

Director, John Ford; staged by William Collier Sr.; screenplay, Maurice Watkins.

Cast: Spencer Tracy (*St. Louis*); Claire Luce (*Judy*); Warren Hymer (*Dannemora Dan*); Humphrey Bogart (*Steve*); William Collier Sr. (*Pop*); Joan Marie Lawes (*Jean*); George MacFarlane (*Jessup*).

Steve is a respectable young man sent to prison for accidental manslaughter. He falls in love with Judy, who has been framed and sent to the prison. A blackmailer jeopardizes the lovers' happiness. Two prison friends, St. Louis and Dannemora Dan, escape from prison, thwart the blackmailer, then sneak back into prison.

Notes: This film was almost canceled when MGM's prestige prison film *Big House* (1930), starring Wallace Beery and Chester Morris, was released first. To compensate, John Ford and gag writer William Collier changed *Up the River* from a melodrama into a comedy.

During the making of this film, Bogart and Tracy began their long-lasting friendship.

Remake: *Up the River* (1938), with Preston Foster and Arthur Treacher as the cons who break in and out of prison, and crooner Tony Martin, who sings three songs, in the Bogart role.

Body and Soul (Fox, 1931) 83 minutes.

Director, Alfred Santell; screenplay, Jules Furthman (from the unproduced and unpublished play, *Squadrons*, by Elliott White Springs and A. E. Thomas, in turn based on the short story "Big Eyes and Little Mouth" by Springs).

Cast: Charles Farrell (*Mal Andrews*); Elissa Landi (*Carla*); Humphrey Bogart (*Jim Watson*); Myrna Loy (*Alice Lester*); Donald Dillaway (*Tap Johnson*); Craufurd Kent (*Major Burke*); Pat Somerset (*Major Knowles*); Ian MacLaren (*General Trafford-Jones*).

A World War I story of American flyers in France. Jim Watson is killed early, shot down while attacking a German observation balloon. His aviator friend Mal Andrews seeks out the dead man's girlfriend Carla, who may be a spy.

Note: Bogart and Farrell fought throughout the two weeks of filming. At the end, Bogart challenged the six-foot-six Farrell to a fight to settle their differences. However, Bogie backed down when Farrell mentioned that he had been a boxing champion in college. So, the two of them talked out their problems, took a vacation on Farrell's boat, and became good friends.

Bad Sister (Universal, 1931) 71 minutes.

Director, Hobart Henley; producer, Carl Laemmle Jr.; screenplay, Raymond L. Schrock and Tom Reed, with dialogue by Edwin H. Knopf (based on the Booth Tarkington story "The Flirt").

Cast: Conrad Nagel (*Dick Lindley*); Sidney Fox (*Marianne Madison*); Bette Davis (*Laura Madison*); ZaSu Pitts (*Minnie*); Slim Summerville (*Sam*); Charles Winninger (*Mr. Madison*); Emma Dunn (*Mrs. Madison*); Humphrey Bogart (*Valentine Corliss*).

Bored rich girl Marianne flirts with Dick Lindley, but falls prey to city slicker Valentine Corliss, who uses the naive girl to swindle local businessmen. Marianne learns her lesson, but when she returns to Dick, he realizes he really loves Marianne's virtuous sister Laura.

Notes: *Bad Sister* is the first of six movies in which Bogart shares screen credit with Bette Davis. The others are *Three on a Match* (1932), *The Petrified Forest* (1936), *Marked Woman* (1937), *Kid Galahad* (1937), and *Dark Victory* (1939).

Bad Sister is a remake of the silent picture *The Flirt* (1922), starring Edward Hearn, Eileen Percy, and Helen Jerome Eddy, with Lloyd Whitlock in the role Bogart would play.

Women of All Nations (Fox, 1931) 72 minutes.

Director, Raoul Walsh; producer, Archibald Buchanan; screenplay, Barry Connors, based on characters created by Laurence Stallings and Maxwell Anderson.

Cast: Victor McLaglen (*Sergeant Flagg*); Edmund Lowe (*Sergeant Quirt*); Greta Nissen (*Elsa*); El Brendel (*Olson*); Fifi Dorsay (*Fifi*); Marjorie

White (*Pee Wee*); T. Roy Barnes (*Marine captain*); Bela Lugosi (*Prince Hassan*); Humphrey Bogart (*Stone*); Joyce Compton (*Kiki*).

The women-chasing Army sergeants Flagg and Quirt, first seen in Fox's *What Price Glory?* (1926), and in *The Cockeyed World* (1929), get fed up with civilian life in Brooklyn and re-enlist. They promptly fall into trouble, romantic and otherwise, in Sweden, Nicaragua, and Egypt. Stone (Bogart) is a fellow Marine.

Note: Raoul Walsh (1887–1980), one of the most versatile of the Warner Bros. directors, would later work with Bogart on *The Roaring Twenties* (1939), *They Drive by Night* (1940), *High Sierra* (1941), and *The Enforcer* (1951—uncredited).

A Holy Terror (Fox, 1931) 53 minutes.

Director, Irving Cummings; screenplay, Ralph Block, Alfred A. Cohen, and Myron Fagan (based on the Max Brand novel *Trailin'*).

Cast: George O'Brien (*Tony Bard*); Sally Eilers (*Jerry Foster*); Rita LaRoy (*Kitty Carroll*); Humphrey Bogart (*Steve Nash*); James Kirkwood (*William Drew*); Stanley Fields (*Butch Morgan*); Robert Warwick (*Thomas Bard*, alias *Thomas Woodbury*).

Millionaire son Tony comes West looking for his father's killer. He falls in love with Jerry, daughter of the rancher/suspect Drew. The ranch foreman, Steve, is also in love with the young woman, and causes trouble. Drew steps in, saves Tony's life, and reveals that he is Tony's true father.

Commented Bogart, "I was too short to be a cowboy, so they gave me elevator shoes and padded out my shoulders. I walked around as though I was on stilts and felt like a dummy" (Joe Hyams, *Bogie*).

"*A Holy Terror* is here to take its meager bow" (*New York Times*, July 20, 1931).

Love Affair (Columbia, 1932) 68 minutes.

Director, Thornton Freeland; adaptation and dialogue, Joe Swerling; continuity, Dorothy Howell (based on a story in *College Humor* by Ursula Parrott).

Cast: Dorothy Mackaill (*Carol Owen*); Humphrey Bogart (*Jim Leonard*); Jack Kennedy (*Gilligan*); Barbara Leonard (*Felice*); Astrid Allwyn (*Linda Lee*); Bradley Page (*Georgie*); Halliwell Hobbs (*Kibbee*); Hale Hamilton (*Bruce Hardy*).

This is the dramatic love story of the blonde heiress Carol and flying instructor Jim. When she discovers that she's actually penniless, she accepts a marriage proposal from Bruce Hardy, thinking to finance her lover's invention. There's misunderstanding all around, which ends with a chase to keep the distraught woman from making a suicide flight.

Note: This was the first film that Bogart had the second lead part, here behind the popular Dorothy Mackaill.

Big City Blues (Warner Bros., 1932) 65 minutes.

Director, Mervyn LeRoy; screenplay, Ward Morehouse and Lillie Hayward (based on the Morehouse play *New York Town*).

Cast: Joan Blondell (*Vida Fleet*); Eric Linden (*Bud Reeves*); Inez Courtney (*Faun*); Evalyn Knapp (*Jo-Jo*); Guy Kibbee (*Hummel*); Lyle Talbot (*Sully*); Gloria Shea (*Agnes*); Walter Catlett (*Gibbony*); Jobyna Howland (*Serena Cartlich*); Humphrey Bogart (*Adkins*).

Small-town youth Bud goes to New York City, meets worldly chorus girl Vida, and is invited to a party where a woman is killed. He is suspected of murder but is eventually cleared. Adkins is one of the likely suspects. (Hint: Keep your eye on Lyle Talbot as "Sully").

"Quite painful to bear" (*New York Times*, October 29, 1931).

Three on a Match (Warner Bros., 1932) 64 minutes.

Director, Mervyn LeRoy; screenplay, Lucien Hubbard; dialog by Kubec Glasmon and John Bright (from a story by Glasmon and Bright).

Cast: Joan Blondell (*Mary Keaton*); Warren William (*Robert Kirkwood*); Ann Dvorak (*Vivian Revere*); Bette Davis (*Ruth Westcott*); Lyle Talbot (*Michael Loftus*); Humphrey Bogart (*Harve, the Mug*); Edward Arnold (*Ace*); Sheila Terry (*Naomi, pianist-singer*); Buster Phelps (*Robert Kirkwood Jr.*); Glenda Farrell (*girl in reform school*).

Drama of three friends—Mary, an actress; Vivian, who marries a rich man; and Ruth, a business woman—and the bad luck that befalls one of them. The Mug is one of the punk hoodlums hired to kidnap the young son of the rich woman.

Remake: *Broadway Musketeers* (1938), with Margaret Lindsay, Ann Sheridan, and Marie Wilson. There is no "Mug" in this version, as the story line was revamped.

Midnight (aka *Call It Murder*) (All-Star/Universal, 1934) 80 minutes.

Director-producer, Chester Erskine; screenplay, Chester Erskine (based on the play by Paul and Claire Sifton).

Cast: Sidney Fox (*Stella Weldon*); O. P. Heggie (*Edward Weldon*); Henry Hull (*Bob Nolan*); Margaret Wycherly (*Mrs. Weldon*); Lynne Overman (*Joe "Leroy" Biggers*); Katherine Wilson (*Ada Biggers*); Richard Whorf (*Arthur Weldon*); Humphrey Bogart (*Garboni*).

Jury foreman Edward Weldon sentences a woman to death for killing her lover. He's hounded by the press and criticized by his own family. But when his own daughter, Stella, murders her lover, the gangster Garboni, Weldon learns the importance of mercy.

Lynne Overman, a friend of Bogart's, got him the supporting role here when the previously assigned screen actor became ill. The *New York Times* slammed Australian actor O. P. Heggie for "suffering at the top of his lungs" but complimented the "admirable" ensemble players.

Note: This film was reissued in the late 1930s as *Call It Murder*, to capitalize on Bogart's then current rise to movie success.

The Petrified Forest (Warner Bros., 1936) 83 minutes.

Director, Archie Mayo; executive producer, Hal B. Wallis; associate producer, Henry Blanke; screenplay, Charles Kenyon and Delmer Daves (based on the play by Robert E. Sherwood).

Cast: Leslie Howard (*Alan Squier*); Bette Davis (*Gabrielle Maple*); Genevieve Tobin (*Mrs. Edith Chisholm*); Dick Foran (*Boze Hertzlinger*); Humphrey Bogart (*Duke Mantee*); Joseph Sawyer (*Jackie*); Porter Hall (*Jason Maple*); Charley Grapewin (*Gramp Maple*); Paul Harvey (*Mr. Chisholm*); Eddie Acuff (*Lineman*).

Alan Squier, a disillusioned, wandering poet, stops at a rundown cafe in the desolate Arizona desert, and befriends the waitress Gabrielle, who dreams of studying art in Paris. Then Duke Mantee, a notorious killer on the run, bursts onto the scene with his gang and holds the occupants of the cafe hostage. Squier sees in the young waitress the artistic spirit he once had. He signs over his life insurance policy to her, so she can go to Paris, and then asks Mantee to kill him. The gangster complies.

"There should be a large measure of praise for Humphrey Bogart who can be a psychopathic gangster more like Dillinger than the outlaw himself" (*New York Times*, February 7, 1936).

"Bogart provides a brilliant picture of a subnormal, bewildered and sentimental killer" (*New York Herald Tribune*, February 7, 1936).

Notes: This was Bogart's breakthrough Hollywood role. When Warner Bros. bought the film rights to the 1935 Broadway hit, they assigned contract tough-guy star Edward G. Robinson to the key gangster part. When Britisher Leslie Howard insisted that he would only make the movie with Bogart (who had costarred with him in the Broadway production), Bogie was given a new beginning in Hollywood.

As Bogart had done on Broadway, he played the rampaging Duke Mantee while sitting in a chair for most of the proceedings.

In 1945, Warner Bros. remade *The Petrified Forest* as the B movie *Escape in the Desert*, substituting Nazis for gangsters, and featuring Philip Dorn, Helmut Dantine (as the "Duke Mantee" counterpart), Jean Sullivan, Irene Manning, and Alan Hale.

Eduardo Ciannelli played Duke Mantee in the *Lux Radio Theatre* production (November 22, 1937), with Herbert Marshall as the poet and Margaret Sullavan as the waitress.

Lawrence Tierney, at the time a big hit as *Dillinger* in Monogram's film of 1945, portrayed Duke Mantee in a new *Lux Radio Theatre* production on April 23, 1945. Ronald Colman and Susan Hayward performed the roles of the poet and the waitress, respectively.

There have been three U.S. television productions, to date, of *The Petrified Forest*:

Lucky Strike Theatre, NBC, October 23, 1950. Black-and-white, 60 minutes. (The name of the show was later changed to *Robert Montgomery Presents*.)

Producer, Robert Montgomery; director, Norman Felton.

Robert Montgomery played Alan Squier, the world-weary poet, with Joan Lorring as Gaby, and Herbert Rudley as Duke Mantee. Montgomery, who usually hosted this anthology series, turned over that chore for this entry to actor Brian Aherne.

Celanese Theatre, ABC, February 20, 1952. Black-and-white, 60 minutes.

Producer-director, Alex Segall; television adaptation, Norman Lessing.

Hollywood favorite David Niven played Alan Squier, with Kim Hunter as Gaby and Lloyd Gough as Duke Mantee.

Producers' Showcase, NBC, May 30, 1955. Color, 90 minutes.

Producer, Fred Coe; director, Delbert Mann; television adaptation, Tad Mosel.

This time around Henry Fonda was the poet, Lauren Bacall was Gaby, and Humphrey Bogart played Duke Mantee for the third time. The supporting cast included Paul Hartman, Jack Warden, Richard Jaeckel, Natalie Schafer, and Jack Klugman.

This was the most expensive, most prestigious production yet of *The Petrified Forest*, and the first in color. *Variety* questioned the need of color in a dramatic production, but conceded that "the added tint values managed to superimpose the desert heat and glare and barrenness" (June 1, 1955). Of Bogart's reinterpretation of the pivotal role of Mantee, *Variety* judged, "Bogart, of course, remains Bogart, but somewhere in the adaptation the part of the killer Mantee shrunk to undemanding and unrewarding opportunities."

Bullets or Ballots (First National/Warner Bros., 1936) 81 minutes.

Director, William Keighley; executive producers, Jack L. Warner and Hal B. Wallis; associate producer, Louis F. Edelman; screenplay, Seton I. Miller (based on an original story by Martin Mooney and Miller).

Cast: Edward G. Robinson (*Johnny Blake*); Joan Blondell (*Lee Morgan*); Barton MacLane (*Al Kruger*); Humphrey Bogart (*Nick "Bugs" Fenner*); Frank McHugh (*Herman*); Joseph King (*Captain Dan McLaren*); Richard Purcell (*Driscoll*).

When top cop Johnny Blake is demoted he goes to work for the mob, then reveals gangland secrets to the police. Nick "Bugs" Fenner, right-hand man to the mob chief, is suspicious of the undercover law enforcer and dies in a shootout with him.

Note: This was the first time Bogart and Robinson killed each other on-camera, but certainly would not be the last!

Two Against the World (aka **One Fatal Hour**) (First National/Warner Bros., 1936) 64 minutes.

Director: William McGann; executive producers, Jack L. Warner and Hal B. Wallis; associate producer, Bryan Foy; screenplay, Michael Jacoby (based on the Louis Weitzenkorn play *Five Star Final*).

Cast: Humphrey Bogart (*Sherry Scott*); Beverly Roberts (*Alma Ross*); Helen MacKellar (*Martha Carstairs*); Henry O'Neill (*Jim Carstairs*); Linda Perry (*Edith Carstairs*); Carlyle Moore Jr. (*Billy Sims*); Virginia Brissac (*Mrs. Marion Sims*).

A muckraking radio station digs up a twenty-year-old murder case which leads to the suicide of two of the principals. Sherry, the crusading station manager, and secretary Alma, join forces to oppose the scandal-crazy broadcast executives.

Note: *Two Against the World* is a remake of the hard-hitting *Five Star Final* (1931), which starred Edward G. Robinson and Marian Marsh and was set in the newspaper world.

China Clipper (First National/Warner Bros., 1936) 85 minutes.

Director, Ray Enright; executive producers, Jack L. Warner and Hal B. Wallis; associate producer, Louis F. Edelman; screenplay, Frank Ward, with additional dialog by Norman Reilly Raine.

Cast: Pat O'Brien (*Dave Logan*); Beverly Roberts (*Jean Logan*); Ross Alexander (*Tom Collins*); Humphrey Bogart (*Hap Stuart*); Marie Wilson (*Sunny Avery*); Henry B. Walthall (*Dad Brunn*); Joseph Crehan (*Jim Horn*); Joseph King (*Mr. Pierson*); Ruth Robinson (*Mother Brunn*).

Inspired by aviator Charles Lindbergh's conquest of the Atlantic Ocean, businessman Dave Logan plans a transpacific airline. His obsession drives away his wife, Jean, alienates his ace flyer, Hap Stuart, and kills his own father with overwork. However, the China Clipper is successful.

"There are some genuine moments of excitement as Bogart nurses the plane across thousands of miles of hostile weather conditions and other hazards, but alas, the film's heart remains grounded, in more ways than one" (Terence Pettigrew; *Bogart: A Definitive Study of His Film Career*).

Note: This marks the first joint screen appearance of Bogart and Pat O'Brien. They later appeared together in *The Great O'Malley* (1937), *San Quentin* (1937), and *Angels with Dirty Faces* (1938).

Isle of Fury (Warner Bros., 1936) 60 minutes.

Director, Frank McDonald; executive producers, Jack L. Warner and Hal B. Wallis; associate producer, Bryan Foy; screenplay, Robert Andrews and William Jacobs (based on the W. Somerset Maugham novel *The Narrow Corner*).

Cast: Humphrey Bogart (*Val Stevens*); Margaret Lindsay (*Lucille Gordon*); Donald Woods (*Eric Blake*); Paul Graetz (*Captain Deever*); Gordon Hart (*Anderson*); E. E. Clive (*Dr. Hardy*); George Regas (*Otar*); Sidney Bracey (*Sam*).

Val Stevens is a fugitive from justice, now reformed, married to Lucille, and living on a South Seas island. He's tracked down by detective Eric Blake, who has second thoughts about arresting him. Bogart wears a mustache and fights an octopus.

Notes: The most amazing thing about *Isle of Fury*—an inept B picture—is that Warner Bros. would cast Bogart in it right after his extraordinary acclaim for *The Petrified Forest*. Bogart, understandably, pretended he couldn't remember this movie whenever he discussed his movie career.

Isle of Fury was first filmed by Warner Bros. in 1933 as *The Narrow Corner*, with Douglas Fairbanks Jr. and Patricia Ellis.

Black Legion (Warner Bros., 1937) 83 minutes.

Director, Archie Mayo; executive producers, Jack L. Warner and Hal B. Wallis; associate producer, Robert Lord; screenplay, Abem Finkel and William Wister Haines (based on a story by Lord).

Cast: Humphrey Bogart (*Frank Taylor*); Dick Foran (*Ed Jackson*); Erin O'Brien-Moore (*Ruth Taylor*); Ann Sheridan (*Betty Grogan*); Robert Barrat (*Brown*); Helen Flint (*Pearl Davis*); Joseph Sawyer (*Cliff Moore*); Addison Richards (*prosecuting attorney*).

Frank Taylor is an embittered factory worker who joins the Black Legion, a "pro-American" Ku Klux Klan–type terrorist organization. When Frank drunkenly reveals Legion secrets to his best friend, Ed Jackson, he's later forced to kill his friend to keep him quiet. When it's uncovered that the "patriotic" Legion was organized by racketeers for their own gain, Frank and other clansmen are sent to prison.

"[Bogart is] dynamic and stirring. The role is one which demands the talents of a [Paul] Muni or a [Edward G.] Robinson. And Bogart has filled it superbly. No more B pix for Bogart!" (*New York Post*, January 18, 1937).

"No more B pix"? How little they knew about Warner Bros.!

Notes: In addition to *Black Legion*, talented, beautiful, deep-voiced Ann Sheridan (also called "the Oomph Girl") also appeared with Humphrey Bogart in *The Great O'Malley* (1937), *San Quentin* (1937), *Angels with Dirty Faces* (1938), *It All Came True* (1940), *They Drive by Night* (1940); *Thank Your Lucky Stars* (1943), and a cameo role in *The Treasure of the Sierra Madre* (1948).

The Ku Klux Klan sued Warner Bros., not for maligning their white-sheeted organization—but for copyright infringement for using their symbol of a white cross on a circular red background with a black square in the center. The court threw out the case, and made the Klan pay the legal costs.

The Great O'Malley (Warner Bros., 1937) 71 minutes.

Director, William Dieterle; executive producers, Jack L. Warner and Hal B. Wallis; associate producer, Harry Joe Brown; screenplay, Milton Krims and Tom Reed (based on the Gerald Beaumont story "The Making of O'Malley").

Cast: Pat O'Brien (*James Aloysius O'Malley*); Sybil Jason (*Barbara Phillips*); Humphrey Bogart (*John Phillips*); Ann Sheridan (*Judy Nolan*); Frieda Inescort (*Mrs. Phillips*); Donald Crisp (*Captain Cromwell*); Henry O'Neill (*defense attorney*).

The actions of overzealous police officer O'Malley drive blue-collar worker John Phillips into crime, and prison. Meanwhile, relegated to being a traffic cop, O'Malley befriends a little girl . . . and discovers that she's the daughter of the man he sent to prison.

Bogart has a memorable screen scene in which he tries to pawn his service medals and the pawnbroker calls them junk. "The only things left to remind me I was once a man," Bogie's character explodes, "and you call them junk!"

Note: *The Great O'Malley* is a remake of the silent film *The Making of O'Malley* (1925). The stars of this First National Pictures production were Milton Sills, Dorothy Mackaill, Helen Rowland, and Warner P. Richmond in the earlier incarnation of the Bogart part.

Marked Woman (First National/Warner Bros., 1937) 96 minutes.

Director, Lloyd Bacon; executive producers, Jack L. Warner and Hal B. Wallis; associate producer, Louis F. Edelman; screenplay, Robert Rossen and Abem Finkel.

Cast: Bette Davis (*Mary Dwight Strauber*); Humphrey Bogart (*District Attorney David Graham*); Lola Lane (*Gabby Marvin*); Isabel Jewell (*Emmy Lou*); Eduardo Ciannelli (*Johnny Vanning*); Rosalind Marquis (*Florrie Liggett*); Mayo Methot (*Estelle Porter*); Jane Bryan (*Betty Strauber*); Allen Jenkins (*Louie*).

The "hostesses" (i.e., prostitutes) of a New York nightclub are terrorized into silence by their gangster boss, Johnny Vanning. When a woman is accidentally killed, her sister Mary threatens exposure. She's beaten and scarred, but she and her co-workers tell their story to the racket-busting District Attorney Graham.

Notes: Mayo Methot appears as one of the nightclub "girls," ridiculed by the mobster boss for looking older than the others. Off-camera, Bogart was then living with wife number two, Mary Philips, but it was assumed that Mayo would soon be his new spouse. This is the only time Methot and Bogart acted together on-camera.

Lloyd Bacon (1890–1955) is the efficient director; he supervised the most films with Bogart. This is the first of seven features they made together.

Kid Galahad (aka The Battling Bellhop) (First National/Warner Bros., 1937) 101 minutes.

Director, Michael Curtiz; executive producers, Jack L. Warner and Hal B. Wallis; associate producer, Samuel Bischoff; screenplay, Seton I. Miller (based on the novel by Francis Wallace).

Cast: Edward G. Robinson (*Nick Donati*); Bette Davis (*Fluff [Louise Phillips]*); Humphrey Bogart (*Turkey Morgan*); Wayne Morris (*Ward Guisenberry*); Jane Bryan (*Marie Donati*); Harry Carey (*Silver Jackson*); William Haade (*Chuck McGraw*); Soledad Jiminez (*Mrs. Donati*).

Fight promoter Nick Donati thinks he really has a boxing champion on his hands when he meets good-hearted Ward Guisenberry—that is until Guisenberry falls in love with the promoter's convent-bred sister. There's also trouble from Turkey Morgan, the slugger's manager who thinks the promoter is double-crossing him. The two—Robinson and Bogart again—eventually kill one another in a memorable gunfight.

Notes: This version of *Kid Galahad* has been shown on television as *The Battling Bellhop*.

Michael Curtiz (1888–1962) would also direct Bogart in *Angels with Dirty Faces* (1938), *Virginia City* (1940), *Casablanca* (1942), *Passage to Marseille* (1944), and *We're No Angels* (1955).

Remakes: *Kid Galahad* is the basis for *The Wagons Roll at Night* (1941), this time with a circus setting, and Bogart playing the man who's much too protective of his young sister (Joan Leslie).

The story was remade yet again, this time by United Artists, as *Kid Galahad* (1962), with Elvis Presley, who has six songs in the movie. Gig Young is in the equivalent of the Bogart role.

A FEW WORDS ON A PICTURES AND B PICTURES

In their peak productive years, the Hollywood studios made A pictures and B pictures. A pictures were more ambitious, more expensive, and featured the lot's then most popular stars. B pictures were produced on smaller budgets, had shorter shooting schedules, and usually headlined personalities on their way out and newcomers on their way up.

Ironically, history has turned up many B-picture gems, while countless A pictures have lost their luster and been relegated to the wee morning hours of Turner Classic Movies on cable TV.

At Warner Bros. in the early 1930s to the mid-1940s, the A department was run by Hal B. Wallis, with the B's handled by Bryan Foy. Wallis would supervise about twenty pictures a year, with Foy grinding out about thirty-five. The studio, based in Burbank, California, was notorious for its penny-pinching, cost-cutting ways. One notable trick: Seven or eight years after one of Wallis's successful A entries, Foy would turn around and make it into a B picture. Moneymakers were redone, with new settings, new titles. Thus *Bordertown* (1935) became *They Drive by Night* (1941), and *The Narrow Corner* (1933) was regurgitated as *Isle of Fury* (1936). *The Maltese Falcon* (1941) story was filmed three times, as was *High Sierra* (1941). The hugely successful *Casablanca* (1942) became a mold into which countless other projects were squeezed.

San Quentin (First National/Warner Bros., 1937) 70 minutes.

Director, Lloyd Bacon; executive producers, Jack L. Warner and Hal B. Wallis; associate producer, Samuel Bischoff; screenplay, Peter Milne and Humphrey Cobb (based on an original story by Robert Tasker and John Bright).

Cast: Pat O'Brien (*Captain Stephen Jameson*); Humphrey Bogart (*Joe "Red" Kennedy*); Ann Sheridan (*May Kennedy*); Barton MacLane (*Lieutenant Druggin*); Joseph Sawyer (*Sailor Boy Hansen*); Veda Ann Borg (*Helen*), James Robbins (*Mickey Callahan*).

Stephen Jameson is yard captain at the high-security San Quentin penitentiary, and is in love with May Kennedy whose brother, "Red," is a prisoner there. The brother's mind is poisoned against Jameson. He escapes to kill him, but is shot. Red's dying plea is for the other convicts to cooperate with the well-meaning guard.

Dead End (United Artists, 1937) 93 minutes.

Director, William Wyler; producer, Samuel Goldwyn; associate producer, Merritt Hulburd; screenplay, Lillian Hellman (based on the play by Sidney Kingsley).

Cast: Sylvia Sidney (*Drina Gordon*); Joel McCrea (*Dave Connell*); Humphrey Bogart (*Baby Face Martin*); Wendy Barrie (*Kay Burton*); Claire Trevor (*Francey*); Allen Jenkins (*Hunk*); Marjorie Main (*Mrs. Martin*); Billy Halop (*Tommy*); Huntz Hall (*Dippy*); Bobby Jordan (*Angel*); Leo Gorcey (*Spit*); Gabriel Dell (*T. B.*); Bernard Punsley (*Milty*).

This film is set within a rich tapestry of city life, on a New York City dead-end street, with tenements on one side and homes of the rich on the other. Dave is an architect who wants to tear down the slums. The shop girl Drina fights to keep her young brother Tommy from becoming a criminal. The neighborhood's most notable graduate is the gangster "Baby Face" Martin, who comes back to see his mother—who denounces him—and an old girlfriend Francey, who is now a syphilis-infected streetwalker.

"This is the finest performance Bogart has ever given—the ruthless sentimentalist who had melodramatized himself from the start" (Graham Greene. *Graham Greene on Film*; New York: Simon and Schuster, 1972).

The London *Film Weekly* in the fall of 1937 wrote of "Bogart's brilliant characterization" and said, "One brief and deeply moving scene [between Bogart and Claire Trevor] is tragic poetry."

Notes: The "Dead End Kids" were graduates of the original 1935 Broadway production. Their popularity in this feature prompted Warner Bros. to put them into six other crime melodramas over the next few years. Some of the group went to Universal Studios and starred in nine entries in a group called The Dead End Kids and Little Tough Guys. In 1940, producer Sam Katzman launched a long-running low-budget series (twenty-two titles) at Monogram Pictures called The East Side Kids. In 1946, Leo Gorcey became the unofficial star of these Monogram quickies. The group was now renamed The Bowery Boys, and they lasted for another forty-eight (!) movies.

Dead End is the first Bogart–Claire Trevor collaboration. They later appeared together in *The Amazing Dr. Clitterhouse* (1938) and *Key Largo* (1948).

Stand-In (Walter Wanger/United Artists, 1937) 90 minutes.

Director, Tay Garnett; producer, Walter Wanger; screenplay, Gene Towne and Graham Baker (based on the Clarence Budington Kelland serialized story in the *Saturday Evening Post*).

Cast: Leslie Howard (*Atterbury Dodd*); Joan Blondell (*Lester Plum*); Humphrey Bogart (*Douglas Quintain*); Alan Mowbray (*Koslofski*); Marla Shelton (*Thelma Cheri*); C. Henry Gordon (*Ivor Nassau*); Jack Carson (*Potts*).

This comedy centers around New York City banker/efficiency expert Atterbury Dodd, who learns the ways of Hollywood and ends up leading the employees in an insurrection against a film studio. Douglas Quintain is the hard-drinking movie producer of the jungle epic *Sex and Satan*.

"*Stand-In* is the greatest *unknown* Bogart film—clever, campy, witty—a rare treat for those lucky enough to see it" (Jeffrey Meyers, *Bogart: A Life in Hollywood*, 1997).

Note: Director Tay Garnett (1894–1977) fought for the casting of Bogart, thinking the change of pace would be good for his career. Producer Walter Wanger (1894–1968) resisted, but finally gave in. One day while watching the dailies, an assistant said to Garnett, "You're crazy if you think you'll make a hero out of him—the son of a bitch lisps!"

Swing Your Lady (Warner Bros., 1938) 79 minutes.

Director, Ray Enright; executive producers, Jack L. Warner and Hal B. Wallis; associate producer, Samuel Bischoff; screenplay, Joseph Schrank and Maurice Leo (based on the play by Kenyon Nicholson and Charles Robinson).

Cast: Humphrey Bogart (*Ed Hatch*); Frank McHugh (*Popeye Bronson*); Louise Fazenda (*Sadie Horn*); Nat Pendleton (*Joe Skopapoulos*); Penny Singleton (*Cookie Shannon*); Allen Jenkins (*Shiner Ward*); Ronald Reagan (*Jack Miller*); and the Weaver family: Leon, Elvirey, and Frank.

Ed Hatch is a quick-buck promoter who arranges a bout between dim-witted wrestler Joe Skopapoulos and Sadie Horn, an amazon from the

Ozarks. When the two contestants fall in love and refuse to fight, Ed tries to break up the romance.

Note: This was Warner Bros.' attempt to imitate Paramount's tremendously successful *Mountain Music* (1937), starring Bob Burns and Martha Raye.

Harry Medved and Randy Dreyfuss include *Swing Your Lady* in their book *The Fifty Worst Films of All Time* (New York: Popular Library, 1978): "[Bogart] approaches the role with all the self-willed enthusiasm of a sophomore half-back playing the final quarter of his big game with a fractured ankle."

In retrospect, *Swing Your Lady* is more notable as an early film assignment for amiable studio contract player Ronald Reagan.

Crime School (First National/Warner Bros., 1938) 86 minutes.

Director, Lewis Seiler; executive producers, Jack L. Warner and Hal B. Wallis; associate producer, Bryan Foy; screenplay, Crane Wilbur and Vincent Sherman (from a story by Wilbur).

Cast: Humphrey Bogart (*Mark Braden*); Gale Page (*Sue Warren*); Billy Halop (*Frankie Warren*); Bobby Jordan (*Squirt*); Huntz Hall (*Goofy*); Leo Gorcey (*Spike Hawkins*); Bernard Punsley (*Fats Papadopolo*); Gabriel Dell (*Bugs Burke*).

Mark Braden is a crusading law official who discovers that the superintendent of a reform school is a sadist. Braden takes over the job himself and wins the rebellious young inmates' trust and respect.

Note: *Crime School* is a remake of *The Mayor of Hell* (1933) starring James Cagney. It was filmed yet again as *Hell's Kitchen* (1939) with Ronald Reagan.

Men Are Such Fools (Warner Bros., 1938) 70 minutes.

Director, Busby Berkeley; executive producers, Jack L. Warner and Hal B. Wallis; associate producer, David Lewis; screenplay, Norman Reilly Raine and Horace Jackson (based on the novel by Faith Baldwin).

Cast: Wayne Morris (*Jimmy Hall*); Priscilla Lane (*Linda Lawrence*); Humphrey Bogart (*Harry Galleon*); Hugh Herbert (*Harvey Bates*); Penny Singleton (*Nancy*); Johnnie Davis (*Tad*); Mona Barrie (*Beatrice Harris*); Marcia Ralston (*Wanda Townsend*).

Busy advertising executive Linda Lawrence decides to marry ex–football hero Jimmy Hall and become a housewife. When Jimmy refuses her help in furthering his career, Linda walks out and returns to her old job. Her boss Harry Galleon proposes marriage, and she accepts—which brings the football hero running.

Note: This film was a change of pace for Busby Berkeley (1895–1976), famous for his kaleidoscopic musical-production numbers in such landmark films as *42nd Street* (1933) and *Gold Diggers of 1933* (1933). Audiences and critics alike agreed that Berkeley should have stuck with the chorus lines. "Sad and aimless," rated the *New York Times* (June 17, 1938).

"The nadir of Bogart's post–*Petrified Forest* film career, and his discomfort is shared by others in this trite, inept production" (Terence Pettigrew, *Bogart: A Definitive Study of His Film Career*, 1977/1981).

The Amazing Dr. Clitterhouse (First National/Warner Bros., 1938) 87 minutes.

Director, Anatole Litvak; executive producers, Jack L. Warner and Hal B. Wallis; producer, Gilbert Miller; associate producer, Robert Lord; screenplay, John Wexley and John Huston (based on the play by Barre Lyndon).

Cast: Edward G. Robinson (*Dr. Clitterhouse*); Claire Trevor (*Jo Keller*); Humphrey Bogart (*Rocks Valentine*); Allen Jenkins (*Okay*); Donald Crisp (*Inspector Lane*); Gale Page (*Nurse Randolph*); Henry O'Neill (*judge*); John Litel (*prosecuting attorney*).

Dr. Clitterhouse, an overzealous psychologist, joins a gang of safecrackers led by Jo Keller to get firsthand knowledge of the criminal mind. After his research is completed, he tries to leave the group. When gang member Rocks Valentine threatens to expose him, the doctor decides to add a final chapter to his book—one on homicide—and poisons Valentine.

Racket Busters (Warner Bros./Cosmopolitan, 1938) 71 minutes.

Director, Lloyd Bacon; executive producers, Jack L. Warner and Hal B. Wallis; associate producer, Samuel Bischoff; screenplay, Robert Rossen and Leonardo Bercovici.

Cast: Humphrey Bogart (*Pete Martin*); George Brent (*Denny Jordan*); Gloria Dickson (*Nora Jordan*); Allen Jenkins (*Horse Wilson*); Walter Abel (*Thomas Alison*); Henry O'Neill (*Governor*); Penny Singleton (*Gladys*); Anthony Averill (*Crane*).

A battle—between a powerful gang chief Pete Martin and racket-smashing prosecutor Thomas Alison—for control of the trucking business, in order to corner the produce market. A defiant, well-intentioned trucker, Denny Jordan, is caught in the middle.

Angels with Dirty Faces (First National/Warner Bros., 1938) 97 minutes.

Director, Michael Curtiz; executive producers, Jack L. Warner and Hal B. Wallis; producer, Sam Bischoff; screenplay, John Wexley and Warren Duff (based on a story by Rowland Brown).

Cast: James Cagney (*Rocky Sullivan*); Pat O'Brien (*Jerry Connolly*); Humphrey Bogart (*James Frazier*); Ann Sheridan (*Laury Ferguson*); George Bancroft (*Mac Keefer*); Billy Halop (*Soapy*); Bobby Jordan (*Swing*); Leo Gorcey (*Bim*); Gabriel Dell (*Pasty*); Huntz Hall (*Crab*); Bernard Punsley (*Hunky*).

The story of two tough East Side New York City boys: Rocky Sullivan, who drifts into crime, and Jerry Connolly, who becomes a priest. Frazier is a crooked lawyer who attempts to cheat Sullivan but is shot by him. The film's climactic scene is deservedly famous: tough-guy Sullivan feigning cowardice on his way to the electric chair, to disillusion the slum kids who idolize him.

Note: This is the first time Bogart costarred with James Cagney, who shoots him, as he does in *The Roaring Twenties* (1939). In the western *The Oklahoma Kid* (1939), Bogart is shot by Cagney's brother (Harvey Stephens).

Sequel: *Angels Wash Their Faces* (1939) with Ann Sheridan and the Dead End Kids in roles similar to the earlier offering, plus Ronald Reagan, Bonita Granville, Margaret Hamilton, and Marjorie Main.

King of the Underworld (Warner Bros., 1939) 69 minutes.

Director, Lewis Seiler; associate producer, Bryan Foy; screenplay, George Bricker and Vincent Sherman (based on the W. R. Burnett novel, *Dr. Socrates*, serialized in *Liberty* magazine).

Cast: Humphrey Bogart (*Joe Gurney*); Kay Francis (*Carol Nelson*); James Stephenson (*Bill Forrest*); John Eldredge (*Niles Nelson*); Jessie Busley (*Aunt Margaret*); Arthur Aylesworth (*Dr. Sanders*); Raymond Brown (*Sheriff*).

Carol and Niles Nelson, a husband-and-wife doctor team, are forced into the lives and crimes of rampaging gangster Joe Gurney. Niles is killed, and the police charge Carol with being an accomplice. She plots the capture of the gang by temporarily blinding the mobsters with eyedrops.

"Bogart's egocentric gangster . . . is just plain silly, but no sillier than the climax, as, temporarily blinded, he lurches around like a headless chicken, popping off shots at people who aren't there" (Terence Pettigrew, *Bogart: A Definitive Study of His Film Career*, 1977/1981).

Notes: Bogart was given star billing in *King of the Underworld*, with Kay Francis given below-title billing—obviously an attempt by Warner Bros. to further humiliate the once reigning queen of the studio.

King of the Underworld is a B-picture remake of *Dr. Socrates* (1935), a major production in which Paul Muni is the doctor with the eyedrops, outwitting vicious hoodlum Barton MacLane.

The Oklahoma Kid (Warner Bros., 1939) 80 minutes.

Director, Lloyd Bacon; executive producers, Jack L. Warner and Hal B. Wallis; associate producer, Samuel Bischoff; screenplay, Warren Duff, Robert Buckner, and Edward E. Paramore (based on a story by Paramore and Wally Klein).

Cast: James Cagney (*Jim Kincaid*); Humphrey Bogart (*Whip McCord*); Rosemary Lane (*Jane Hardwick*); Donald Crisp (*Judge Hardwick*); Harvey Stephens (*Ned Kincaid*); Hugh Sothern (*John Kincaid*); Charles Middleton (*Alec Martin*); Ward Bond (*Wes Handley*).

This western concerns the opening of Oklahoma's Cherokee Strip to settlers in 1895. Whip McCord and his gang hold up a stage, but then the notorious Oklahoma Kid robs them. When McCord learns that the Kid is the son of prominent citizen John Kincaid, McCord frames the father and incites a mob to lynch him. The Kid tracks down the gang one by one.

Notes: Bogart's all-black outfit in this feature was the inspiration for the screen persona of low-budget western actor Lash LaRue (1917–1996), who dressed in black. Coincidentally, Lash also had problems with a lisp.

Cagney steals the picture when he sings "I Don't Want to Play in Your Yard."

Dark Victory (First National/Warner Bros., 1939) 106 minutes.

Director, Edmund Goulding; associate producer, David Lewis; screenplay, Casey Robinson (based on the play by George Emerson Brewer Jr. and Bertram Bloch).

Cast: Bette Davis (*Judith Traherne*); George Brent (*Dr. Frederick Steele*); Humphrey Bogart (*Michael O'Leary*); Geraldine Fitzgerald (*Ann King*); Ronald Reagan (*Alec Hamn*); Henry Travers (*Dr. Parsons*); Cora Witherspoon (*Carrie Spottswood*).

Fast-living heiress Judith Traherne is operated on for a brain tumor, and falls in love with the doctor, Frederick Steele. When she discovers she has only ten months to live, she returns to her carefree life. Her Irish horse trainer, Michael O'Leary, who is secretly in love with her, urges her to find happiness while there is still time.

"Bogart, wonder of wonders, is simply a horse trainer, with a thick but not phony Irish brogue. After a while you stopped expecting him to whip out a rod. . . . You accepted him as a horse trainer. That's acting" (*New York Post*, April 2, 1939).

Notes: *Dark Victory* was first presented on Broadway in 1934, with Tallulah Bankhead as the spoiled society girl, and Earle Larrimore as the doctor. There was no horse trainer in this original production. *Lux Radio Theatre* did an adaptation of the play in 1938, starring Barbara Stanwyck and Melvyn Douglas . . . and it was this presentation that attracted the attention of producer Hal B. Wallis and Warner Bros., who then bought the property for Bette Davis.

Lux Radio Theatre broadcast *Dark Victory* in 1940, this version based on the movie. Bette Davis re-created her movie role, while Spencer Tracy stepped in as the doctor. Fred Shields was in Bogart's screen part as the horse trainer.

Remakes: *Stolen Hours* (1963), with Susan Hayward, Michael Craig, and Edward Judd. This United Artists version eliminated the role Bogart had played. A 1976 NBC-TV production of *Dark Victory* starred Elizabeth Montgomery as the dying heiress, Anthony Hopkins as her physician, and a supporting cast including Michele Lee, Michael Lerner, and Vic Tayback.

You Can't Get Away with Murder (First National/Warner Bros., 1939) 78 minutes.

Director, Lewis Seiler; associate producer, Samuel Bischoff; screenplay, Robert Buckner, Don Ryan, and Kenneth Gamet (based on the play *Chalked Out*, by Warden Lewis E. Lawes and Jonathan Finn).

Cast: Humphrey Bogart (*Frank Wilson*); Billy Halop (*Johnnie Stone*); Gale Page (*Madge Stone*); John Litel (*Attorney Carey*); Henry Travers

(*Pop*); Harvey Stephens (*Fred Burke*); Harold Huber (*Scappa*); Joseph Sawyer (*Red*).

Small-time crook Frank Wilson introduces teenager Johnnie Stone to a life of crime. When the two wind up in prison, the older man plots to kill the frightened boy before he can reveal the truth about past dirty deeds.

Commenting on the waste of talent, the *New York Times* (March 25, 1939) wrote, "Warners' most valuable stock players like Humphrey Bogart . . . are held not so much by five-year contracts, as by five-year sentences."

HOW DO YOU KILL A GUY LIKE THAT BOGART?!

Along the way, Humphrey Bogart made a number of comments about his early Hollywood movie career, along the lines of, "In my first thirty-four films, I was shot in twelve, electrocuted or hanged in eight, and was a jailbird in nine. I was the Little Lord Fauntleroy of the lot."

Actually, his totals aren't quite accurate. Here are the statistics by method of death, in chronological order.

Gunshot

- *Body and Soul* (As a World War I pilot; shot by the Germans.)

- *Midnight* (As a gangster; killed by girl friend Sidney Fox.)

- *The Petrified Forest* (As a gangster; shot down off-camera by the police.)

- *Bullets or Ballots* (As a gangster; he and cop Edward G. Robinson shoot each other.)

- *Kid Galahad* (As a gangster/fight manager; he and fight promoter Edward G. Robinson blast one another.)

- *San Quentin* (As an escaped prisoner; mowed down by the cops.)

- *Dead End* (As a hoodlum; done in by good guy Joel McCrea.)

- *Angels with Dirty Faces* (As a crooked lawyer; gunned down by cheated client Cagney.)

- *King of the Underworld* (As a gangster; killed in gunfire with the police.)

- *The Oklahoma Kid* (As a western bad guy; done in by Cagney's brother.)

- *The Roaring Twenties* (As a bootlegger; eliminated by Cagney.)

- *The Return of Dr. X* (As an executed murderer brought back to life; killed by the police.)

- *Invisible Stripes* (As a bank robber; taken out by other mobsters.)

- *Virginia City* (As a half-breed Mexican bandit; shot by the cavalry.)

- *High Sierra* (As an aging gangster; gunned down by the cops.)

- *The Big Shot* (As a gangster; he and a crooked lawyer kill each other.)

- *Passage to Marseille* (As a World War II French journalist; liquidated by the Nazis.)

- *Tokyo Joe* (As a nightclub owner; killed by Japanese criminal Sessue Hayakawa in post–World War II Japan.)

- *The Desperate Hours* (As an escaped criminal; shot by the police.)

Poisoning
- *The Amazing Dr. Clitterhouse* (As a gangster; he's poisoned by Edward G. Robinson, who wants to see what it feels like to kill another person.)

Electrocution
- *The Return of Doctor X* (As Doctor Xavier; he is put to death by electrocution for an illegal experiment that killed a baby—and is returned to life, where he is shot down by the police . . . wait a minute, doesn't that constitute double jeopardy?)

- *You Can't Get Away with Murder* (As a killer trapped by the deathbed confession of one of his victims; he has been sentenced to electrocution.)

Death by Lion
- *The Wagons Roll at Night* (As the jealous carnival owner who sends a rival to his death in the lion's cage . . . and then changes his mind.)

Decapitated (off-screen)
- *The Treasure of the Sierra Madre* (As a paranoid American gold prospector in Mexico, who doesn't hear the Mexican bandits creeping up behind him.)

Death by Hand Grenade
- *Sirocco* (As a gun-running American in Damascus who decides, too late, to do a good deed.)

The Roaring Twenties (Warner Bros., 1939) 106 minutes.

Director, Raoul Walsh; executive producer, Hal. B. Wallis; associate producer, Samuel Bischoff; screenplay, Jerry Wald, Richard Macaulay, and Robert Rossen (based on a story by Mark Hellinger).

Cast: James Cagney (*Eddie Bartlett*); Priscilla Lane (*Jean Sherman*); Humphrey Bogart (*George Hally*); Gladys George (*Panama Smith*); Jeffrey Lynn (*Lloyd Hart*); Frank McHugh (*Danny Green*); Paul Kelly (*Nick Brown*); Elisabeth Risdon (*Mrs. Sherman*).

Three soldier buddies go their way at the end of the first World War. Lloyd Hart becomes a lawyer, George Hally a bootlegger, and

Eddie Bartlett drives a taxi. The men drift into the bootleg-liquor business, become successful, and then get caught up in gang warfare. Two of them fall in love with Jean Sherman. Then they start shooting at each other.

The Return of Dr. X (First National/Warner Bros., 1939) 62 minutes.

Director, Vincent Sherman; executive producers, Jack L. Warner and Hal B. Wallis; associate producer, Bryan Foy; screenplay, Lee Katz (based on the story "The Doctor's Secret" by William J. Makin).

Cast: Wayne Morris (*Walter Barnett*); Rosemary Lane (*Joan Vance*); Humphrey Bogart (*Marshall Quesne*, alias *Dr. Xavier*); Dennis Morgan (*Dr. Michael Rhodes*); John Litel (*Dr. Francis Flegg*) Lya Lys (*Angela Merrova*), Huntz Hall (*Pinky*).

The police investigate a series of murders in which the victims are drained of their blood. The trail leads to a physician experimenting with restoring life to corpses through injections of rare blood . . . and to Dr. Xavier—a killer who has been legally executed but then was brought back to life. Now he seeks out young girls for their life-sustaining blood.

Said Bogie, "If it'd been [studio bosses] Jack Warner's blood or Harry [Warner]'s, I wouldn't have minded as much. The trouble was, they were drinking mine and I was making this stinking movie" (Richard Gehman, *Bogart*, 1965).

"Bogart, leering evilly but self-consciously behind his Marcel Marceau complexion and two-tone crew cut, is like a banshee amusing himself between funerals" (Terence Pettigrew, *Bogart: A Definitive Study of His Film Career*, 1977/1981).

Note: *The Return of Doctor X* is not a sequel to the horror classic *Dr. X* (1932), just a blatant attempt to capitalize on it.

Invisible Stripes (Warner Bros./First National, 1939) 82 minutes.

Director, Lloyd Bacon; executive producer, Hal B. Wallis; associate producer, Louis F. Edelman; screenplay, Warren Duff (from a story by Jonathan Finn, based on a book by Warden Lewis E. Lawes).

Cast: George Raft (*Cliff Taylor*); Jane Bryan (*Peggy*); William Holden (*Tim Taylor*); Humphrey Bogart (*Chuck Martin*); Flora Robson (*Mrs. Taylor*); Paul Kelly (*Ed Kruger*); Lee Patrick (*Molly*); Henry O'Neill (*Parole Officer Masters*); Frankie Thomas (*Tommy*).

Two convict friends are released from prison: Cliff intends to go straight but it's hard to find legitimate work; Chuck goes back to his old criminal ways. Cliff joins Chuck's gang "just to buy a garage for his younger brother," but the die is cast. Both men are killed in a shootout.

Virginia City (Warner Bros./First National, 1940) 121 minutes.

Director, Michael Curtiz; executive producer, Hal B. Wallis; associate producer, Robert Fellows; screenplay, Robert Buckner.

Cast: Errol Flynn (*Kerry Bradford*); Miriam Hopkins (*Julia Hayne*); Randolph Scott (*Vance Irby*); Humphrey Bogart (*John Murrell*); Frank McHugh (*Mr. Upjohn*); Alan Hale (*Olaf "Moose" Swenson*); Guinn "Big Boy" Williams (*Marblehead*).

Set in Nevada, this western revolves around five million dollars in gold bullion secretly being sent to help the Confederacy in the last days of the Civil War. Union officer Kerry Bradford is ordered to stop the shipment, which is guarded by Vance Irby. Julia Hayne is a Southern spy attracted to both men. John Murrell is a half-breed Mexican leading a huge band of bandits, and is killed by the cavalry.

Bogart wears a mustache which, as in *Isle of Fury* (1936), was an aesthetic mistake.

It All Came True (Warner Bros./First National, 1940) 97 minutes.

Director, Lewis Seiler; executive producers, Jack L. Warner and Hal B. Wallis; associate producer, Mark Hellinger; screenplay, Michael Fessier and Lawrence Kimble (based on "Bigger Than Life" by Louis Bromfield).

Cast: Ann Sheridan (*Sarah Jane Ryan*); Jeffrey Lynn (*Tommy Taylor*); Humphrey Bogart (*Grasselli/Chips Maguire*); ZaSu Pitts (*Miss Flint*); Una O'Connor (*Maggie Ryan*); Jessie Busley (*Norah Taylor*); John Litel (*Mr. Roberts*); Grant Mitchell (*Mr. Salmon*); Felix Bressart (*Mr. Boldini*).

This comedy has cop killer "Chips" Maguire hiding out in a boardinghouse filled with colorful eccentrics. When he sees an amateur night in the parlor, he suggests the place be turned into a nightclub.

Note: The screenwriters had trouble deciding whether the Bogart character was a good guy or a bad one, and this ambivalence shows in the final celluloid product.

"JUST CALL ME TWO-GUN LOUIE! OR IS IT TWO-GUN LEFTY? OR IS IT FEATHERS MALONE? SAY . . . JUST WHAT IS MY NICKNAME?"

Can you match Bogie's colorful on-screen nicknames to the correct movie?

1. "Turkey" Morgan	a. *All Through the Night*
2. "Red" Kennedy	b. *The Amazing Dr. Clitterhouse*
3. "Baby Face" Martin	c. *The Big Shot*
4. "Rocks" Valentine	d. *Bullets or Ballots*
5. "Whip" McCord	e. *Dead End*
6. "Chuck" Martin	f. *Dead Reckoning*
7. "Chips" Maguire	g. *Invisible Stripes*
8. "Gloves" Donahue	h. *It All Came True*
9. "Duke" Berne	i. *Kid Galahad*
10. "Duke" Mantee	j. *The Oklahoma Kid*
11. "The Mug"	k. *The Petrified Forest*
12. "Bugs" Fenner	l. *San Quentin*
13. "Rip" Murdock	m. *Three on a Match*

Answers: 1-i, 2-l, 3-e, 4-b, 5-j, 6-g, 7-h, 8-a, 9-c, 10-k, 11-m, 12-d, 13-f.

Brother Orchid (Warner Bros./First National, 1940) 91 minutes.

Director, Lloyd Bacon; executive producer, Hal B. Wallis; associate producer, Mark Hellinger; screenplay, Earl Baldwin (from a story by Richard Connell).

Cast: Edward G. Robinson (*Little John Sarto*); Ann Sothern (*Flo Addams*); Humphrey Bogart (*Jack Buck*); Donald Crisp (*Brother Superior*); Ralph Bellamy (*Clarence Fletcher*); Allen Jenkins (*Willie the Knife*).

Racket boss "Little John" Sarto goes to Europe in search of "class," and returns to find his mob taken over by grasping Jack Buck. Wounded in a gunfight, Sarto takes refuge in a monastery where he is soon won over by the humility of the religious brothers, and by their "class." When he learns that the religious order is in trouble because his old gang has stopped them from selling their flowers, he heads back to the city to take care of business.

They Drive by Night (Warner Bros./First National, 1940) 93 minutes.

Director, Raoul Walsh; executive producer, Hal B. Wallis; associate producer, Mark Hellinger; screenplay, Jerry Wald and Richard Macaulay (based on the novel *The Long Haul* by A. I. Bezzerides).

Cast: George Raft (*Joe Fabrini*); Ann Sheridan (*Cassie Hartley*); Ida Lupino (*Lana Carlsen*); Humphrey Bogart (*Paul Fabrini*); Gale Page (*Pearl Fabrini*); Alan Hale (*Ed Carlsen*); Roscoe Karns (*Irish McGurn*); John Litel (*Harry McNamara*); George Tobias (*George Rondolos*).

The two Fabrini brothers work hard in the trucking business. Joe goes to work for the top man, Ed Carlsen, and attracts the attention of the boss's wife Lana. When Joe spurns her, she kills her husband and blames him. Paul Fabrini hates the road; he falls asleep at the wheel, crashes, and loses an arm.

Note: This is a remake of *Bordertown* (1935) with Paul Muni and Bette Davis. The leading man did not have a brother in that version.

High Sierra (Warner Bros./First National, 1941) 100 minutes.

Director, Raoul Walsh; executive producer, Hal B. Wallis; associate producer, Mark Hellinger; screenplay, John Huston and W. R. Burnett (based on the novel by Burnett).

Cast: Ida Lupino (*Marie Garson*); Humphrey Bogart (*Roy Earle*); Alan Curtis (*Babe Kozak*); Arthur Kennedy (*Red Hattery*); Joan Leslie (*Velma*); Henry Hull (*Doc Banton*); Henry Travers (*Pa Goodhue*); Jerome Cowan (*Healy*); Barton MacLane (*Jake Kranmer*).

The last days of old-style gangster Roy Earle. He's sprung from prison to engineer a major holdup. The robbery is pulled off, and Roy makes his getaway with Marie, a dance-hall hostess. But then his two henchmen are killed, the mastermind behind the robbery dies of a heart attack, and the police are hot on Roy's trail. Earle puts Marie on a bus, then heads for a mountain pass, hoping to make it out of California. He's trapped on a mountain peak by the law. "Mr. Bogart plays the leading role with a perfection of hard-boiled vitality" (*New York Times*, January 25, 1941).

"One of the finest performances of a fine actor. . . . He is at once savage and sentimental; fatalistic and filled with half-formulated aspirations. . . . His steady portrayal, even more than Raoul Walsh's staccato staging, is what makes the melodrama something more than merely exciting" (*New York Herald Tribune*, January 25, 1941).

Note: Ida Lupino was given star billing in this Warner Bros. project because of the rave reviews she'd received for her mad scene in *They Drive by Night* (1940).

Remakes: The western *Colorado Territory* (Warner Bros., 1949), with Joel McCrea and Virginia Mayo, directed by Raoul Walsh; and *I Died a*

Thousand Times (Warner Bros., 1955) a CinemaScope color version, with Jack Palance and Shelley Winters.

The Wagons Roll at Night (Warner Bros./First National, 1941) 84 minutes.

Director, Ray Enright; executive producers, Jack L. Warner and Hal B. Wallis; associate producer, Harlan Thompson; screenplay, Fred Niblo Jr. and Barry Trivers (based on the novel *Kid Galahad* by Francis Wallace).

Cast: Humphrey Bogart (*Nick Coster*); Sylvia Sidney (*Flo Lorraine*); Eddie Albert (*Matt Varney*); Joan Leslie (*Mary Coster*); Sig Ruman (*Hoffman the Great*); Cliff Clark (*Doc*); Charley Foy (*Snapper*); Frank Wilcox (*Tex*); John Ridgely (*Arch*).

Carnival owner Nick Coster keeps his personal life a secret—few know he has a convent-bred younger sister, Mary. Nick trains grocery clerk Matt to be a lion tamer, but is upset when the young man meets and falls in love with Mary. Nick urges Matt into the cage of a mad lion. When his sister begs him to save her lover, Nick goes into the cage and dies in place of the grocery clerk.

"[Bogart is] badly hampered in a ridiculously fustian villain role" (*New York Times*, May 10, 1941).

Remakes: *The Wagons Roll at Night* is a close variation of *Kid Galahad* (1937), in which Bogart was featured. The story was rehashed again as *Kid Galahad* (1962), starring Elvis Presley, with Gig Young in the parallel Bogart assignment.

The Maltese Falcon (Warner Bros./First National, 1941) 100 minutes.

Director, John Huston; executive producer, Hal B. Wallis; associate producer, Henry Blanke; screenplay, John Huston (based on the Dashiell Hammett novel).

Cast: Humphrey Bogart (*Sam Spade*); Mary Astor (*Brigid O'Shaughnessy*); Gladys George (*Iva Archer*); Peter Lorre (*Joel Cairo*); Barton MacLane (*Lieutenant Dundy*); Lee Patrick (*Effie Perine*); Sydney Greenstreet (*Casper Gutman*); Ward Bond (*Detective Tom Polhaus*); Jerome Cowan (*Miles Archer*); Elisha Cook Jr. (*Wilmer Cook*).

Tough San Francisco private eye Sam Spade encounters a mysterious, beautiful woman, Brigid O'Shaughnessy, and an assortment of other memorable characters—including a very fat individual named Gutman, an effete little man wearing perfume, and a nervous gunman named

Wilmer—as he tracks down his partner's killer and a priceless jeweled antique statuette of a falcon.

"Perfection" (*Variety*, October 1, 1941). "A knockout job, a classic in its field . . . with Humphrey Bogart contributing one of the finest performances of his career" (*New York Herald Tribune*, October 4, 1941).

Notes: This property had been filmed by Warner Bros. twice before— as *The Maltese Falcon* (1931) with Ricardo Cortez as Sam Spade, Bebe Daniels as the femme fatale; and as *Satan Met a Lady* (1936), with Warren William, Bette Davis, and Allison Skipworth as the detective, the mystery woman, and the grasping crook, respectively.

John Huston and screenwriter Howard Koch later collaborated on an original screenplay called *Three Strangers*, written for Bogart, Greenstreet, Lorre, and Mary Astor, as an unofficial *Maltese Falcon*–type thriller. The story is of a search for unattainable wealth, again, this time revolving around a winning lottery ticket. The eventual movie, directed by Jean Negulesco, was a 1946 Warner Bros. release. However, the dream billing didn't happen: Greenstreet and Lorre were the male leads, with Geraldine Fitzgerald in the Astor part.

With *The Maltese Falcon*, John Huston cast his father, Walter Huston, in an unbilled appearance as Captain Jacobi, the wounded seafarer who brings the black bird statuette to Sam Spade's office.

Bogart and Peter Lorre were best of friends. They also costarred in *All Through the Night* (1942), *Casablanca* (1942), *Passage to Marseille* (1944), and *Beat the Devil* (1954).

Remakes: There was a George Segal movie called *The Black Bird* (Columbia, 1975) which was a takeoff, or a spoof, or *something*, on *The Maltese Falcon*—but it didn't work on any level. Of fleeting interest was the casting of Peter Lorre as a gunman named Wilmer (a slight change from his role in the original), and Lee Patrick as a secretary called Effie (a role she was more comfortable with in the 1941 production).

One final note: Writer Dashiell Hammett (1899–1961), the acknowledged father of the hard-boiled detective story, was under constant fire from his book publisher and editors to tone down the rough street language of his characters. So when he published *The Maltese Falcon* in 1931, he sneaked one past them: the word *gunsel*—meaning gunman, right? Wrong. It's a word going back to Elizabethan England, identifying someone on the receiving end of a homosexual liaison. The fall-guy gunman Wilmer, played by Elisha Cook Jr., is identified as a gunsel. The Bogart character in *Across the Pacific* (1942) even refers to a "Jap gunsel."

All Through the Night (Warner Bros./First National, 1942) 107 minutes.

Director, Vincent Sherman; producer, Jerry Wald; executive producer, Hal B. Wallis; screenplay, Leonard Spigelgass and Edwin Gilbert (based on a story by Leonard Q. Ross [Leo Rosten] and Spigelgass).

Cast: Humphrey Bogart (*Gloves Donahue*); Conrad Veidt (*Hall Ebbing*); Kaaren Verne (*Leda Hamilton*); Jane Darwell (*Ma Donahue*); Frank McHugh (*Barney*); Peter Lorre (*Pepi*); Judith Anderson (*Madame*); William Demarest (*Sunshine*); Jackie Gleason (*Starchie*); Phil Silvers (*waiter*); Barton MacLane (*Marty Callahan*).

Gangster "Gloves" Donahue and his bumbling underlings stumble over a nest of Nazis planning to blow up a battleship in New York Harbor. It's played mainly for laughs and for the action sequences, with the patriotic speeches turning up on schedule.

Notes: The Bogart biography by A. M. Sperber and Eric Lax sees this film as "in some zany ways a dry run for *Casablanca*." The co-writers of that classic, Philip and Julius Epstein, were brought in to touch up the script for this one.

The first choice for the male lead in *All Through the Night* was the charismatic, fast-talking Broadway columnist Walter Winchell, who wanted to accept the part, but couldn't fit it into his busy media schedule.

First choice for the female lead was Austrian import Luise Rainer, the two-time (1936 and 1937) Oscar-winning actress, who was hopeful of a screen comeback. Instead, the role went to Kaaren "Whatever happened to. . . ?" Verne, the former Mrs. Peter Lorre.

The Big Shot (Warner Bros./First National, 1942) 82 minutes.

Director, Lewis Seiler; producer, Walter MacEwen; screenplay, Bertram Millhauser, Abem Finkel, and Daniel Fuchs.

Cast: Humphrey Bogart (*Duke Berne*); Irene Manning (*Lorna Fleming*); Richard Travis (*George Anderson*); Susan Peters (*Ruth Carter*); Stanley Ridges (*Martin Fleming*); Minor Watson (*Warden Booth*); Chick Chandler (*Dancer*); Joseph Downing (*Frenchy*).

Duke Berne, once a big-shot gangster but now a three-time loser, reluctantly becomes part of an armored-car robbery. His former sweetheart

Lorna keeps him from joining the holdup, but he's implicated and jailed anyway. Duke breaks out of prison to kill the criminal mastermind, but both men die in the climactic gunfight.

Note: Both George Raft, now in the last months of his dying contract with Warner Bros., and Mary Astor, had passed on this property. Then Vincent Sherman was replaced as director at the last minute by Lewis Seiler, who, reports have it, had to be reminded to appear on the set before the stars. To say that Bogart saved this movie from being just another gangster rerun is, unfortunately, not saying much.

> "You pay for your sins on television reruns today. Some pictures were acclaimed as great successes—and look at them now!"
> —Edward G. Robinson (quoted in Ezra Goodman's *Bogey: The Good-Bad Guy*, 1965)

Across the Pacific (Warner Bros./First National, 1942) 97 minutes.

Director, John Huston; producers, Jerry Wald and Jack Saper; screenplay, Richard Macaulay (based on the novel *Aloha Means Goodbye* by Robert Carson).

Cast: Humphrey Bogart (*Richard Thomas "Rick" Leland*); Mary Astor (*Alberta Marlowe*); Sydney Greenstreet (*Dr. Lorenz*); Charles Halton (*A. V. Smith*); Victor Sen Yung (*Joe Totsuiko*); Roland Got (*Sugi*); Lee Tung Foo (*Sam Wing On*); Frank Wilcox (*Captain Morison*).

Rick Leland is a secret agent who poses as a court-martialed soldier selling his services to the highest bidder—even to the Japanese, planning to bomb the Panama Canal. On a ship bound for Japan by way of Panama, Leland meets Japanese sympathizer Dr. Lorenz, and mystery woman Alberta Marlowe. Rick uncovers the plot to bomb the Panama Canal and single-handedly prevents the attack.

Notes: The original idea behind this project had been to continue the story of *The Maltese Falcon*, picking up the main characters from where they left off. But there were too many problems; like: What do you do with Brigid O'Shaughnessy (Mary Astor), who is "taking the fall" and going to prison?

Most of the Japanese characters on-screen here are portrayed by Chinese actors, as many Japanese-Americans were being put into internment camps because of the war scare.

If you want to get picky about it—or geographically correct—this movie should have been called *"Across the Atlantic,"* as most of the action occurs on the Atlantic side of the Canal.

Casablanca (Warner Bros./First National, 1942) 102 minutes.

Director, Michael Curtiz; producer, Hal B. Wallis; screenplay, Julius J. and Philip G. Epstein and Howard Koch (based on the unproduced play *Everybody Comes to Rick's,* by Murray Burnett and Joan Alison).

Cast: Humphrey Bogart (*Richard "Rick" Blaine*); Ingrid Bergman (*Ilsa Lund*); Paul Henreid (*Victor Laszlo*); Claude Rains (*Capt. Louis Renault*); Conrad Veidt (*Major Heinrich Strasser*), Sydney Greenstreet (*Señor Farrari*); Peter Lorre (*Ugarte*); Dooley Wilson (*Sam*); S. Z. Sakall (*Carl*); Madeleine LeBeau (*Yvonne*); John Qualen (*Berger*); Leonid Kinskey (*Sascha*); Helmut Dantine (*Jan Brandel*); Curt Bois (*pickpocket*); Marcel Dalio (*Emil, the Croupier*).

During World War II, refugees fleeing the Nazis head for Casablanca in North Africa, which was the jumping-off point for America. In Casablanca, everybody comes to Rick's Café Americain, where one can find just about anything: liquor, gambling, music, companionship. From out of the past, Rick's one true love, Ilsa, shows up at the cafe one night—but she's married to Victor Laszlo, a resistance fighter the Nazis are looking for. Rick makes his wrenching choice between love and duty, in one of the cinema's most famous and most-quoted endings.

"[Warner Bros.] used Bogart's personality, so well established in other brilliant films, to inject a cold point of tough resistance to evil" (*New York Times,* November 27, 1942).

"*High Sierra* and *The Maltese Falcon* made him a star; it remained for *Casablanca* to make him a myth" (Andrew Sarris, "Here's Looking at You, Bogie," in *The Village Voice,* February 14, 1977).

Notes: After the enormous success of *Casablanca,* there were countless attempts to duplicate the film, or to be associated with it, or just to use elements that might remind viewers of it.

One way was to utilize other imported leading ladies, like the Swedishborn Ingrid Bergman playing opposite Bogart on-screen. Some examples are:

Michele Morgan (from France) in *Passage to Marseille* (1944)
Florence Marly (from Czechoslovakia) in *Tokyo Joe* (1949)

Marta Toren (from Sweden) in *Sirocco* (1951)
Gina Lollobrigida (from Italy) in *Beat the Devil* (1954)

Remakes: There have been various unofficial remakes of *Casablanca*, including two with Bogart himself: *To Have and Have Not* (1944) and *Key Largo* (1948).

Other unofficial remakes, and their leading men, include *Tequila Sunrise* (1988), with Mel Gibson; *Havana* (1990), with Robert Redford; and *Caboblanco* (1981), with Charles Bronson.

Some Rick Blaines:

Alan Ladd starred in the *Lux Radio Theatre* production of *Casablanca* (CBS, January 24, 1944; 60 minutes). Others in the cast were Hedy Lamarr (*Ilsa*), John Loder (*Victor Laszlo*), Edgar Barrier (*Captain Renault*), Norman Field (*Major Strasser*).

Paul Douglas headlined in the *Lux Video Theatre* version (CBS, March 3, 1955; 60 minutes). Also appearing were Arlene Dahl (*Ilsa*), Hoagy Carmichael (*Sam*), Carl Esmond (*Victor Laszlo*), John Hoyt (*Captain Renault*), and Ivan Triesault (*Major Strasser*).

Charles McGraw, playing a character called Rick Jason for some reason, starred in another television version of *Casablanca*, which was presented as one-third of *Warner Bros. Presents*, an hourlong ABC series alternating with *Cheyenne* and *King's Row*. The *Casablanca* section aired in eleven episodes, from September 13, 1955, to April 24, 1956. Regulars in the show included two actors from the original 1942 feature: Marcel Dalio, who was the croupier in the film, now played Captain Renault; and Dan Seymour, Abdul the doorman in the original movie, was now Farrari. Clarence Muse played Sam the piano man in this TV series.

David Soul starred in a 1982 *Casablanca* series on CBS-TV that lasted just five episodes, between April 10 and September 3. Other regulars on the hourlong show were played by Hector Elizondo (*Captain Renault*), Reuven Bar-Yotam (*Farrari*), Ray Liotta (bartender *Sasha*), Scatman Crothers (*Sam*), and Patrick Horgan (*Major Strasser*). This production of *Casablanca* was special in that it used the sets from the original film.

Action in the North Atlantic (Warner Bros./First National, 1943) 127 minutes.

Director, Lloyd Bacon; producer, Jerry Wald; screenplay, John Howard Lawson; additional dialog, A. I. Bezzerides and W. R. Burnett (based on the novel by Guy Gilpatric).

Cast: Humphrey Bogart (*First Mate Joe Rossi*); Raymond Massey (*Captain Steve Jarvis*); Alan Hale (*Boats O'Hara*); Julie Bishop (*Pearl*); Ruth Gordon (*Mrs. Jarvis*); Sam Levene (*Chips Abrams*); Dane Clark (*Johnny Pulaski*).

In World War II, a deadly game of cat and mouse is played by the convoy ship *Sea Witch* and a German submarine. At first, the ship eludes the sub, but then it's attacked by German planes. When Captain Jarvis is wounded, first mate Joe Rossi takes command. The ship fakes a fire, which lures the sub to the surface, whereupon the *Sea Witch* rams it.

Note: It was in this picture that a new contract player, by the name of Bernie Zanville, first worked with Bogart. The studio insisted on changing Zanville's name, coming up with the usual list which included Zane Clark. Bogart suggested, instead, Dane Clark, and a friendship between them was started.

Sahara (Columbia, 1943) 97 minutes.

Director, Zoltan Korda; producer, Harry Joe Brown; screenplay, John Howard Lawson and Zoltan Korda; adaptation by James O'Hanlon (from an original story by Philip MacDonald, based on an incident in the 1937 Soviet feature film, *The Thirteen*).

Cast: Humphrey Bogart (*Sergeant Joe Gunn*); Bruce Bennett (*Waco Hoyt*); J. Carrol Naish (*Guiseppe*); Lloyd Bridges (*Fred Clarkson*); Rex Ingram (*Tambul*); Richard Nugent (*Captain Jason Halliday*); Dan Duryea (*Jimmy Doyle*), Carl Harbord (*Marty*), Kurt Krueger (*Captain Von Schletow*).

During World War II, in the Libyan Desert, an American tank crew is led by Sergeant Gunn. They are holed up in an abandoned fort, fighting off a battalion of Germans desperate for water . . . who are unaware that the well is dry.

"This story is told so expertly, detail by detail, that the whole unlikely affair seems believable. Humphrey Bogart is the only well-known actor in the picture. To say that he is as good as the rest of the cast is high praise" (*Time* magazine, October 18, 1943).

Note: The most intriguing aspect of *Sahara* is its writing credits (see above).

Remakes: *Sahara* is often listed as a remake of John Ford's psychological drama *The Lost Patrol* (1934).

Passage to Marseille (Warner Bros./First National, 1944) 109 minutes.

Director, Michael Curtiz; producer, Hal B. Wallis; screenplay, Casey Robinson and Jack Moffitt (based on the novel *Men Without Country* by Charles Nordhoff and James Norman Hall).

Cast: Humphrey Bogart (*Matrac*); Claude Rains (*Captain Freycinet*); Michele Morgan (*Paula*); Philip Dorn (*Renault*); Sydney Greenstreet (*Major Duval*); Peter Lorre (*Marius*); George Tobias (*Petit*); Helmut Dantine (*Garou*); John Loder (*Manning*); Victor Francen (*Captain Malo*); Vladimir Sokoloff (*Grandpère*); Eduardo Ciannelli (*Chief Engineer*).

World War II in France. French journalist Matrac is framed for murder and sent to the Devil's Island penal colony. He and four other convicts—Renault, Marius, Petit, and Garou—escape in a canoe and are picked up by a French freighter. When word is received that France has fallen to the Nazis, the convicts help put down a mutiny on the ship. Later, they join a Free French bomber squadron.

London's *Today's Cinema* reported in 1944: "The crackling action and the patriotic motif will appeal powerfully to the generality of cinemagoers. Humphrey Bogart plays Matrac with a species of tortured concentration which does reveal something of the character's thwarted idealism."

Notes: There was controversy and condemnation over the scene in which Bogart machine-guns the surviving helpless crew of a wrecked German plane. The sequence was cut from prints distributed in Europe.

Also, the city is incorrectly spelled in the title as "*Marseille*." It should be "*Marseilles*."

To Have and Have Not (Warner Bros./First National, 1944) 100 minutes.

Producer-director, Howard Hawks; screenplay, Jules Furthman and William Faulkner (based on the novel by Ernest Hemingway).

Cast: Humphrey Bogart (*Harry Morgan*); Walter Brennan (*Eddie*); Lauren Bacall (*Marie*); Dolores Moran (*Helene de Brusac*); Hoagy Carmichael (*Cricket*); Walter Molnar (*Paul de Brusac*); Sheldon Leonard (*Lieutenant Coyo*); Marcel Dalio (*Gerard*); Dan Seymour (*Captain Renard*).

During World War II in the Caribbean, Harry Morgan hires out his small cabin cruiser to take wealthy sportsmen on fishing trips. When he's asked to smuggle French underground leader Paul de Brusac to safety, he refuses. But then love—and various characters trying to push him around—brings out the political animal in him and forces him to choose sides.

According to *Today's Cinema* in early 1945: "Bogart . . . dominates the portrayal and the artistes. Harry is another of those curiously intense characterizations in which he is so renowned a specialist . . . excellent melodramatic entertainment."

Note: This was the first screen pairing of Bogart and Bacall, which set off sparks. Director Hawks said afterward: "Without [Bogart's] help, I couldn't have done what I did with Bacall. Not many actors would sit around and wait while a girl steals a scene. But he fell in love with the girl and the girl with him, and that made it easy."

Remakes: *The Breaking Point* (1950), with John Garfield and Patricia Neal; and *The Gun Runners* (1958), with Audie Murphy and Patricia Owens. Both films kept the Caribbean setting of the original Hemingway novel and the 1944 Bogart-Bacall feature.

Conflict (Warner Bros./First National, 1945) 86 minutes.

Director, Curtis Bernhardt; producer, William Jacobs; screenplay, Arthur T. Horman and Dwight Taylor (based on a story by Robert Siodmak and Alfred Neumann).

Cast: Humphrey Bogart (*Richard Mason*), Alexis Smith (*Evelyn Turner*); Sydney Greenstreet (*Dr. Mark Hamilton*); Rose Hobart (*Kathryn Mason*); Charles Drake (*Professor Norman Holdsworth*); Grant Mitchell (*Dr. Grant*); Patrick O'Moore (*Detective Egan*); Ann Shoemaker (*Nora Grant*).

An unhappy marriage ends in death, when Richard Mason cleverly (he thinks) murders his wife Kathryn. Then strange things begin to happen which make it look as if the spouse is still alive. But it's a game being played by shrewd psychiatrist Dr. Hamilton to catch a murderer.

"Bogart plays the unlucky killer with his usual proficient intensity. There is enough talent and ambition involved in *Conflict* to make another *Double Indemnity* [1944], which is roughly what its makers were trying for. But the picture is too ornate to be of genuine psychological interest, and too slow to be thoroughly exciting" (*Time* magazine, August 13, 1945).

Note: *Conflict* is a lesser Warner Bros. effort. There is speculation that perhaps the movie was made to capitalize on the well-known real-life conflict between Bogart and wife Mayo Methot.

The Big Sleep (Warner Bros./First National, 1946) 114 minutes.

Producer-director, Howard Hawks; screenplay, William Faulkner, Leigh Brackett, and Jules Furthman (based on the novel by Raymond Chandler).

Cast: Humphrey Bogart (*Philip Marlowe*); Lauren Bacall (*Vivian Sternwood Rutledge*); John Ridgely (*Eddie Mars*); Martha Vickers (*Carmen Sternwood*); Dorothy Malone (*Bookstore owner*); Peggy Knudsen (*Mona [Mrs. Eddie] Mars*); Regis Toomey (*Bernie Ohls*); Charles Waldron (*General Sternwood*); Charles D. Brown (*Norris*); Bob Steele (*Canino*); Elisha Cook Jr. (*Harry Jones*); Louis Jean Heydt (*Joe Brody*); Sonia Darrin (*Agnes*); Dan Wallace (*Owen Taylor*); Tom Rafferty (*Carol Lundgren*); Theodore Von Eltz (*Arthur Geiger*).

This film details the adventures of private detective Philip Marlowe, who is hired by a millionaire to deal with a blackmailer, but becomes very involved with the lives and crimes of the man's two daughters: the nymphomaniac Carmen, and the seductive, wisecracking Vivian.

"A violent, smoky cocktail shaken together from most of the printable misdemeanors and some that aren't—one of those Raymond Chandler Specials which puts you, along with the cast, into a state of semi-amnesia through which tough action and reaction drum with something of the nonsensical solace of hard rain on a tin roof" (James Agee, *The Nation*, August 31, 1946).

Remake: *The Big Sleep* (1978), updated and set in London, starring Robert Mitchum and Sarah Miles.

The Big Sleep was filmed in late 1944 and early 1945. Lauren Bacall then made *Confidential Agent* (Warner Bros., 1945) with Charles Boyer, which was released first. When she received devastatingly bad reviews for *Agent*, Warner Bros. decided to shoot new scenes for *The Big Sleep* that would play up the provocative, insolent Bacall so popular from *To Have and Have Not*.

A year after *The Big Sleep* had wrapped, the cast and crew reassembled to shoot eighteen minutes of new footage. A like amount of footage was then deleted from the first version . . . including a scene in which Bogart explains who killed whom.

The new version was released to wide acclaim, Bacall's screen reputation was saved, and *The Big Sleep* became famous for its incomprehensible plot: Who did kill the chauffeur?

Director Howard Hawks defended the movie (quoted in William Meyer: *Warner Bros. Directors*; New Rochelle, NY: Arlington House, 1978), saying "[The plot] didn't matter at all. I say neither the author, the writer, nor myself knew who had killed whom. It was all what made a good scene. I can't follow it. I saw some of it on television last night, and it had me thoroughly confused."

The intial, 1945 version of *The Big Sleep*, which had been shown at the time only to American servicemen overseas, was discovered and restored by the UCLA Film and Television Archive and exhibited in the United States for the first time in 1997.

Most fans of the film agree that the plot is irrelevant anyway, that what counts is the excitement, the erotic byplay and wisecracks between the characters, the charged atmosphere.

For those who still insist on "Whodunit?" here is . . .

The Big Sleep Explained

Soldier-of-fortune Shawn Regan (a major character never seen in the film) is hired by wealthy General Sternwood (Charles Waldron). Sternwood has two beautiful daughters with "corrupt blood": sexy, spoiled Carmen (Martha Vickers) and the cool, insolent Vivian (Lauren Bacall).

Carmen loves Regan but he treats her like a child. Instead, he becomes involved with the wife (Peggy Knudsen) of gambling tycoon Eddie Mars (John Ridgely), so jealous Carmen kills him. Mars hides the body, and sends blackmail demands to Vivian, who pays to protect her sister.

At the same time, Carmen also attracts the attentions of the Sternwood's chauffeur Owen Taylor (Dan Wallace)—and, at the same time, she is the subject of pornographic photos (perhaps taken while she was zonked out of her mind on drugs), and is being blackmailed by Arthur Geiger (Theodore Von Eltz), owner of a bookstore selling pornography from the back room.

The chauffeur kills Geiger for blackmailing Carmen. Taylor, in turn, is eliminated by Joe Brody (Louis Jean Heydt), to get those valuable photos of Carmen. Brody is the boyfriend of Agnes

(Sonia Darren), the woman who works in Geiger's bookstore and doesn't know about first editions when Marlowe asks her about *Ben-Hur*.

Marlowe follows Vivian to Brody's apartment. Brody goes to answer the doorbell, and is killed by Carol Lundgren (Tom Rafferty, in leather jacket), Geiger's "shadow" (lover?) who thinks that Brody killed Geiger.

Agnes, busy lady that she is, is also friends with Harry Jones (Elisha Cook Jr.) who is killed by Eddie Mars's scary gunman Canino (Bob Steele) to prevent him from telling Marlowe what he knows about Shawn Regan.

Canino traps Marlowe at the garage and is about to shoot him but, with Vivian's help, Marlowe kills him first.

Marlowe then lures Eddie Mars to a showdown and tricks him into being machine-gunned by his own men.

Any questions?

Dead Reckoning (Columbia, 1947) 100 minutes.

Director, John Cromwell; producer, Sidney Biddell; screenplay, Oliver H. P. Garrett and Steve Fisher; adaptation, Allen Rivkin (based on a story by Gerald Adams and Sidney Biddell).

Cast: Humphrey Bogart (*Rip Murdock*); Lizabeth Scott (*Coral Chandler*); Morris Carnovsky (*Martinelli*); Charles Cane (*Lieutenant Kincaid*); William Prince (*Johnny Drake*); Marvin Miller (*Krause*); Wallace Ford (*McGee*); James Bell (*Father Logan*).

Ex-paratrooper Rip Murdock investigates the murder of a friend, and encounters an ice-water blonde, Coral Chandler, for whom men may have committed homicide—and who may have done some killing on her own.

An obvious (though unsuccessful) attempt to make another *The Maltese Falcon*, the ex-paratrooper hero even tells the blonde: "You're going to fry! A guy's pal is killed, he ought to do something about it."

The Two Mrs. Carrolls (Warner Bros./First National, 1947) 99 minutes.

Director, Peter Godfrey; producer, Mark Hellinger; screenplay, Thomas Job (based on the play by Martin Vale).

Cast: Humphrey Bogart (*Geoffrey Carroll*); Barbara Stanwyck (*Sally Carroll*); Alexis Smith (*Cecily Latham*); Nigel Bruce (*Dr. Tuttle*); Isobel Elsom (*Mrs. Latham*); Patrick O'Moore (*Charles Pennington*); Ann Carter (*Beatrice Carroll*); Anita Bolster (*Christine*).

This melodrama of a woman in distress is set in England. Sally marries artist Geoffrey Carroll and slowly uncovers the details of the mysterious death of the *first* Mrs. Carroll.

When *The Two Mrs. Carrolls* opened in England in mid-1945, the *London Times* offered, "The characters Mr. Humphrey Bogart normally plays are happier knocking girls about than poisoning them in the intervals of talking about art, and as Geoffrey, he is equally unconvincing as artist, madman, and murderer. The setting is an English cathedral town as Warner Brothers imagine it, and a curious place it is, almost as curious as the failure of a film with an exciting idea to be in any way exciting itself."

Dark Passage (Warner Bros./First National, 1947) 106 minutes.

Director, Delmer Daves; producer, Jerry Wald; screenplay, Delmer Daves (based on the novel *The Dark Road* by David Goodis).

Cast: Humphrey Bogart (*Vincent Parry*); Lauren Bacall (*Irene Jansen*); Bruce Bennett (*Bob Rapf*); Agnes Moorehead (*Madge Rapf*); Tom D'Andrea (*Sam*); Clifton Young (*Baker*); Douglas Kennedy (*Detective*).

Vincent Parry is framed for the murder of his wife. He escapes from San Quentin, changes his face with plastic surgery, and then seeks the real killer, while the police search for him. He is aided by Irene Jansen, a young woman who believes in his innocence. Irene hides Vincent in her apartment, and, because they're Bogie and Bacall, they fall in love.

"A suspenseful and surprising melodrama," said the *Motion Picture Herald* (September 6, 1947). The British *Monthly Film Bulletin* in the fall of 1947 disagreed: "An overlong and at times rather tedious thriller. Humphrey Bogart lacks something of his customary vigor."

Notes: This film noir thriller begins with a subjective point of view—we see everything through the eyes of Vincent Parry. The audience does not see the face of Humphrey Bogart until sixty-two minutes into the feature, when the bandages from plastic surgery are removed from his face.

Sequel: *Dark Passage* is sometimes listed as the source of *The Fugitive* (ABC-TV series, 1963–67), starring David Jansen, and the film version of *The Fugitive* (1993), with Harrison Ford, but that really seems to be stretching things—how many dozens of movies have there been about a guy hunting for his wife's killer?

The Treasure of the Sierra Madre (Warner Bros./First National, 1948) 126 minutes.

Director, John Huston; producer, Henry Blanke; screenplay, John Huston (based on the novel by B. Traven [pseudonym of Ret Marut]).

Cast: Humphrey Bogart (*Fred C. Dobbs*); Walter Huston (*Howard*); Tim Holt (*Curtin*); Bruce Bennett (*Cody*); Barton MacLane (*McCormick*); Alfonso Bedoya (*Gold Hat*); Bobby [Robert] Blake (*Mexican boy*); Jack Holt (*bum* in *flophouse*).

Dobbs and Curtin are two American drifters on the bum in Mexico. Howard is a grizzled old-timer wise in the ways of men and gold. The three men pool their resources and go looking for gold. They find their precious treasure, but suspicions cloud their minds and two of them are destroyed by greed and madness.

"This story and Huston's whole handling of it are about as near to folk art as a highly conscious artist can get; both also approach the global appeal, to the most and least sophisticated members of an audience, which the best poetic drama and nearly all the best movies have in common" (James Agee, *The Nation*, January 31, 1948).

Notes: Ann Sheridan is said to have made a brief appearance, heavily disguised as a streetwalker, in the film, as a good-luck gesture to director friend John Huston. If you spot her, please let me know.

B. Traven, the mystery-shrouded author of *The Treasure of the Sierra Madre* (1935), had wanted Lewis Stone ("Judge Hardy" from MGM's Andy Hardy movie series) for the part of Fred C. Dobbs.

Key Largo (Warner Bros./First National, 1948) 101 minutes.

Director, John Huston; producer, Jerry Wald; screenplay, Richard Brooks and John Huston (based on the play by Maxwell Anderson.)

Cast: Humphrey Bogart (*Frank McCloud*); Edward G. Robinson (*Johnny Rocco*); Lauren Bacall (*Nora Temple*); Lionel Barrymore (*James Temple*); Claire Trevor (*Gaye Dawn*); Thomas Gomez (*Curly Hoff*).

Ex–Army officer Frank McCloud seeks out the family of a World War II buddy, and finds them in a hotel on a Florida key. Before long, racketeer Johnny Rocco and his gang hold the group hostage in the hotel. McCloud agrees to help the gangsters escape to Cuba by boat, then, out on the ocean, he kills them one by one.

"A bang-up thriller of the old gangster school" (*New York Herald Tribune*, July 17, 1948).

Note: Claire Trevor won the Academy Award for Best Supporting Actress for her portrayal of the gangster's drunken mistress—a characterization that was probably based on Bogart's third wife, actress-singer Mayo Methot (see chapter 6: The Main Players in the Life of Humphrey Bogart, *Four Wives and One Mistress*).

Knock on Any Door (Santana Productions/Columbia, 1949) 100 minutes.

Director, Nicholas Ray; producer, Robert Lord; associate producer, Henry S. Kesler; screenplay, Daniel Taradash and John Monks Jr. (based on the novel by Willard Motley).

Cast: Humphrey Bogart (*Andrew Morton*); John Derek (*Nick Romano*); George Macready (*Kerman*); Allene Roberts (*Emma*); Susan Perry (*Adele Morton*); Mickey Knox (*Vito*); Barry Kelley (*Judge Drake*); Cara Williams (*Nelly*).

Andrew Morton is a lawyer who survived the mean streets of Chicago, and now feels compelled to help a young tough, Nick Romano, accused of killing a cop.

Notes: In January of 1948, Bogart realized a dream of independent filmmaking when he formed his own company, Santana Productions, named after his yacht. *Knock on Any Door* was the first of five Santana movies.

Knock on Any Door is the source of one of the most familiar quotes of the late 1940s–early 1950s, and which is still heard: "Live fast, die young and leave a good-looking corpse"—the motto of doomed Nick Romano.

Marlon Brando was interested in appearing in this film, in the Nick Romano role, when it involved the participation of two important producers: Mark Hellinger and David O. Selznick. When Hellinger died, in 1947, Selznick dropped out—and so did Brando.

Tokyo Joe (Santana Productions/Columbia, 1949) 88 minutes.

Director, Stuart Heisler; producer, Robert Lord; associate producer, Henry S. Kesler; screenplay, Cyril Hume and Bertram Millhauser (adapted by Walter Doniger, from the story by Steve Fisher).

Cast: Humphrey Bogart (*Joe Barrett*); Alexander Knox (*Mark Landis*); Florence Marly (*Trina*); Sessue Hayakawa (*Baron Kimura*); Jerome Courtland (*Danny*); Gordon Jones (*Idaho*).

After the end of World War II, the American Joe Barrett returns to Tokyo, where he once owned a nightclub and had a wife. The club is in other hands now, as is his wife, who is remarried and has a child. However, the little girl is Joe's, and he's forced to smuggle Japanese war criminals to save her. The Axis wrongdoers are caught, the girl is rescued, but Joe pays with his life.

Notes: The borrowings from *Casablanca* (1942) are pretty blatant, starting with the nightclub and the mysterious American in a foreign land. And Florence Marly seems made up to look like Lauren Bacall.

This film has a scene of Bogart rolling on the floor, practicing martial arts on an unwilling friend, that's as clumsy and funny as his fight with the fake octopus in *Isle of Fury* (1936).

Chain Lightning (Warner Bros./First National, 1950) 94 minutes.

Director, Stuart Heisler; producer, Anthony Veiller; screenplay, Liam O'Brien and Vincent Evans (based on a story by J. Redmond Prior).

Humphrey Bogart (*Matt Brennan*); Eleanor Parker (*Jo Holloway*); Raymond Massey (*Leland Willis*); Richard Whorf (*Carl*); James Brown (*Major Hinkle*); Roy Roberts (*General Hewitt*); Morris Ankrum (*Ed Bostwick*); Fay Baker (*Mrs. Willis*).

After World War II, former bomber pilot Matt Brennan gets a job with a plane manufacturer who's eager to sell the Air Force a new jet before its safety features have been thoroughly tested. After the plane's designer is killed perfecting an escape device, Matt risks his life to prove that it's safe.

"Humphrey Bogart, having by now exhausted almost all forms of ground-level strong-arm stuff, takes to the stratosphere in *Chain Lightning*. As long as he is aloft, flying everything from a B-17 during the war to a jet plane afterwards, there is plenty of zip in the film. It gets pretty sad when it comes down to earth though" (*The New Yorker*, March 4, 1950).

In a Lonely Place (Santana Productions/Columbia, 1950) 94 minutes.

Director, Nicholas Ray; producer, Robert Lord; associate producer, Henry S. Kesler; screenplay, Andrew Solt (adapted by Edmund North, from the novel by Dorothy B. Hughes).

Cast: Humphrey Bogart (*Dixon Steele*); Gloria Grahame (*Laurel Gray*); Frank Lovejoy (*Brub Nicolai*), Carl Benton Reid (*Captain Lochner*); Art Smith (*Mel Lippman*); Jeff Donnell (*Sylvia Nicolai*); Martha Stewart (*Mildred Atkinson*); Hadda Brooks (*nightclub singer*).

Hollywood screenwriter Dixon Steele, known for his violent temper, is suspected of murder. He's cleared by Laurel Gray, a beautiful blonde neighbor in his apartment building. The two become friends, then lovers . . . until Laurel sees the violence and jealousy Dixon is capable of. The real killer is found, but the couple recognize that their affair is over.

"[Like the young Method actors] Bogart revealed that he, too, was willing to plumb his own dark depths, and in doing so he gave his most subtle, disturbing performance" (Joshua Mooney, "Greatish Performances: Humphrey Bogart in *In a Lonely Place*," *Movieline* magazine, June 1998).

Notes: There seems to be much of Bogart in the tortured, resentful character of Dixon Steele, and in the references to people and places in his life.

Real-life restaurateur and friend Mike Romanoff appears in the movie, as himself. Bogart had wanted Lauren Bacall for the female lead, but Warner Bros. wouldn't release her for this Columbia Pictures production.

The Enforcer (United States Pictures/Warner Bros., 1951) 87 minutes.

Director, Bretaigne Windust [and Raoul Walsh, uncredited]; producer, Milton Sperling; screenplay, Martin Rackin.

Cast: Humphrey Bogart (*Martin Ferguson*); Zero Mostel (*Big Babe Lazich*); Ted De Corsia (*Joseph Rico*); Everett Sloane (*Albert Mendoza*); Roy Roberts (*Captain Frank Nelson*); Lawrence Tolan (*Duke Malloy*); King Donovan (*Sergeant Whitlow*); Bob Steele (*Herman*).

This fast-paced, stark drama concerns crusading district attorney Martin Ferguson trying to build a case against the mastermind of Murder, Inc.—an infamous murder-for-hire organization—and is notable for its use of a large number of familiar and forceful character actors.

Note: *The Enforcer* marked the end of an era: it was the forty-seventh and last feature film Bogart made for Warner Bros. (The first was *Big City Blues* in 1932.)

Sirocco (Santana Productions/Columbia, 1951) 98 minutes.

Director, Curtis Bernhardt; producer, Robert Lord; associate producer, Henry S. Kesler; screenplay, A. I. Bezzerides and Hans Jacoby (based on the novel *Coup de Grace* by Joseph Kessel).

Cast: Humphrey Bogart (*Harry Smith*); Marta Toren (*Violette*); Lee J. Cobb (*Colonel Feroud*); Everett Sloane (*General LaSalle*); Gerald Mohr (*Major Leon*); Zero Mostel (*Balukjian*); Nick Dennis (*Nasir Aboud*); Onslow Stevens (*Emir Hassan*).

Harry Smith is a gunrunner in 1925 French-occupied Damascus —an American without a past or strong political beliefs. (Sound familiar?) When he's finally motivated to take sides, to save an innocent police officer, he's killed as his reward.

One of the rebel leaders calls him "an oddity—an American in Damascus, with no morals, no political convictions." And if that doesn't tell you that you're in *Casablanca* territory, listen as kept lady Marta Toren relates how she's never loved her protector (Lee J. Cobb) and that she's always wanted him dead. In response, Bogie snarls, "You're a schweet kid!"

"The story follows a pattern familiar since *Casablanca*. The plot development is slow and lacks conviction, as does the Damascus atmosphere. Bogart himself, walking about the catacombs in a raincoat, gives a performance so emotionless and expressionless as to suggest a parody of his own acting technique" (British *Monthly Film Bulletin*, July 1951).

The African Queen (Horizon-Romulus/United Artists, 1951) Color, 105 minutes.

Director, John Huston; producer, S. P. Eagle [Sam Spiegel]; screenplay, James Agee and John Huston [and Peter Viertel, uncredited] (based on the novel by C. S. Forester).

Cast: Humphrey Bogart (*Charlie Allnut*); Katharine Hepburn (*Rose Sayer*); Robert Morley (*Reverend Samuel Sayer*); Peter Bull (*Captain of the* Louisa); Theodore Bikel (*First Officer of the* Louisa).

A romantic adventure set in Africa at the beginning of World War I— the story of how a grizzled, gin-swilling boat captain and a "crazy, psalm-singing skinny old maid" find love and sink a German gunboat.

"Vastly exciting. As for Bogart, he has shaken himself out of the routine performance he has been giving lately and gone back to being the actor he was years ago" reported the London *Sunday Times*, February 1952.

Notes: Humphrey Bogart won the Academy Award as Best Actor of the Year for his performance.

The African Queen is Bogart's sixty-fifth feature film, and his first in color.

Katharine Hepburn wrote a charming book about her experiences on the Dark Continent: *The Making of the African Queen: Or How I Went to Africa with Bogart, Bacall and Huston and Almost Lost My Mind* (New York: Knopf, 1987). Cinematographer Jack Cardiff has a chapter on the film in his memoirs, *Magic Hour* (London/Boston: Faber and Faber, 1996). Peter Viertel, who worked on the screenplay, wrote the novel *White Hunter, Black Heart* (Garden City, NY: Doubleday, 1953) which is a barely-disguised account of the filming, with an alarming portrait of John Huston as a dangerously obsessive hunter. (See Appendix 2: The Annotated, Opinionated Bibliography of Humphrey Bogart for further details.)

The African Queen had originally been bought by Columbia Pictures as a project for Charles Laughton and his actress wife Elsa Lanchester. Warner Bros. later acquired the screen rights from Columbia, intending to film the story with Bette Davis and David Niven.

Remakes: There were two attempts to turn *The African Queen* into a television series. In 1962, Four Star/NBC produced a pilot starring James Coburn and Glynis Johns; this aired on April 3, 1962. A 1977 version, from Viacom/CBS, featured Warren Oates and Mariette Hartley, and was seen on March 18, 1977. Neither project was heard from again after the unmemorable pilots were aired.

Deadline—U.S.A. (Twentieth Century–Fox, 1952) 87 minutes.

Director, Richard Brooks; producer, Sol C. Siegel; screenplay, Richard Brooks.

Cast: Humphrey Bogart (*Ed Hutchinson*); Ethel Barrymore (*Mrs. John Garrison*); Kim Hunter (*Nora*); Ed Begley (*Frank Allen*); Warren Stevens (*George Burrows*); Paul Stewart (*Harry Thompson*); Martin Gabel (*Tomas Rienzi*); Joe De Santis (*Herman Schmidt*); Joyce MacKenzie (*Kitty Garrison Geary*); Audrey Christie (*Mrs. Willebrandt*); Fay Baker (*Alice Garrison Courtney*); Jim Backus (*Jim Cleary*).

This is a newspaper movie, gangster movie, and romance all in one, and crusading newspaper editor Ed Hutchinson is fighting three battles at the same time. He's desperate to save the paper itself, as its indifferent owners want to sell it to the rival paper. He's pushing his staff to the limit to expose murderous vice king Tomas Rienzi. And he still loves his ex-wife Nora, who is planning to remarry.

"One of the most authentic and exciting newspaper dramas to come along in many a month . . . packed with touches which give it life." Bogart's performance is "assured throughout" (Vincent Canby, *Motion Picture Herald*, March 15, 1952).

Battle Circus (Metro-Goldwyn-Mayer, 1953) 90 minutes.

Director, Richard Brooks; producer, Pandro S. Berman; screenplay, Richard Brooks (based on a story by Allen Rivkin and Laura Kerr).

Cast: Humphrey Bogart (*Major Jed Webbe*); June Allyson (*Lieutenant Ruth McCara*); Keenan Wynn (*Sergeant Orevil Statt*); Robert Keith (*Lieutenant Colonel Hillary Whalters*); William Campbell (*Captain John Rustford*).

The work of a M.A.S.H. unit (Mobile Army Surgical Hospital) behind the front lines during the Korean War. Major Webbe is an Army surgeon and Lieutenant McCara a nurse. As portrayed by Bogart and Allyson, it's a totally unbelievable romance, with no on-screen chemistry between the costars. However, there are fascinating documentary details of the hospital being quickly dismantled and reassembled elsewhere.

According to the *London Times* in mid-1953, "The formula of mixing war and romance, of using the battlefield and the casualty station as background for the amorous maneuvers of conventional hero and heroine . . . is distasteful. In one or two semi-documentary scenes the film achieves interest and dignity but such scenes are all too few" (*London Times*).

Note: The picture was originally called *M.A.S.H. 66*—not to be confused with the Robert Altman film *M*A*S*H* (1970), or the beloved long-running television series of the same name (CBS, 1972–83), based on the Altman film. Neither of the latter would want to be associated with *Battle Circus*.

Beat the Devil (Santana-Romulus/United Artists, 1954) 93 minutes.

Director, John Huston; associate producer, Jack Clayton; screenplay, John Huston and Truman Capote (based on the novel by James Helvick).

Cast: Humphrey Bogart (*Billy Dannreuther*); Jennifer Jones (*Gwendolen Chelm*); Gina Lollobrigida (*Maria Dannreuther*); Robert

Morley (*Petersen*); Peter Lorre (*O'Hara*); Edward Underdown (*Harry Chelm*); Bernard Lee (*C. I. D. inspector*).

A wildly disparate group of adventurers, scoundrels, and crooks—most of the cast—are bound for Africa, where they hope to corner the uranium market. In the meantime, they're stranded in a small Italian town, then caught on a sinking ship, then arrested by an Arab police officer infatuated with Rita Hayworth.

"The main irritation of *Beat the Devil* is that it promises everything and, sure enough, everything is there if only somebody would put it all together" (Terence Pettigrew, *Bogart: A Definitive Study of His Film Career*, 1977/1981).

"As elaborate a shaggy dog story as have ever been told. A sort of a screwball classic" (*Time* magazine, May 8, 1954).

Notes: This movie is variously seen as a misguided attempt at a *Maltese Falcon*–type thriller . . . or as a *Maltese Falcon* spoof. Take your pick.

On his way to Europe, after the film's release, a customs official supposedly warned Bogie that if he made another movie like *Beat the Devil*, he wouldn't be allowed back in the country. "I won't want to come back," the movie star retorted.

The Caine Mutiny (A Stanley Kramer Company Production/Columbia, 1954) Color, 125 minutes.

Director, Edward Dmytryk; producer, Stanley Kramer; screenplay, Stanley Roberts; additional dialogue by Michael Blankfort (based on the novel by Herman Wouk).

Cast: Humphrey Bogart (*Captain Philip Francis Queeg*); Jose Ferrer (*Lieutenant Barney Greenwald*); Van Johnson (*Lieutenant Steve Maryk*); Fred MacMurray (*Lieutenant Tom Keefer*); Robert Francis (*Ensign Willie Keith*); May Wynn (*May Wynn*); Tom Tully (*Captain DeVries*); E. G. Marshall (*Lieutenant Commander Challee*); Lee Marvin (*Meatball*).

Captain Philip Francis Queeg is skipper of the destroyer *Caine*, stationed at Pearl Harbor after the beginning of World War II. Some of his officers consider him paranoid and cowardly and, during a typhoon, take control of the ship. During the court-martial that follows, Queeg comes apart on the witness stand.

"Bogart is not convincing as Captain Queeg, for his forte is projecting conviction, not uncertainty. The court-martial itself, which is exploited so dramatically on the stage, is thrown away in the film" (Henrietta Lehman, *Films in Review*, June–July, 1954).

"Bogart adds a quality of almost noble despair to the Captain's sufferings" (*Time* magazine, June 28, 1954).

Notes: Producer Stanley Kramer said of working with the star (quoted in Ezra Goodman's *Bogey, The Good-Bad Guy*, 1965): "Bogart was not too pleasant to me the first time I met him. . . . He has the damnedest facade of any man I've ever met in my life. He's playing Bogart all the time, but he's really a big, sloppy bowl of mush. I believe that the facade is a defense mechanism.

"During rehearsals, he'd complain in a loud voice: 'You can't expect me to remember these long speeches,' but when we got around to shooting them, he was letter perfect. He's supposed to be difficult, but he isn't at all.

"I knew I not only had the right guy but he would go all the way. Nobody ever came through better than Bogart did."

Author Herman Wouk himself dramatized the trial sequence from his 1951 novel, and presented it on Broadway in January of 1954 as *The Caine Mutiny Court Martial*. Lloyd Nolan starred as Captain Queeg, with Henry Fonda as Greenwald, and John Hodiak as Maryk. The production was directed by Charles Laughton. The play ran for 405 performances, and has the distinction of playing simultaneously with the movie—which has to be a first, and a last.

Sabrina (Paramount, 1954) 113 minutes.

Director-producer, Billy Wilder; screenplay, Billy Wilder, Samuel Taylor, and Ernest Lehman (based on the play *Sabrina Fair* by Taylor).

Cast: Humphrey Bogart (*Linus Larrabee*); Audrey Hepburn (*Sabrina Fairchild*); William Holden (*David Larrabee*); Walter Hampden (*Oliver Larrabee*); John Williams (*Thomas Fairchild*); Martha Hyer (*Elizabeth Tyson*); Marcel Dalio (*Baron*); Francis X. Bushman (*Mr. Tyson*).

Sabrina, the chauffeur's daughter, is infatuated with David, the playboy son of the rich Larrabee household. After a sojourn in Paris, a more worldly Sabrina returns home to Long Island, New York, to win the man of her dreams. The older and wiser brother Linus, a businessman, tries to steer the girl away from David, but is himself attracted to her. Hepburn and Wilder were both nominated for Academy Awards.

In reviewing the picture in September 1954, the *London Times* decided, "A gay trifle of a film which chatters away without making a bore of itself. Mr. Bogart is only too successful in considering himself past the age for romantic love."

Remake: *Sabrina* (1995), with Harrison Ford in the Bogart role, Julia Ormond in the Hepburn part, and Greg Kinnear in the Holden role.

The Barefoot Contessa (Figaro Inc./United Artists, 1954) Color, 128 minutes.

Director, Joseph L. Mankiewicz; producer, Forrest E. Johnston; screenplay, Joseph L. Mankiewicz.

Cast: Humphrey Bogart (*Harry Dawes*); Ava Gardner (*Maria Vargas*); Edmond O'Brien (*Oscar Muldoon*); Marius Goring (*Alberto Bravano*); Valentina Cortesa (*Eleanora Torlato-Favrini*); Rossano Brazzi (*Vincenzo Torlato-Favrini*); Elizabeth Sellars (*Jerry*).

This film unfolds the melodramatic life of Maria Vargas, a beautiful Spanish dancer who becomes a famous movie star. She dallies with many men, but finds love with a Spanish count. When she discovers that her husband is impotent, she decides to give him a child by another man. (Bad idea). Harry Dawes is the has-been movie director hired to direct a film starring Maria.

"The film has a few startlingly good lines and situations, and several embarrassingly bad ones, but even the neat lines, Bogart's expert delivery and some effectively acid scenes fail to make *Contessa* much more than an international set soap opera" (*Time* magazine, October 18, 1954).

Note: Actress Linda Darnell (1921–1965), who had an affair with Joseph L. Mankiewicz, claimed that she was the inspiration for the role of Maria Vargas. The director-writer himself has said that the role of Maria was based on Rita Hayworth (1918–1987), the Brooklyn-born Hollywood legend who was discovered dancing in Mexico, became a movie star, and had numerous love affairs and husbands, including actor/filmmaker Orson Welles and Moslem prince Ali Khan.

We're No Angels (Paramount, 1955) Color, 103 minutes.

Director, Michael Curtiz; producer, Pat Duggan; screenplay, Ronald MacDougall (based on the play *La Cuisine des Anges* by Albert Husson).

Cast: Humphrey Bogart (*Joseph*); Aldo Ray (*Albert*); Peter Ustinov (*Jules*); Joan Bennett (*Amelie Ducotel*); Basil Rathbone (*Andre Trochard*);

Leo G. Carroll (*Felix Ducotel*); John Baer (*Paul Trochard*); Gloria Talbot (*Isabelle Ducotel*).

A comedy of three convicts—Joseph, Albert, and Jules—who escape from Devil's Island, and take shelter with a family whose kindness wins them over. The carefree trio of con men and killers proceed to solve the family's domestic problems.

"The charm seems sometimes thinned to the vanishing point," reported the *London Financial Times* in mid-1955. "The three rogues . . . look terribly hard put to it having to be endlessly whimsical and droll. Mr. Bogart, favoring understatement, wildly throws his part away."

Remake: *We're No Angels* (1989), with Robert De Niro and Sean Penn (three convicts whittled down to two, along with the humor).

The Left Hand of God (Twentieth Century–Fox, 1955) Color, 87 minutes.

Director, Edward Dmytryk; producer, Buddy Adler; screenplay, Alfred Hayes (based on the novel by William E. Barrett).

Cast: Humphrey Bogart (*Jim Carmody*); Gene Tierney (*Anne Scott*); Lee J. Cobb (*Mieh Yang*); Agnes Moorehead (*Beryl Sigman*); E. G. Marshall (*Dr. David Sigman*); Jean Porter (*Mary Yin*); Carl Benton Reid (*Reverend Cornelius*).

In China, during World War II, Jim Carmody shows up at an isolated Catholic mission. He's dressed as a priest, though clearly not comfortable as such . . . especially when he begins to fall in love with nurse Anne Scott. Eventually it's revealed that Carmody is an American flyer who had been working for Chinese warlord Mieh Yang and escaped from him in the clothes of a priest. This production was shot in CinemaScope, which only magnified the film's melodramatic shortcomings.

"There are a number of scenes and incidents that strain the imagination. While at first glance, it's difficult to picture Bogart as a priest, his smooth portrayal of a spurious man of cloth is a compliment to his acting" (*Variety*, August 24, 1955).

The Desperate Hours (Paramount, 1955) 112 minutes.

Director-producer, William Wyler; associate producer, Robert Wyler; screenplay, Joseph Hayes (based on his novel and play).

Cast: Humphrey Bogart (*Glenn Griffin*); Fredric March (*Dan Hilliard*); Arthur Kennedy (*Jesse Bard*); Martha Scott (*Eleanor Hilliard*); Dewey

Martin (*Hal Griffin*); Gig Young (*Chuck*); Mary Murphy (*Cindy Hilliard*); Richard Eyer (*Ralphie Hilliard*).

Three escaped convicts take over a suburban home at gunpoint and hold the family captive. The drama evolves into a battle of nerves, and wits, between gang leader Glenn Griffin and Dan Hilliard, head of the household.

"A thriller that jabs so shrewdly and sharply at sensibility that the moviegoer's eye might feel that it has not so much been entertained as used for a pin cushion. Bogart gives a piteously horrible impression of the essential criminal" (*Time* magazine, October 10, 1955).

"Bogart has the honesty to meet his death scene as a small beaten man without any of the false movie bravado that sometimes glorifies crime. It is one of his greatest performances" (*Hollywood Reporter*, September 14, 1955).

Remake: *The Desperate Hours* (1990), with Mickey Rourke as the escaped convict, and Anthony Hopkins as the beleaguered family man.

The Harder They Fall (Columbia, 1956) 109 minutes.

Director, Mark Robson; producer, Philip Yordan; screenplay, Philip Yordan (based on the novel by Budd Schulberg).

Cast: Humphrey Bogart (*Eddie Willis*); Rod Steiger (*Nick Benko*); Jan Sterling (*Beth Willis*); Mike Lane (*Toro Moreno*); Max Baer (*Buddy Brannen*); Jersey Joe Walcott (*George*); Edward Andrews (*Jim Weyerhause*); Harold J. Stone (*Art Leavitt*).

Eddie Willis is an ex-sportswriter hired to sell a gentle giant, Toro Moreno, as a great boxer, when his fights are actually fixed by the crooked syndicate of promoters. When Toro is brutally defeated in a match that nets thousands of dollars for the syndicate—but only $49 for the boxer—Eddie gives the fighter his share of the winnings. He vows to expose the promoters.

"A hunk of red, raw meat, it has the most intense acting duel in many years, that between Bogart and Steiger, in which the latter has an initial advantage as the script's aggressor and uses it, and his brilliant talent, like a whip. But Bogart rides the tiger, gives better than he gets, and turns in his most outstanding performance since *The Petrified Forest*" (Jaik Rosenstein, *Hollywood Reporter*, March 23, 1956).

Note: The character of Toro Moreno is based on the boxer Primo Carnera (1906–1967) who, with the help of mobsters, became Heavyweight

Champion of the World. He lost the title in a brutal fight with an honest champion—Max Baer. In *The Harder They Fall*, the unsullied victor is called Buddy Brannen, but he's played by . . . Max Baer himself. Primo Carnera appeared in a few movies, including *Mighty Joe Young* (1949), as one of the strongmen monkeying around in a tug of war with Joe.

Other Movie Appearances

The Dancing Town (Paramount, October 27, 1928) Two reels.
    Director, Edmund Lawrence; screenplay, Rupert Hughes.
    Cast: Helen Hayes, Humphrey Bogart.
    An early sound film in Paramount's "Great Stars and Authors" series of short subjects. No complete copy is known to exist.

Broadway's Like That (Vitaphone/Warner Bros., 1930) 10 minutes.
    Director-in-chief, Murray Roth; story and dialogue, Stanley Rauh.
    Cast: Ruth Etting; Humphrey Bogart; Joan Blondell.
    Bogart is a city slicker who deceives nice girl Etting, who breaks into song when her heart is broken. The soundtrack for this early film has been lost.

Swingtime in the Movies (Vitaphone/Warner Bros., 1938) Technicolor, 20 minutes.
    Director/writer, Crane Wilbur; original songs, M. K. Jerome, Jack Scholl.
    Cast: Fritz Feld, Kathryn Kane, John Carroll, Charley Foy, Jerry Colonna, Helen Lynd, and Irene Franklin.
    A lively, behind-the-scenes look at moviemaking with numerous Warner Bros. luminaries making uncredited cameo appearances: Humphrey Bogart, George Brent, Gabriel Dell, John Garfield, Leo Gorcey, Huntz Hall, Billy Haloop, Priscilla Lane, Rosemary Lane, Pat O'Brien, and Marie Wilson.

In This Our Life (Warner Bros./First National, 1942) 97 minutes.
    Director, John Huston; producer, Hal B. Wallis in association with David Lewis; screenplay, Howard Koch (based on the novel by Ellen Glasgow).
    Cast: Bette Davis, Olivia de Havilland, George Brent, Dennis Morgan, Charles Coburn.

Walter Huston has a few lines as a bartender, but Bogart and other *Maltese Falcon* cast members were said to have made unbilled cameo appearances in this overblown feature film. If you spot them, let me know.

Thank Your Lucky Stars (Warner Bros./First National, 1943) 127 minutes.

Director, David Butler; producer, Mark Hellinger; screenplay, Norman Panama, Melvin Frank, and James V. Kern (based on an original story by Everett Freeman and Arthur Schwartz).

This patriotic all-star musical revue features Warners' top stars as themselves. Humphrey Bogart does a skit in which he's intimidated by roly-poly S. Z. "Cuddles" Sakall. Also featured are Eddie Cantor, Bette Davis, Olivia de Havilland, Errol Flynn, John Garfield, Joan Leslie, Ida Lupino, Dennis Morgan, Ann Sheridan, Dinah Shore, and Alexis Smith.

Report from the Front (1944) 3 minutes.

This trailer was prepared by the Red Cross Drive Committee of the Motion Picture Industry. Bogart and his then wife Mayo Methot appear in film clips showing them entertaining American troops in North Africa. Bogart appeals for donations, which would then be collected in theaters.

Hollywood Victory Caravan (1945) 20 minutes.

Director, William Russell; screenplay, Melville Shavelson.

This short was produced jointly by the War Activities Committee and the Treasury Department and Paramount Pictures. It involves the adventures of a young woman on a trainload of stars headed for a Washington rally. Bogart delivers an appeal for Victory Loan bonds.

Others on hand in the patriotic endeavor included Bing Crosby, Bob Hope, Betty Hutton, Alan Ladd, Diana Lynn, Olga San Juan, Barbara Stanwyck, and Marjorie Weaver.

Two Guys from Milwaukee (Warner Bros./First National, 1946) 90 minutes.

Director, David Butler; producer, Alex Gottlieb; screenplay, Charles Hoffman and I. A. L. Diamond.

Cast: Dennis Morgan, Jack Carson, Joan Leslie, Janis Paige, S. Z. Sakall.

A Balkan prince (Dennis Morgan) visiting New York hides his identity so he can see the "real" America. He learns about democracy and "the common man," and loses his throne in the process. In the final scene, he finds a seat on a plane beside his dream girl, Lauren Bacall (as herself) . . . but then a jealous Humphrey Bogart kicks him out.

Never Say Goodbye (Warner Bros., 1946) 97 minutes.

Director, James V. Kern; producer, William Jacobs; screenplay, Ben Barzman, Norma Barzman, and I. A. L. Diamond.

Cast: Errol Flynn, Eleanor Parker, S. Z. Sakall, Forrest Tucker, Lucile Watson, Hattie McDaniel.

In this marital comedy, after the couple heads for divorce court the husband decides he wants his wife back.

Errol Flynn does an imitation of Humphrey Bogart, with the voice of the real Bogart on the soundtrack.

Always Together (Warner Bros./First National, 1948) 78 minutes.

Director, Frederick de Cordova; producer, Alex Gottlieb; screenplay, Phoebe Ephron, Henry Ephron, and I. A. L. Diamond.

Cast: Robert Hutton, Joyce Reynolds, Cecil Kellaway.

Dying millionaire Kellaway leaves his fortune to secretary Reynolds, a movie addict who marries poor boy Hutton without telling him of her riches. But the millionaire doesn't die, and wants his money back. The secretary imagines life as a movie, replete with Warner Bros. stars.

Bogart appears in a takeoff on the classic tearjerker *Stella Dallas*, as an outcast father, weeping against a rainy windowpane. *Time* magazine thought this sequence the best thing in the movie.

Road to Bali (Paramount, 1952) Color, 90 minutes.

Director, Hal Walker; producers, Daniel Dare and Harry Tugend; screenplay, Frank Butler, Hal Kanter, and William Morrow (from a story by Harry Tugend).

Cast: Bing Crosby, Bob Hope, Dorothy Lamour.

This sixth film in the popular "Road to . . ." comedy series was the first one in color. An actual clip from *The African Queen* (1951) is used, showing Bogart pulling the boat through the marsh.

U.S. Savings Bond Trailer (1952) 2 minutes.

A special trailer made by MGM, with Bogart presenting the Series E savings bonds. Featured in the movie-theater newsreels of July 25 and 26.

The Love Lottery (Ealing, 1953) Color, 89 minutes.

Director, Charles Crichton; producer, Monja Danischewsky; screenplay, Harry Kurnitz (from a story by Zelma Bramley Moore and Charles Neilson-Terry).

Cast: David Niven, Peggy Cummins, Anne Vernon, Herbert Lom, Hugh McDermott.

This British film comedy has movie star David Niven as the prize in an international lottery. Bogart appears in a cameo as himself, probably as a favor to friend Niven.

A Star Is Born (Warner Bros., 1954) 154 minutes.

Director, George Cukor; producer, Sidney Luft; associate producer, Vern Alves; screenplay, Moss Hart, Alan Campbell, and Robert Carson.

Cast: Judy Garland, James Mason, Jack Carson, Charles Bickford, Tommy Noonan.

In a scene with Judy Garland singing in a cafe, we hear a drunk call out, "Sing 'Melancholy Baby'!" That's Bogie, as a good-luck gesture to Judy, who was a neighbor, and also one of the original members of the Holmby Hills Rat Pack. At one point Bogart had been mentioned as a candidate for the part ultimately claimed by James Mason.

Take Me Out to the Ballgame (1955) 10 minutes.

Cast: William Frawley, Humphrey Bogart, Bob Hope, and baseball commissioner Ford Frick.

A promotional film in which the stars extol the pleasures of baseball, America's great national pastime. Segments are televised during the 1955 World Series games (New York Yankees vs. Brooklyn Dodgers).

Bogie on Video

Out of Humphrey Bogart's first forty movies—the fortieth being the breakthrough *High Sierra*—twenty-five are not currently available on home video, DVD, etc. Of that group, only two are really missed: the hard-hitting social drama *Black Legion*, and Bogart's first comedy *Stand-In*.

Of the twenty-seven titles made after *Casablanca*, only *Deadline—U.S.A.* is missing.

If you have difficulty finding a particular title, most video stores will order it. The popular paperback video guides—*VideoHound's Golden Movie Retriever* (Detroit, MI: Visible Ink Press, 1999) and *Leonard Maltin's Movie & Video Guide* (New York: Signet Books, 1999)—both have listings of mail-order sources.

These titles are currently available:

Across the Pacific, MGM
Action in the North Atlantic, MGM
The African Queen, Fox

(There is also a Commemorative Edition, which includes a copy of Katharine Hepburn's 1987 book on the making of *The African Queen*, and a copy of the original shooting script.)

All Through the Night, MGM
Angels with Dirty Faces, MGM
The Barefoot Contessa, MGM, Fox
Battle Circus, MGM
The Big Sleep, MGM, Fox
Brother Orchid, MGM
Bullets or Ballots, MGM
The Caine Mutiny, Columbia
Casablanca, MGM

(There is also a Fiftieth Anniversary Edition of *Casablanca*, digitally remastered. It includes the original theatrical trailer and a documentary on the making of the film. In addition, Rhino Records packages the video with an original soundtrack CD.)

Chain Lightning, MGM
Conflict, MGM
Dark Passage, MGM
Dark Victory, MGM
Dead End, MGM
Dead Reckoning, Columbia
The Desperate Hours, Paramount
The Enforcer, Republic

The Harder They Fall, Columbia
High Sierra, Fox
In a Lonely Place, Columbia
Key Largo, MGM, Fox
Kid Galahad, MGM
Knock on Any Door, Columbia
The Left Hand of God, Fox
The Maltese Falcon, MGM, Fox
Marked Woman, MGM
Midnight, Critics Choice Video
The Oklahoma Kid, MGM
Passage to Marseille, Fox
The Petrified Forest, MGM, Fox
The Roaring Twenties, MGM, Fox
Sabrina, Paramount
Sahara, Columbia
Sirocco, Columbia
They Drive by Night, MGM
Three on a Match, MGM
To Have and Have Not, Columbia
Tokyo Joe, Columbia
The Treasure of the Sierra Madre, MGM, Fox
The Two Mrs. Carrolls, MGM
Virginia City, MGM
We're No Angels, Paramount

All the Other Films Bogart Didn't Make

In *Dark Victory*, Bogart had a successful change of pace as the Irish-accented horse trainer who makes romantic overtures to the young heiress who learned she only had a few months to live. He was so liked that he was awarded the lead in Bette Davis's next project, the Civil War period drama *The Old Maid* (Warner Bros., 1939). He would play the object of affection of the two women who loved him, acted by Davis and Miriam Hopkins, but would die early, to become a haunting memory that lingers on to both women.

While watching the dailies, production supervisor Hal B. Wallis realized he'd made a casting mistake—Bogart just was not the type to haunt passionate women. So Bogart was sidelined, and George Brent substituted. Now *there's* an actor to haunt a love-sick memory!

◆　　◆　　◆

Other studios also liked what they saw in *Dark Victory*. Over at Twentieth Century–Fox, head honcho Darryl F. Zanuck visualized Bogart in their remake of Paul Muni's 1929 hit *The Valiant*. And Universal had the really wild idea of casting Bogart opposite Mae West and W. C. Fields in *My Little Chickadee* (1940). Independent producer Walter Wanger (for whom Bogart had made *Stand-In*), was casting a film to star his beautiful actress wife Joan Bennett, and thought Bogart would be ideal for it.

Warner Bros. rejected all three offers: Bogart was needed for the gangster role in *It All Came True*, and for the half-breed bandit in the western *Virginia City*. They were shot at the same time, with Bogart running back and forth between soundstages—literally.

Neither project did anything for his screen career.

◆　　◆　　◆

Lewis Milestone, who had directed *All Quiet on the Western Front* (1930), asked for Bogart for his screen version of *Of Mice and Men* (1939), taken from the John Steinbeck novel. Bogart begged to be allowed to do it, his first meaty role since *Dead End*, but instead Warner Bros. put him into *The Roaring Twenties*. With Burgess Meredith and Lon Chaney Jr. in the leading roles, *Of Mice and Men* won popular acclaim, and an Oscar nomination for Best Picture.

◆　　◆　　◆

Irwin Shaw's *The Gentle People: A Brooklyn Fable*, a dramatic fantasy about the rising threat of Fascism, was one of the most important Broadway successes of 1939. Having a solid record of transforming Broadway hits to the screen, Warner Bros. bought the movie rights. Ida Lupino, memorable in both *They Drive by Night* and *High Sierra*, was given the female lead. Bogart felt he deserved the star part of the racketeer, after his *High Sierra* success, but Lupino surprised a lot of people when she refused to appear again with Bogart, saying he'd been too rough with her on *High Sierra*. Later, much later, she would deny the statement, saying it was the studio's doing, that they didn't like her *or* Bogart *or* Errol Flynn, because their growing popularity threatened the studio's control over them.

The Gentle People was released under the generic title of *Out of the Fog* (1941), starring Ida Lupino, with John Garfield in the part Bogart had wanted. In hindsight, it would have been a better project with Bogart, as Garfield was inherently too likable to be terrorizing innocent little people.

•   •   •

Then . . . Bogart was cast in *Manpower* (1941) at the Burbank, California, lot. It was a drama about two men fighting over leading lady Marlene Dietrich, and again a costar refused to work with him. This time it was screen tough-guy George Raft who insisted that Bogart be dropped from the movie; and since Raft was then the bigger star on the lot, that's what happened. Edward G. Robinson replaced Bogart, after which Raft began to make Edward G. Robinson's life miserable. A fistfight erupted between the two, which was caught by news photographers.

•   •   •

When Sidney Kingsley's new play *Detective Story* began tryouts in Philadelphia, in late 1948, Bogart was there to cheer him on. The actor had had one of his earliest successes in the 1937 movie version of the playwright's *Dead End*. Now Bogart was eager to buy the movie rights for the new play for his own production company, Santana. Kingsley was agreeable, visualizing how terrific Bogart would be as the overly conscientious police detective, but Paramount Pictures made a bigger money offer that the playwright could not refuse.

William Wyler directed the film version of *Detective Story* (1951), which featured an outstanding ensemble cast headed by Kirk Douglas, and received an Oscar nomination for Best Picture.

•   •   •

In 1952, Bogie missed out on another Broadway hit, William Inge's *Come Back, Little Sheba*, when Warner Bros. refused to buy the movie rights. Paramount picked it up and starred Shirley Booth and Burt Lancaster in the acclaimed 1952 screen adaptation.

Ironically, the movie was produced by Hal B. Wallis, who had left Warner Bros. in 1944 after supervising many of that studio's greatest films, including *Casablanca*.

+   +   +

In the mid-1950s, John Huston acquired the screen rights to Rudyard Kipling's "The Man Who Would Be King," a rousing adventure story of two daredevil British soldiers who try to bamboozle a remote Asian country out of its treasure. A script was written, locations were chosen, the budget was raised, and Humphrey Bogart and Clark Gable were set to star as the raffish pair Daniel Dravot and Peachy Carnehan.

But when Bogart died in January 1957, Huston shelved the screen project. A few years later he tried to revive it again, and then Clark Gable died (November 1960). Later, the persistent Huston once again attempted to make the film, this time with Richard Burton and Peter O'Toole . . . and then with Richard Burton and Michael Caine . . . but couldn't get backing. A decade later, producer John Foreman learned of the long-stalled Huston project, and found the necessary funding. The movie was released by Columbia Pictures in 1975, with Sean Connery and Michael Caine in the leads, and became a critical and commercial success.

+   +   +

John Huston and Humphrey Bogart might have collaborated on yet another project in the 1950s, time willing. Henry Blanke, who produced a number of Bogart's better pictures at Warner Bros., tells of driving to Santa Barbara with John Huston to see the star on his boat, to discuss his playing the lead role of a film version of Herman Melville's Captain Ahab in *Moby Dick*.

"Bogey said he didn't know. It was great and wonderful, but it was like playing Shakespeare or like poetry. He was actually a little bit afraid" (quoted in Goodman, *Bogey: The Good-Bad Guy*).

John Huston's production of *Moby Dick*, with Gregory Peck as the obsessed Captain Ahab, was a 1956 Warner Bros. release. John Barrymore had starred in a 1930 film of *Moby Dick*, as well as in an earlier silent version, for the brothers Warner. Patrick Stewart starred in a 1998 television adaptation for Hallmark Home Entertainment.

◆   ◆   ◆

After completing *The Barefoot Contessa* in 1954, Bogart was looking for new screen projects for Santana, his own film production company. He was interested in a movie adaptation of Frank Harris's memoir, *Reminiscences of a Cowboy*, but questioned whether he could play a loud, tough, boisterous frontiersman, and dropped the idea.

The project made it to the screen, without Bogie as "Cowboy" (Columbia, 1958). Warner Bros. veteran Delmer Daves directed. Jack Lemmon played the tenderfoot and Glenn Ford appeared as the tough cattle boss, the screen role Bogart might have played.

◆   ◆   ◆

Producer Sam Spiegel, who launched *The African Queen* in 1951, wanted Bogart for his production of his epic set in World War II, *The Bridge on the River Kwai* (Columbia, 1957). The star would play the American commando sent to blow up the bridge built by British POWs in the Asian jungle. Bogie was intrigued, but he was already committed to another Columbia project, *The Harder They Fall*. The role went to Bogie's old nemesis William Holden. The film won the Academy Award for Best Picture.

◆   ◆   ◆

After completing *The Harder They Fall* in 1956, Bogart and Lauren Bacall began planning a new movie together, *Melville Goodwin, U.S.A.*, from the 1952 novel by J. P. Marquand. Marquand was acclaimed for his novels of proper Bostonians trying to survive in the twentieth century.

Melville Goodwin, U.S.A. was the story of a hard-bitten Army general who has an affair with a notable newspaperwoman. Milton Sperling was to produce, H. C. Potter was to direct, and the screenplay was being written by Roland Kibbee.

Because of Bogart's failing health, *Melville Goodwin* only got as far as wardrobe tests, in January 1956, with some clowning around by the two stars, playfully bumping butts. Snippets of the footage are seen in the 1988 *Bacall on Bogart* TV documentary (on the PBS-TV series *Great Performances*).

When Bogart and Bacall dropped out of the project, the novel was filmed as *Top Secret Affair* (Warner Bros., 1957) with Kirk Douglas and Susan Hayward.

Chapter 11

The Warner Bros. Cast of Characters

The Warner Bros. "Murderers' Row"

During the 1930s and 1940s, Warner Bros. made the most gangster films, and had the best lineup of appropriate actors—"Murderers' Row"—to star in them: Paul Muni, Edward G. Robinson, James Cagney, John Garfield, and Humphrey Bogart. That was roughly the official lineup: a project would be offered first to Muni, then to Robinson, and down the line. When George Raft signed on, he became number one. Bogart got a number of projects by attrition—after everyone else had turned them down.

Interestingly, Bogart seems not to have developed any sort of camaraderie with these actors. You might expect them to be pals just from sharing a common background on the New York City stage. Perhaps it had something to do with the "Murderers' Row" pecking order: All the actors at the top had chalked up various screen successes, while Bogie was still fighting to prove himself.

• • •

Paul Muni (1895–1967) was Warner Bros.' top star, their prestige actor. His most memorable characterizations are in the jolting dramas *Scarface: The Shame of a Nation* (1932), as a Caponelike gangster, and in *I Am a*

Fugitive from a Chain Gang (1932). But he preferred the on-screen biographies of historical characters: *The Story of Louis Pasteur* (1936), *The Life of Emile Zola* (1937), and *Juarez* (1939).

Muni and Bogart never appeared together on film. Bogart did star in *King of the Underworld*, a remake of Muni's 1935 *Dr. Socrates*. Muni was in the original stage production of *Key Largo*, in the role Bogart would do in the movie version. After George Raft rejected *High Sierra* (1941), Warner Bros. assigned it to Paul Muni, who was willing do it, in order to star in a promised biography of Beethoven. But the studio canceled that idea—they rolled Beethoven over, so to speak—so Muni tore up his contract. As a result, Bogey got *High Sierra* by default.

• • •

Edward G. Robinson (1893–1973) created a prototype for gangsters in 1930 with *Little Caesar*. He proved to be a versatile actor, but is best remembered as one of the screen's great bad guys.

Robinson and Bogart shared screen billing five times, all for Warner Bros.: In *Bullets or Ballots* (1936), Bogart dies trying to kill undercover cop Robinson. In *Kid Galahad* (1937), both men expire in a blazing gunfight. The next year, Robinson poisons Bogart in *The Amazing Dr. Clitterhouse* just to see what it feels like. In *Brother Orchid* (1940), Bogart takes control of the gang when Robinson is away in a monastery. The tables are finally turned in 1948, when Bogey shoots cruel mobster Robinson in *Key Largo*.

Robinson described the process in his autobiography *All My Yesterdays* (New York: Hawthorne, 1973): "Bogie and I carried on a charade in each picture. Almost inevitably both of us would get killed at the end of the films in which we worked together. Because we were both rotten, we had to get our just desserts. [Censorship czar] Will Hays and his successors said so in the motion picture code. The charade followed a precise pattern. When I was the reigning star, Bogie would be slain first, and I'd live another reel before I got it. As the years passed and Bogie became the reigning star and I was demoted to character roles, I'd get the bullet first and Bogie would live out another reel before he was struck down for his sins."

In his book, Robinson also analyzes his costar: "Bogie had a manner, a personality—yes, an immense talent—that made him almost immortal. For all his outward toughness, insolence, braggadocio, and contempt . . . there came through a kind of sadness, loneliness, and heartbreak (all of which were very much part of Bogie the man.) I always felt sorry for him—sorry that he imposed upon himself the facade of the character with which he had become identified."

Edward G. Robinson's other films include *Dr. Ehrlich's Magic Bullet* (1940), *The Sea Wolf* (1941), *Double Indemnity* (1944), *Scarlet Street* (1945), *All My Sons* (1948), *House of Strangers* (1949), *A Bullet for Joey* (1955), *The Ten Commandments* (1956), *A Hole in the Head* (1959), *Two Weeks in Another Town* (1962), *The Prize* (1963), *Cheyenne Autumn* (1964), *The Cincinnati Kid* (1965), *Never a Dull Moment* (1968), and *Soylent Green* (1973).

●　　●　　●

Bogart's stardom dates from 1941's *High Sierra*, fifteen years after his first screen appearance. **James Cagney** (1899–1986) became a screen luminary a year after he hit Hollywood, as the arrogant, hypertensive gangster in *The Public Enemy* (1931). It was a type of role he would play many times.

Cagney and Bogart crossed paths in three movies for Warner Bros. In *Angels with Dirty Faces* (1938), gangster Cagney gets even with crooked lawyer Bogart. In the western *The Oklahoma Kid* (1939), Bogart almost shoots Cagney, before he's gunned down by Cagney's brother Ned (Harvey Stephens.) In the action drama *The Roaring Twenties* (1939), Cagney kills Bogart but Bogart's men gun down Cagney who then dies, memorably, on the church steps.

"Each [Bogart and Cagney] had perfected his own version of the fanged killer's smile, and a good deal of *The Roaring Twenties* developed into a sort of grinning contest" (Kenneth Tynan, *Playboy* magazine, June 1966).

Cagney was a versatile actor who won the 1942 best actor Oscar for his portrayal of entertainer George M. Cohan in *Yankee Doodle Dandy*. His other films include *Blonde Crazy* (1931), *Lady Killer* (1933), the Busby Berkeley musical *Footlight Parade* (1933), Shakespeare's *A Midsummer Night's Dream* (1935), *The Bride Came C.O.D.* (1941), *White Heat* (1949), *What Price Glory?* (1952), *Love Me or Leave Me* (1955), *Mister Roberts* (1955), *Man of a Thousand Faces* (1957), *The Gallant Hours* (1960), director Billy Wilder's nonstop comedy *One, Two, Three* (1961), and filmmaker Milos Forman's complex historical drama *Ragtime* (1981).

Cagney loved sailing, like Bogart, and had his own boat, *The Martha*. You'd think they would have been friends. Doug Warren spells it out in

James Cagney: The Authorized Biography (New York: St. Martin's Press, 1983): "There was no enmity between them. They just didn't hit it off."

But Cagney was quoted as saying that when it came to real-life fighting, Bogart was about as tough as Shirley Temple.

And Bogart described Cagney in *The Oklahoma Kid* thusly: "In that ten-gallon hat, he looked like a mushroom."

But there was no enmity.

HUMPHREY BOGART AND THE STRANGE CASE OF GEORGE RAFT, THE DISAPPEARING ACTOR

George Raft (1895–1980), was born George Ranft in the Hell's Kitchen tenement area on the West Side of midtown New York City. He played in the streets with friend Owney Madden, who later became a powerful gang boss.

A street fighter, Raft was briefly a professional boxer. He hung around the Broadway clubs listening to the music. Inspired by the success of his songwriter friend Billy Rose, he practiced to be a dancer. He worked in "tearooms" where idle women paid for dances and other intimate favors. Rudolph Valentino was a fellow dancer-for-hire.

In the early 1920s, Raft entered big-time vaudeville as "The Fastest Dancer in the World." Fred Astaire thought he was extraordinary. Raft married a woman with whom he had sex only once, because she had lied about her virginity. But she refused to give the Catholic Raft a divorce from 1923 until her death in 1970.

Raft frequented clubs popular with such gangsters as Al Capone, Lucky Luciano, etc. The real stuff. He patterned his style after the cunning and suave gangster-gambler Arnold Rothstein.

In 1919, Prohibition turned Owney Madden into an efficient gangster businessman, supplying the East Coast with beer. Raft ran errands for Madden, and would sometimes drive one of the cars protecting Madden's beer trucks. "George Raft's relationship with Madden and other notorious friends was a crucial part of his life," says biographer Lewis Yablonsky (*George Raft*; New York: McGraw-Hill, 1974).

The character that George Raft portrayed on-screen, says Yablonsky, was a composite of the gangsters he'd known. "He was extraordinarily convincing in his screen portrayals because he absorbed every gangster nuance, every smirk of restrained violence and ever-present menace.

Maybe he played the roles too well . . . for he often overidentified with his parts, and this produced inner confusion."

Raft danced his way from ballrooms to nightclubs to Broadway, where he appeared with the brassy club hostess and entertainer Texas Guinan. He accompanied Guinan to Hollywood, appearing in her film *Queen of the Night Clubs* (1929).

Howard Hawks's 1932 film *Scarface: The Shame of a Nation* made Raft a star, as a coin-flipping gunman. He did occasional movies as a dancer, but essentially established his reputation as a cinema tough-guy.

The parallel lives of Humphrey Bogart and George Raft began in 1939 when Raft terminated his contract at Paramount, where he had frequently been suspended for refusing movie assignments. Raft said that he did not want to play gangsters on-screen anymore—so he signed a contract with Warner Bros., the studio that *specialized* in gangster movies. His contract with the brothers Warner began exactly one day before filming was to start on *Each Dawn I Die* (1939), a prison drama set to star James Cagney and Humphrey Bogart. Raft now had higher priority on Warner Bros.' tough-guy parts, so he was handed the Bogart role in *Each Dawn I Die*.

For Warner Bros., Raft and Bogart later appeared together as ex-cons in *Invisible Stripes* (1939), and as brother truckers in *They Drive by Night* (1940), and were said to be sociable to each other off-screen.

George Raft was considered for, or actually cast in, a number of projects that he rejected, and which then went to Humphrey Bogart by default. Raft biographer James Robert Parish wrote, "Little did Bogart realize it at the time [of the filming of *Dead End* in 1937], but Raft was later to be responsible for turning Bogart into a motion picture superstar" (*The George Raft File: The Unauthorized Biography*; New York: Drake, 1974).

Raft turned down screen role after role. His on-set disruptions delayed shooting, ran up production costs, and created bad public relations. He was known to take a role, go on payroll during preproduction, and then refuse to shoot—while still pocketing the salary. Yet the studio behaved as if Raft embodied dependability itself, renewing his options and raising his per-picture fees without a murmur.

Raft became a star because of his affiliation with gangsters—and stayed a star because studio boss Jack L. Warner was fearful of this affiliation—but then Raft scuttled his career because he didn't want to make movies that might cause viewers to think he was associated with the underworld.

Here then is the George Raft "Oops!" list of what might have been:

- *Dead End* (1937). Raft did not like the vicious character of "Baby Face" Martin in this adaptation of Sidney Kingsley's prize-winning Broadway play, saying that Martin should be made more sympathetic.

He particularly didn't like the script's depiction of the gangster's mother (played by Marjorie Main in both the stage and screen versions), who slaps him and calls him a "yellow dog." Raft's own mother was very dear to him. When Raft rejected *Dead End*, producer Samuel Goldwyn reluctantly cast Bogart, who was widely hailed for his portrayal.

- *It All Came True* (1940). Raft said no to this pleasant little B picture with Ann Sheridan. It's the story of a gangster hiding out in a boardinghouse of retired entertainers, who turns the place into a nightclub and then turns himself in. The part went to Bogie.

- *High Sierra* (1941). No, said Raft—because he did not want to play a criminal on-camera again and, furthermore, he did not want to die in the story's climax.

The part of soft-hearted killer Roy Earle was then offered to Paul Muni, who rejected it, as did Warner Bros.' Cagney and Robinson and even John Garfield. Director Raoul Walsh took credit for suggesting Bogart for the role instead.

John Huston, who co-wrote the screenplay, was never one to mince words: "Everything was intended for George Raft at that time, and I was not among George Raft's greatest admirers. I thought he was a clown, walking around in his white suit with the padded shoulders and form-fitting hips, and bodyguards. . . . He refused everything that was thrown at him. And he refused *High Sierra*. You know, he was really an ignorant man. Poor devil."

- *The Wagons Roll at Night* (1941). Raft said no because this was a remake (of *Kid Galahad*) and his contract ruled out remakes. It's too bad Bogart himself couldn't have said no as this is one of the studio's dumber efforts. Bogart plays the owner of a circus who tries to commit murder with a lion.

- *Manpower* (1941). Filming for this action drama actually began with George Raft and Humphrey Bogart as costars. However, problems soon arose that ended with Raft demanding Bogart be fired. Edward G. Robinson was assigned as the replacement—but then he and Raft soon came to physical blows. Raft no doubt did Bogart a favor by having him kicked off this production.

- *The Maltese Falcon* (1941). Raft said no because he did not want to be directed by the inexperienced John Huston, whose first feature this was, and because Raft didn't think it an important project—and his contract promised that he would not appear in remakes (this was the third time around for this property).

The details of Raft's goof and Bogart's success were widely reported. A leading man went from star to laughingstock in short order.

- *All Through the Night* (1942). Raft was actually second choice for this comedy of gangsters versus Nazis, with Bogart in third place. Jack Warner's first choice for leading man? The charismatic columnist Walter Winchell. Winchell was willing, but just could not find the time.

- *The Big Shot* (1942). Raft rejected this one, a dreary variation on the aging gangster, because he did not want to do movie gangsters anymore. The fact that the project was assigned to Bogart, fresh from his success with *The Maltese Falcon*, is inexplicable—what would it take for the studio to realize what they had on their hands? Bogie did what he could, which was not much.

- *Casablanca* (1942). There are stories that Raft rejected the part of Rick Blaine because he recognized his own unsuitability for the movie role. However, there is enough research to show that he was never even considered, that it was Bogart's part from the beginning. Studio records spell it out in a memo from studio head Jack L. Warner to producer Hal B. Wallis:

"What do you think of using Raft for *Casablanca?*" Warner asked. "Bogart is ideal for it, and it is being written for him," Wallis replied.

Raft did make his own halfhearted version of *Casablanca*—a lackluster entry called *Background to Danger* (1943), in which he plays an American agent playing cat and mouse with the Nazis, in World War II Turkey. Peter Lorre and Sydney Greenstreet were featured, in case any viewer might miss the *Casablanca* connection.

Raft's foolish ways had to catch up with him someday. His career began its decline in the mid-1940s. He made films in Europe in the early 1950s. He had a syndicated TV series, *I'm the Law* (1952–53), and lost his shirt. He was a celebrity host at a casino in Havana but then Fidel Castro shut it down in 1959. He was hired to manage a high-life gambling joint in England, but was denied entry into the country because of his low-life friends. And then Uncle Sam hounded him for back taxes.

He did cameo appearances and bit parts, most memorably in Billy Wilder's *Some Like It Hot* (1959), and most lamentably in *Sextette* (1978) with his old friend Mae West. Allied Artists made a low-budget film of his life, *The George Raft Story* (1961) with Ray Danton in the title role.

George Raft's final professional appearance was in *Sam Marlowe, Private Eye* (1980), adapted from the spoof novel *The Man with Bogart's Face*, the story of a comically serious private eye who undergoes plastic surgery to look like Humphrey Bogart. (Is that a poetic postscript, or just one more of George Raft's suicidal bad judgments?)

Raft boasted that he never read scripts: "Tell it to me!" he would demand. James Robert Parish reports (*The George Raft File*, 1974) that Raft frequently had to have his lines read to him. Jack L. Warner suggested that Raft did not know *how* to read—which opens up all kinds of interesting speculations.

George Raft and his gangster friend Owney Madden are characters in *The Cotton Club*, Francis Coppola's 1984 tribute to colorful gangsters and Harlem nightlife. Bob Hoskins appears as Madden, and Richard Gere plays the character based on George Raft.

There's a final Bogart-Raft tie-in. Back in the early 1930s, Owney Madden took over management of would-be boxer Primo Carnera, a gentle giant who looked fierce but was totally incompetent in the ring. Carnera won every fight because every opponent was paid to take a dive. For Carnera's first big match in Madison Square Garden, a million-dollar bout, his opponent was allegedly drugged, supposedly by George Raft (according to Raft chronicler Lewis Yablonsky in *George Raft*, 1974). Carnera became World Heavyweight Champion in 1933. After he was almost killed by an honest fighter, Primo Carnera finally was returned to

Italy while he could still stand up. The Carnera story was novelized in Budd Schulberg's *The Harder They Fall*—which was the basis for Humphrey Bogart's last feature film at Columbia Pictures (1957).

The movies George Raft *did* make include *Scarface* (1932)—probably his most notable film, in which he's Gino Rinaldo, tossing a nickel in the air; *The Bowery* (1933); *Bolero* (1934) and *Rumba* (1935), in which he dances spectacularly with Carole Lombard; *The Glass Key* (1935); *Souls at Sea* (1937), in which he gives what many consider his best performance; *Spawn of the North* (1938); *Each Dawn I Die* (1939), a prison drama with Jimmy Cagney; *They Drive by Night* (1940), a classic study of truck drivers, with Bogart; *Manpower* (1941); *Broadway* (1942), a movie loosely based on the life of Raft himself; a series of low-budget crime and spy films; and then, cameo roles in such prestige outings as *Around the World in 80 Days* (1956), *Some Like It Hot* (1959), *Ocean's Eleven* (1960), and *Casino Royale* (1967).

Other Costars

Bette Davis (1908–1989) made her film debut in *Bad Sister* (Universal, 1931), which was only Bogart's fourth feature. By the end of the decade, Davis was queen of the Warner Bros. lot. However, Bogart had made several quality movies but was still being assigned to clinkers like *Swing Your Lady* (1938) and *The Return of Dr. X* (1939) at the Burbank lot. After *Bad Sister*, Bogart and Davis shared screen billing in five more Hollywood features for Warner Bros.: *Three on a Match* (1932), *The Petrified Forest* (1936), *Marked Woman* (1937), *Kid Galahad* (1937), and *Dark Victory* (1939). The two also made cameo appearances as themselves in *Thank Your Lucky Stars* (1943), an all-star variety picture.

In addition, Bogart began filming for the period tearjerker, *The Old Maid* (1939), as the love interest of Bette Davis and Miriam Hopkins, but then the studio felt he was not romantic enough and replaced him with George Brent.

Bette Davis disliked Bogart from the start, and never changed her opinion, even when they were doing good on-camera work together. Gossip columnist Louella Parsons asked her, "How can you act so well with him if, as you say, you dislike Bogie so?"—to which Davis replied, "Because that's what I am—an actress! I'll whip up an acting storm with Lucifer himself if it's worth it to me!"

✦   ✦   ✦

Sydney Greenstreet (1879–1954) costarred in five projects for Warner Bros. with Bogart: *The Maltese Falcon* (1941), *Across the Pacific* (1942), *Casablanca* (1942), *Passage to Marseille* (1944), and *Conflict* (1945).

The three-hundred-pound Greenstreet was born in Sandwich, England, and died in Los Angeles at age seventy-five, from diabetes and Brights' disease, shortly after retiring from films. Greenstreet was a busy stage actor in England and America, and vowed never to make a movie. Ironically, this great screen villain had specialized in comedy, often playing amusing butlers. John Huston persuaded him to play Kasper Gutman in *The Maltese Falcon* thus making his film debut at age sixty-one.

The rotund Greenstreet was paired with the short Peter Lorre in nine movies (they were a sort of Abbott and Costello of murder and intrigue): *The Maltese Falcon* (1941), *In This Our Life* [cameos] (1942), *Casablanca* (1942), *Background to Danger* (1943), *Passage to Marseille* (1944), *The Mask of Dimitrios* (1944), *The Conspirators* (1944), *Three Strangers* (1946), and *The Verdict* (1946)—all for Warner Bros. Naturally, they were also in the all-star *Hollywood Canteen* (1944), (who wasn't?).

✦   ✦   ✦

Humphrey Bogart didn't get along with handsome leading man **William Holden** (1918–1981) from the very beginning, when they met on the set of the 1939 gangster drama *Invisible Stripes* at Warner Bros.

That movie starred George Raft as an ex-convict fighting to keep his disillusioned kid brother (Holden) from a life of crime as exemplified by another ex-con, played by Bogart, who leads a gang of bank robbers. Both ex-cons are killed in a police shootout, but the kid brother turns out all right, running a garage.

Bogart was thirty-nine and making his thirty-fifth movie; he resented being billed in the credits *after* leading man Holden, a twenty-one-year-old in only his second starring role after his widely praised leading part in *Golden Boy* (1939)—with above-the-title billing, moreover.

Invisible Stripes turned out to be a "routine" but classy gangster film that had no noticeable effect on the careers of the stars, regardless of the billing sequence.

Eighteen years later, in 1954 at Paramount, Bogart and Holden costarred—and clashed—for the romantic comedy *Sabrina*, also starring Audrey Hepburn, and directed by Billy Wilder. Bogart and Holden play brothers in a wealthy Long Island family: When the chauffeur's daughter Sabrina (Hepburn) falls in love with the playboy brother (Holden), the Bogart character seeks to distract her but falls in love with her and wins the young lady instead.

The film began production without a finished script, which made Bogart, a perfectionist, nervous. He knew he had been second choice for the role, after Cary Grant had turned it down, and now he suspected director Wilder and Holden of conspiring against him—rewriting the script so Holden would get the girl.

Bogie openly criticized Holden's and Hepburn's acting. He was also outraged that Holden, a married man, was having an after-work affair with Hepburn. Holden, something of a puritan, and a hypocrite (as he was himself a heavy drinker), frequently denounced Hollywood parties and nightclubs, and even singled out Bogie's informal little social group, dubbed "the Rat Pack." Said Holden, "It might sound stuffy and dull, but it is quite possible for people to have social intercourse without resorting to a rat pack and even to drink or do anything without resorting to a rat pack."

William Holden had been discovered acting in a college play (in Pasadena, a few miles east of Hollywood) by a talent scout from Paramount. He was an extra in one film, had a single line in the next one, and then starred in *Golden Boy* (1939). He won the Oscar for Best Actor for *Stalag 17* (1953). His other notable movies include *Sunset Boulevard* (1950), *Born Yesterday* (1951), *Executive Suite* (1954), *The Country Girl* (1954), *Picnic* (1955), *Love Is a Many-Splendored Thing* (1955), *The Bridge on the River Kwai*, (1957), *The Wild Bunch* (1969), *Network* (1976), and *S.O.B.* (1981).

◆　　◆　　◆

Peter Lorre (1904–1964) and Humphrey Bogart were best friends who shared a sharp and mordant sense of humor. Bogart sympathized with Lorre's morphine addiction, as his own father had been similarly afflicted.

Lorre will always be associated with Humphrey Bogart, if only because they both appear in the ageless classic *Casablanca* (1942). The two also costarred in *The Maltese Falcon* (1941), *All Through the Night* (1942),

Passage to Marseille (1944), and *Beat the Devil* (1954), the last one for United Artists.

Lorre was born in Hungary, studied acting in Vienna, Austria, and made his stage debut in Zurich, Switzerland. He was virtually unknown when the famous German director Fritz Lang chose him for the leading role in M (1931), as a sinister yet pathetic child murderer. The film, and its star, created a sensation.

Fleeing the Nazis, Lorre wound up in Hollywood in 1935. His American debut was in *Mad Love* (1935) at MGM, as the love-crazed surgeon who grafts the hands of a killer onto a concert pianist. He later starred in a series of low-budget films as the Oriental detective "Mr. Moto." His best movies were made at Warner Bros. in the 1940s, where the short actor was often popularly paired with the hulking Sydney Greenstreet. He also appeared in *Arsenic and Old Lace* (1944), *20,000 Leagues Under the Sea* (1954), *Silk Stockings* (1957), *Tales of Terror* (1962), and *The Comedy of Terrors* (1964), the latter two with that other master of the macabre, Vincent Price.

◆   ◆   ◆

Ida Lupino's (1918–1995) association with Bogart brings up questions and controversies that have yet to be resolved.

They both appear in *They Drive by Night* (1940), Bogey as a trucker, Lupino as the murderous wife of the owner (Alan Hale) of the trucking company, but they have no on-camera scenes together.

Lupino, however, has a going-mad sequence, which audiences and critics always love. To capitalize on all this attention, the studio gave her top billing in *High Sierra* (1941), although that movie is clearly Bogart's. During the filming, Bogart supposedly spent time with Lupino, giving her acting tips. But then—speaking of madwomen—Bogart's third wife Mayo Methot showed up on location in eastern California's Sierra Nevada Mountains, suspecting the worst of the Bogart-Lupino relationship. Mayo may have been right.

Soon after, Warner Bros. bought the rights to Irwin Shaw's Broadway hit drama *The Gentle People: A Brooklyn Fable*, (released as *Out of the Fog*, in 1941) and cast Ida Lupino in the female lead. Bogart asked for the starring male role, rightly feeling he deserved it after the success of *High Sierra*. However, Lupino shocked the industry by refusing to appear with Bogart, claiming he'd been cruel to her while filming *High Sierra*. She later denied the statement, claiming it was all Warner Bros.' fault, that they were pitting the stars against each other, to keep them from making too many demands on the studio.

When William Donati was interviewing the actress, then in her late seventies (for *Ida Lupino: A Biography*; Lexington, KY: The University Press of Kentucky, 1996), he noted two photos atop her television set: one of her parents; the other of the actress with Humphrey Bogart.

Ida Lupino was born in London of a theatrical family dating back to the seventeenth century. She entered the business at age fifteen when she accompanied her mother to an audition and got the part instead; she had been attending the Royal Academy of Arts. She was brought to the United States by Paramount, then later went to Warner Bros. where she typically played cynical, hardened women (who sometimes crack up in the courtroom). She was not happy with her career as an actress, referring to herself as "a poor man's Bette Davis."

In the early 1950s, Ida Lupino turned to writing, producing, and directing her own movies, and became one of the most successful women filmmakers in Hollywood history. These titles include *Not Wanted* (1949), *Never Fear* (1950), *Outrage* (1950), *Hard, Fast and Beautiful* (1951), *The Hitch-Hiker* (1953), and *The Bigamist* (1953.) At one time she was married to radio and film leading man Howard Duff, and together they costarred in the sophisticated television series, *Mr. Adams and Eve* (1957–58), which led to her nine-year involvement with television shows, during which time she directed episodes of *The Twilight Zone*, *The Untouchables*, *The Fugitive*, *Bewitched*, and *Gilligan's Island*, among others.

◆   ◆   ◆

Bette Davis was in six movies featuring Humphrey Bogart . . . but so was **Ann Sheridan** (1915–1967): *Black Legion* (1937), *The Great O'Malley* (1937), *San Quentin* (1937), *Angels with Dirty Faces* (1938), *It All Came True* (1940), and *They Drive by Night* (1940)—all for Warner Bros. Bette Davis also appeared in a cameo role in Warners' all-star production *Thank Your Lucky Stars* (1943) . . . and so did Ann Sheridan. But, Ann Sheridan is said to have done a second cameo in a Bogie movie, an uncredited appearance in *The Treasure of the Sierra Madre* (1948), as a good-luck gesture to director John Huston. Thus far, no one's been able to spot her in the release print of that Warner Bros. film.

Ann Sheridan was one of the screen's great self-assured, wisecracking, "get outta my way" dames. Born Clara Lou Sheridan, in Texas, she was spotted at a beauty contest, and was brought to Hollywood by Paramount Pictures. She usually appeared in small parts in small films until Warner Bros. lured her away, named her "the Oomph Girl" and made her a star. Her best film is *Kings Row* (1942), but she's more than memorable in *Dodge City* (1939), *Torrid Zone* (1940), *I Was a Male War Bride* (1949), and others. She was married three times—to actors Edward Norris, George Brent, and Scott McKay.

The Directors

Of the Warner Bros. stable of directors, **Lloyd Bacon** (1890–1955) worked with Humphrey Bogart the most often, with seven collaborations: *Marked Woman* (1937), *San Quentin* (1937), *Racket Busters* (1938), *The Oklahoma Kid* (1939), *Invisible Stripes* (1939), *Brother Orchid* (1940), and *Action in the North Atlantic* (1943.)

Bacon entered the movies in 1913 as a performer, and became a popular foil to comic genius Charlie Chaplin. Bacon graduated to supporting actor in 1919, and became a director in 1921. His first important feature film was the 1928 *The Singing Fool* with Al Jolson, the first full-dialogue talkie.

As a director, Bacon was known for his solid craftsmanship, which allowed him to direct everything from musicals to action dramas. He's credited with a number of enjoyable professional films, but Bacon's best did not equal that of Michael Curtiz or Howard Hawks or Raoul Walsh.

Bacon's other movies include the song-and-dance entries *42nd Street* (1933) and *Cain and Mabel* (1936), the comedy *Boy Meets Girl* (1938), and the drama *Knute Rockne, All American* (1940)—all for Warner Bros.

•   •   •

Richard Brooks (1912–1992), director, screenwriter, novelist, is counted as one of Bogart's closest friends from the time they met in late 1946. Just out of the Marines, Brooks had sent his novel *The Brick Foxhole* (1945) to producer Mark Hellinger, who passed it along to Bogart. Both men liked the novel—a grim story of a soldier killed by another soldier because he is homosexual—but agreed that it was too strong for the movies. *The Brick Foxhole* was eventually filmed as *Crossfire* (1947), retooled as a war drama about a soldier killed by a fellow soldier because he is Jewish.

In 1951, Richard Brooks published *The Producer*, a Hollywood novel with a character based on Humphrey Bogart. Biographer Jeffrey Meyers (*Bogart: A Life in Hollywood*) endorses this book as "the most perceptive imaginative work on Bogart."

Richard Brooks and Humphrey Bogart worked together on three projects: *Key Largo* (1948), for which Brooks and John Huston co-wrote the screenplay, from Maxwell Anderson's Broadway hit; *Deadline—U.S.A.* (1952), a newspaper drama with Bogart as a crusading editor, written and directed by Brooks; and *Battle Circus* (1953), written and directed by Brooks, set in a M.A.S.H. unit during the Korean War.

In *Deadline—U.S.A.*, made for Twentieth Century–Fox, Brooks capitalized on the Bogart persona of a tough man with integrity: there's an interrogation scene between the newspaper editor and a gangster which tries to be a carbon copy of the scene in *Casablanca* where Rick Blaine is questioned by the German Major Strasser (Conrad Veidt).

It's hard to guess what Brooks had in mind with the lackluster *Battle Circus*, made at MGM.

As he went on, Brooks's features became more dynamic, more hard-hitting, and thus more successful. He won an Academy Award for his screenplay of *Elmer Gantry* (1960), and was nominated for Oscars as the writer of *The Blackboard Jungle* (1955), as director and co-writer of *Cat on a Hot Tin Roof* (1958), as director and writer of *The Professionals* (1966), and as director and writer of *In Cold Blood* (1967).

◆ ◆ ◆

Casablanca (1942) is always listed as the greatest achievement of director **Michael Curtiz** (1888–1962), but he did other outstanding work, in a prolific career that lasted almost fifty years, making movies in Hungary, Denmark, Germany, Austria, and Burbank, California.

Curtiz and Bogart also worked together on Warner Bros.' *Kid Galahad* (1937), *Angels with Dirty Faces* (1938), *Virginia City* (1940), *Passage to Marseille* (1944), and Paramount's *We're No Angels* (1955). The director was known for bullying his crew and his actors, but Bogart fought back when he felt strongly about how a scene should be played. On at least one occasion, production head Hal B. Wallis had to be called in to mediate disputes between director and actor.

Curtiz was born in Budapest. He entered films as an actor in his early twenties, and began directing soon after. In 1917 he was made production head of Hungary's largest studio. He gained an international reputation that attracted the attention of Jack L. Warner.

Curtiz made over one hundred films for Warner Bros., working in a wide range of genres, worlds, and histories, all on the studio backlots: romantic adventures (*Captain Blood*, 1935, and *The Adventures of Robin Hood*, 1938, co-directed with William Keighley); historical epics (*Noah's Ark*, 1929, and *The Egyptian*, 1954); westerns (*Dodge City*, 1939, and *The Comancheros*, 1961); musicals (*Yankee Doodle Dandy*, 1942, and *White Christmas*, 1954); dramas (*Mildred Pierce*, 1945, and *Young Man with a Horn*, 1950); humor (*Life with Father*, 1947); and horror classics (*The Mystery of the Wax Museum*, 1933). *Casablanca* was his sixty-fifth American film.

In co-screenwriter Howard Koch's account, *Casablanca: Script and Legend*, he remembers an exchange with Michael Curtiz over the problem of script alterations: "Curtiz did what was so often the practice of producers and directors. He started giving out the incomplete script to various colleagues on the lot. Inevitably, their reactions varied, and Mike's attitude toward the story shifted with the changing winds. When I protested that some of the suggested changes were illogical and out of character, he would answer impatiently, 'Don't worry what's logical. I make it go so fast no one notices.'"

◆   ◆   ◆

Howard Hawks (1896–1977) directed Bogart in two outstanding films: *To Have and Have Not* (1944) and *The Big Sleep* (1946). He must also be credited with the discovery of Lauren Bacall and the creation of her sexy, cool, and sarcastic screen persona—supposedly shaping her into a copy of his then own sophisticated wife, Slim.

The repartee between Bogart and Bacall in these two movies, and in others from the same director, is a Hawks trademark. It's always between two hard-edged but likable characters, and filled with sly sexual innuendo. (He: "You look like a slow starter." She: "It depends on who is in the saddle.")

Hawks himself had been a professional race-car driver, a pilot in the first World War, and a designer of planes before he decided he wanted to make movies. He sold a script to Fox Pictures (*The Road to Glory*, 1926) on condition that he direct it—an approach copied fifty years later by Sylvester Stallone with *Rocky* (1976).

Hawks's other films include *The Dawn Patrol* (1930), *The Criminal Code* (1931), *Scarface: The Shame of a Nation* (1932), *Bringing Up Baby* (1938), *His Girl Friday* (1940), *Sergeant York* (1941), *Red River* (1948), *Gentlemen Prefer Blondes* (1953), and *Rio Bravo* (1959).

◆   ◆   ◆

The collaboration between director-writer **John Huston** (1906–1987) and Humphrey Bogart is one of the most significant in the annals of Hollywood.

Theirs was seen as a father-son relationship, that Bogart had an intense desire to be respected by Huston, a strong, quietly dominating man who always sat at the head of the table, literally and figuratively.

Huston was a colorful, "most unforgettable character I ever met" type who was, at one time or another, a boxer, an officer in the Mexican cavalry, and a newspaper reporter. He was the son of venerable actor Walter Huston (1884–1950), who, at his son's urging, appeared without his dentures to play a grizzled old prospector in *The Treasure of the Sierra Madre*.

The Maltese Falcon (1941) was Huston's first directorial challenge, Warner Bros.' reward for ten years of outstanding screenplays, including *Murders in the Rue Morgue* (1932), *The Amazing Dr. Clitterhouse* (1938), *Jezebel* (1938), *Juarez* (1939), and *Dr. Ehrlich's Magic Bullet* (1940).

Huston's major films are, by and large, the same as Bogart's major films. However, Huston also made *The Asphalt Jungle* (1950), *The Red Badge of Courage* (1951), *Moulin Rouge* (1953), *Moby Dick* (1956), *The Misfits* (1961), *The Night of the Iguana* (1964), *The Man Who Would Be King* (1975), and *Prizzi's Honor* (1985). He also killed time with a large number of unworthy projects, such as *The Barbarian and the Geisha* (1958), *The List of Adrian Messenger* (1963), *The Bible . . . In the Beginning* (1966), *Reflections in a Golden Eye* (1967), *The Mackintosh Man* (1973), *Victory* (1981), and so on.

These are the Huston/Bogart collaborations:

- *The Amazing Dr. Clitterhouse* (1938). Bogart was featured in this gangster screenplay by John Wexley and John Huston.

- *High Sierra* (1941). Bogart's breakthrough role, as an old-style gangster running out of time, in an adaptation of W. R. Burnett's novel, with a screenplay by Huston and Burnett.

- *The Maltese Falcon* (1941). With the success of *High Sierra*, Huston was given his first chance to direct, and he chose Dashiell Hammett's novel (which Warner Bros. had filmed twice before). Huston also wrote the screenplay, and selected Bogart to star as the cynical shamus.

- *Across the Pacific* (1942) reunited four of the stars from *The Maltese Falcon*. Huston directed.

- *The Treasure of the Sierra Madre* (1948). Written and directed by Huston, his father Walter Huston and Humphrey Bogart played well off each other in this classic study of greed.

- *Key Largo* (1948). Another attempt at the dynamics of *The Maltese Falcon*, with Bogart and Bacall. Directed by John Huston, screenplay by Richard Brooks and Huston.

- *The African Queen* (1951). Huston directed Bogart and Katharine Hepburn, and co-wrote the crackling screenplay with James Agee and (uncredited) Peter Viertel.

- *Beat the Devil* (1954). Bogart and company in a spoof—ready or not—of *The Maltese Falcon*, with a screenplay by Huston and Truman Capote.

- Huston wanted Bogart and Clark Gable for *The Man Who Would Be King*, a project he wasn't able to launch until 1975, eighteen years after Bogie's death. Huston had also wanted Bogart for his production of *Moby Dick* (1956), but Bogie declined and Gregory Peck played the obsessed Captain Ahab.

◆   ◆   ◆

Raoul Walsh (1887–1980) was another of Warner Bros.' dependable journeyman directors, like Michael Curtiz and Howard Hawks. And, like John Huston, Walsh saw much of the world—as a sailor, and a cowboy—before learning about movies. He entered films in 1912 as an actor: he plays the assassin John Wilkes Booth in D. W. Griffith's *The Birth of a Nation* (1915). He married Griffith actress Miriam Cooper.

As a director, Raoul Walsh is one of the best cinematic storytellers. He worked in many genres, but always concentrated on putting the story over. His best films were probably the virile, outdoor action dramas and adventures which usually have moments of tenderness—*High Sierra*, Bogart's breakthrough film, being a good example, with Bogie as a hardened killer who dreams of a better life. (Walsh would remake the bitter tale as a western, *Colorado Territory*, 1949, with Joel McCrea in Bogart's old role.)

Walsh's other popular tough-with-a-soft-spot movies include *The Bowery* (1933), with Wallace Beery and George Raft; *The Strawberry Blonde* (1941), with James Cagney; *They Died with Their Boots On* (1941), with Errol Flynn; *White Heat* (1949), with Cagney as an aging gangster with a mother fixation; *Captain Horatio Hornblower* (1951), with Gregory Peck; and *Band of Angels* (1957), with Clark Gable.

Walsh also directed Humphrey Bogart in *Women of All Nations* (Fox, 1931), as well as *The Roaring Twenties* (1939), *They Drive by Night* (1940), and made uncredited directorial contributions to *The Enforcer* (1951)—all Warner Bros. projects.

●   ●   ●

Bogart and **Billy Wilder** (b. 1906) detested each other with a passion.

Bogart's friend/agent Irving "Swifty" Lazar urged the actor to do *Sabrina* (1954), a lightweight look at love among the rich, thinking it would help the star's career to show moviegoers that he could do sophisticated comedy. Bogie hated the project from the beginning, knowing he had been second choice (after Cary Grant turned it down). Bogart felt that Wilder and costars William Holden and Audrey Hepburn were in cahoots against him, and gave interviews in which he attacked his celebrated co-workers. Bogart also made fun of the Jewish Wilder's accent and called him a Nazi. *Time* magazine quoted Bogart as saying, "Wilder is the kind of Prussian German with a riding crop. He's the type of director I don't like to work with. This picture *Sabrina* is a crock of shit anyway." It was suggested that Bogart was carrying over the paranoia of the last character he had played, Captain Queeg in *The Caine Mutiny* (Columbia, 1954).

Billy Wilder was proud of his Jewish heritage, and mourned the loss of his mother and other family members to the Nazi concentration camps.

Thus, naturally, he would object to being called a Nazi just because he was German. Wilder once physically attacked Romain Gary when that French writer referred to him as a Nazi. The cosmopolitan Wilder worked hard at becoming an American, and at losing his German accent.

In his biography of Wilder, Maurice Zolotow writes, "Billy Wilder is the kind of man who will not speak ill of the dead but he makes exceptions in the cases of Bogart and Marilyn Monroe."

Billy Wilder's feature films are characterized by their cynicism and often biting humor: *Double Indemnity* (1944), *The Lost Weekend* (1945), *Sunset Boulevard* (1950), *Ace in the Hole*, aka *The Big Carnival* (1951), *Witness for the Prosecution* (1957). His comedies have a touch of the vulgar, a touch of Wilder cynicism: *The Seven Year Itch* (1955), *Some Like It Hot* (1959), *The Apartment* (1960), *One, Two, Three* (1961), *Kiss Me, Stupid* (1964), *The Fortune Cookie* (1966). *Sabrina*, though an atypical Wilder film and starring a miscast Humphrey Bogart, was a financial success for Paramount Pictures.

Billy Wilder won the 1945 Oscar for Best Director for *The Lost Weekend*, and one for Best Screenplay (with Charles Brackett). Wilder and Brackett shared a second Best Screenplay Oscar for *Sunset Boulevard* (1950). In 1960, Wilder won the Best Director award for *The Apartment*, and shared the Academy Award for Best Screenplay with frequent co-writer I. A. L. Diamond.

The Writers

Humphrey Bogart and novelist **Louis Bromfield** (1896–1956), met on the set of *It All Came True* (1940), a gangster comedy based on Bromfield's novel *Better Than Life*. Being partial to the company of writers, Bogart became friends with Bromfield. Bromfield lived on a 715-acre home, called Malabar Farm, near Mansfield, Ohio. Bogart and his third wife, Mayo Methot, visited him there, and later Bogart and his fourth wife, Lauren Bacall, were married on Malabar Farm.

Louis Bromfield won the Pulitzer Prize in 1924 for *The Green Bay Tree*. He published thirty-four books in thirty-three years. Three others were also made into movies: *The Rains Came*, filmed in 1939 and again in 1955 as *The Rains of Ranchipur*; *McLeod's Folly*, filmed as *Johnny Come Lately* (1943); and *Mrs. Parkington* (1944).

✦　　✦　　✦

Mark Hellinger (1903–1947) was a rough-and-tumble New York columnist and reporter. He wrote short stories, plays, and screenplays with varying degrees of success. When he became a film producer, he specialized in such gritty, hard-hitting dramas as *The Killers* (1946), *Brute Force* (1947), and *The Naked City* (1948), which, in a radical departure, was filmed not on a studio backlot, but on the mean streets of New York City.

Hellinger's association with Bogart includes credit as author of the original story of *The Roaring Twenties* (1939); associate producer on *It All Came True*, *Brother Orchid*, and *They Drive by Night* (all in 1940); associate producer on *High Sierra* (1941), a breakthrough film for Bogart; and producer of *The Two Mrs. Carrolls* (1947), an overwrought thriller which was basically a Barbara Stanwyck vehicle.

In early 1947, Hellinger formed a production company with Bogart to film the short stories of Ernest Hemingway. Such a company would have meant artistic and financial independence for both men, but the heavy-drinking Hellinger died in December of the same year, while the firm was still in the dreaming stage.

✦　　✦　　✦

Bogart had great respect and admiration for **Nunnally Johnson** (1897–1977), another writer pal. You can see Johnson and the Bogarts, along with Marilyn Monroe, in the widely-reproduced publicity photos from the premiere of *How to Marry a Millionaire* (1953). Bogie was touched that his friend had tailored a role for Lauren Bacall in that screen comedy, which Johnson wrote and produced.

Born in Columbus, Georgia, Nunnally Johnson began his career there as a newspaper reporter, and graduated to the *New York Herald Tribune*. He began writing screenplays in 1933, and quickly became one of the best, turning out *House of Rothschild* (1934), *Kid Millions* (1934), *The Prisoner of Shark Island* (1936), and *Jesse James* (1939). He later added producing to his achievements at his Twentieth Century–Fox base: *The Grapes of Wrath* (1940), *Three Came Home* (1950), *My Cousin Rachel* (1952) and directed such films as *The Three Faces of Eve* (1957).

Chapter 12

Casablanca

Shall we do a quick recount?

Bogie made seventy-five feature films, of which at least forty are generally considered insignificant, mediocre, god-awful, or otherwise no damn good. He made a number of others you can never remember if you've seen . . . until you sit through them again and wonder why you wasted your time.

Then, of course, he made still others—at least six, maybe ten, maybe more—that regularly show up on all the "best" lists: Best American Films, All-Time Favorites, Critics' Choice, Festival Favorites . . . yadda yadda. Whatever.

Casablanca (1942) was number two, after *Citizen Kane* (1941), in the American Film Institute's much ballyhooed 1998 promotion of America's "100 Best Movies." But who do they think they're fooling? The American Film Institute is probably as out of touch as its other neighbors in Washington, D.C. Ask any average movie-watcher how many times he's seen *Citizen Kane*, and the answer will probably be, "Huh?" The AFI put *Citizen Kane* as number one because it's "Art" and you're *supposed* to prefer it over popular entertainments like *King Kong* (1933) and *Star Wars* (1977). However, ask the same film fan how many times he's seen *Casablanca*, and you'll get a "can't remember" shrug.

Being *the* movie, there's been an awful lot written about it. Is there anything new—or less familiar—to say? Let's give it a shot.

The Twelve Best Things about Casablanca that You Might Not Have Heard Already

1. Hungarian-born director Michael Curtiz (1888–1962) received Academy Award nominations for *Angels with Dirty Faces* (1938) and *Yankee Doodle Dandy* (1942). On March 2, 1944, at Grauman's Chinese Theatre on Hollywood Boulevard, Michael Curtiz finally won the Academy Award for Best Director, for *Casablanca*. Here is his acceptance speech:

   "So many times I have a speech ready, but no dice. Always a bridesmaid, never a mother. Now I win, I have no speech."

2. The influential Italian philosopher-theorist Umberto Eco (b. 1932), explained the appeal of *Casablanca* by showing how the movie combines many different story elements, motifs, themes, and styles. Eco concludes that "*Casablanca* has succeeded in becoming a cult movie because it is not *one* movie. It is *The Movies*."

3. "Here's looking at you, kid," was Humphrey Bogey's contribution to the *Casablanca* screenplay. And he liked the word "kid" so much, he used it again. In *Dead Reckoning* (1947), he calls Lizabeth Scott "kid" twice. "Hello, kid," he says to Florence Marly in *Tokyo Joe* (1949). And in *Sirocco* (1951), he snarls at mean Marta Toren, "You're a shweet kid!"

4. Have you heard the "homosexual love story" theory?

   Consider that Captain Renault (played by Claude Rains) tells Ilsa (Ingrid Bergman), "He is the kind of man that . . . well, if I were a woman, and *I* were not around, I should be in love with Rick." And after Bogie's Rick gives up Ilsa, at the airport finale, he and Renault walk off into the fog together, talking of a beautiful friendship.

This "seductive" theory is discussed by movie critic Richard Corliss in "Casablanca: An Analysis of the Film," in Howard Koch's *Casablanca: Script and Legend*.

In *Cult Movies* Danny Peary writes about the Rick-Renault relationship, and adds this comment: "Never has there been a more romantic ending." And, in his book *Suspects*, David Thomson has Rick and Louis going to Marrakech after the war, where "Louis took the best care of him." Take it for what it's worth.

5. Of all the talented writers in all the studios in Hollywood, it was Warner Bros. executive producer Hal B. Wallis who came up with the immortal last line: "Louis, I think this is the beginning of a beautiful friendship."

6. Lena Horne was considered for the part of the piano player— as were Ella Fitzgerald and singer-pianist Hazel Scott. The role went to Arthur "Dooley" Wilson, a drummer who did not know how to play the piano. "As Time Goes By" was performed off-camera by studio pianist Elliot Carpenter, as Dooley went through the motions on-camera.

7. At the Academy Awards ceremony, when *Casablanca* was announced as winner for Best Picture, producer Hal B. Wallis stood up and started for the stage of Grauman's Chinese Theatre . . . but Jack L. Warner, the head of Warner Bros., jumped to his feet, ran to the front, and accepted the trophy before Wallis could. And he kept it! According to reports, Warner the mogul would not even let Wallis be *photographed* with the Best Picture Oscar.

8. Did you catch the goof with Ilsa's wardrobe? She refers to the blue dress she wore that last day in Paris, when the Germans marched in. However, when Rick gets around to remembering (in flashback) those final hours in Paris, we see that she's wearing a suit.

9. At the time, the early 1940s, Ingrid Bergman was under contract to mogul David O. Selznick, who had brought the Swedish

actress to America in 1939. Julius J. and Philip G. Epstein, the twin brothers working on the *Casablanca* script, were delegated to sell Selznick on the promise of the new screen project, to get him to loan Ingrid Bergman to Warner Bros.

The Epsteins visited Selznick at his Culver City, California, white mansion (seen in the credits of Selznick feature-film releases), and proceeded to outline the movie's plot—which really hadn't been worked out yet—while Selznick ate his lunch. Julius Epstein fumbled around with the narrative for some time, before finally conceding, "Oh, what the hell! It's going to be a lot of shit like *Algiers* [the 1938 United Artists movie]."

That was enough for Selznick, who agreed to Bergman's participation in the wartime thriller.

Note: At the time, Bergman was also wanted for Paramount's *For Whom the Bell Tolls* (1943). It was touch-and-go as to which screen production would be ready first to start shooting. When Bergman finished work on *Casablanca* on August 3, 1942, the phone rang—Paramount calling to say that she had the part in *For Whom the Bell Tolls*, and could she please report to work immediately?—right then, if possible.

The irony is that the Paramount project was regarded as a big, important, classy Ernest Hemingway movie (in color, and with an intermission, for chrissakes!), while *Casablanca* was just another black-and-white title on the Warner Bros. weekly schedule. Over fifty years later, the one movie is enjoyed over and over, and the other is a chore to sit through even once.

10. The best more-than-a-movie analysis:

"*Casablanca* made Bogart; Bogart made *Casablanca*. Whether in a white dinner jacket or in a trench coat and snap-brim fedora, he became a new and timely symbol of the post–Pearl Harbor American: tough but compassionate, skeptical yet idealistic, betrayed yet ready to believe again, and, above all, a potentially deadly opponent" (A. M. Sperber and Eric Lax, *Bogart*).

11. When *Casablanca* was first shown in Germany, after World War II, all references to the Nazis—all of Conrad Veidt's scenes—had

been deleted. The movie, twenty minutes shorter, had been re-edited and had narration added which now turned Rick's Café Americain into a nightclub in which there was drug-dealing. The complete *Casablanca* was not seen in Germany until the mid-1970s.

12. The best *Casablanca*-as-religion analysis:
    "It's just a movie, but it's more than that. It's become something that people can't find in values today. And they go back to *Casablanca* as they go back to church, political church, to find something that is gone from our values today" (Howard Koch, *Casablanca* screenwriter).

Bogie/Rick Plays It Again and Again —on Madison Avenue

Casablanca's setting, characters, and classic lines have become part of the American consciousness. Just look at the endless number of advertisements which play off the classic film to sell everything from ceiling fans to blank videotape to layer cakes. Here are some of the better examples.

Brown & Gold Lighting (1980). An illustration depicts the interior of Rick's Café Americain, with piano, parrot, large ceiling fan, shadow on the wall of a man in hat and trench coat. The text reads, "As time glows by. . . . Cool your summer days and nights with our beautiful, energy-efficient ceiling fans."

Busch Gardens' the Dark Continent Theme Park (1975). A color photo reproduces a *Casablanca* setting: a Bogart look-alike (correctly holding his cigarette the Bogie way), a pretty Ingrid Bergman type, a cringing Peter Lorre type, a suave Claude Rains type, an overweight Sydney Greenstreet type. The headline: "It's still the same old story. In Florida." The ad is promoting a Tampa theme park that reproduces the best of yesteryear's Africa: Moroccan village, Tangiers Theatre, Zagora Café, etc.

CasaBlanca Fan Company (1982). Featuring Bogart look-alike Robert Sacchi (identified in the ads).

- Black and white photo, reproducing the airport farewell, with Rick saying to Ilsa: "Sorry, Kid, but I just can't say goodbye to all my CasaBlanca fans." And in the text: "A kiss is just a kiss, but a CasaBlanca fan isn't just another pretty fan."

- Black and white photo, with a morose Rick in white dinner jacket, and a solicitous Sam standing behind him: "You know, a dame will let you down every time, but a CasaBlanca fan will always hang true." And in the text: "It's not just how they [fans] look, it's how they perform as time goes by. Turn 'em on again, Sam."

Casablanca Records and Film Works (1978). Full-page ad in the entertainment trade paper *Variety*, 1978, with an illustration of a Bogart-wannabe in trench coat and dangling cigarette, in a Rick's Café American setting. Headline: "Return to Casablanca."

Gentleman's Quarterly magazine (1978). Illustration of a seated Rick, with a drink. The advertising copy reads, " 'Here's looking at you, kid.' You've got style and class and savvy. Did it come natural or is it GQ? If not, subscribe: 'So do it right now, before time goes by and you forget. Here's looking at you, kid. You've done alright.'"

Haggar Menswear (1979). Color photo, re-creating a *Casablanca* street scene: a grimacing Bogart type up front, a suave Renault, a mystery lady in black, a fat man in a fez . . . and right in the middle is a handsome model in a light-blue three-piece Dacron suit. The advertising copy asks, "Was he the final stitch in a tapestry of doom?" But then it answers that he has savvy and class and can take care of himself—he doesn't need Rick's help.

London Fog Trench Coat (1972). A color photo re-creating a *Casablanca*-type scene: Jerry Lacy as Bogart, wearing a trench coat, stands beside a piano with a black piano player, while a fat man in white suit and fez glowers from the corner. Headline: "Play it again, London Fog." Text: "It's not the same old story. London Fog has updated the classic trench coat look with Imaginit—a new woven fabric with the stretch, shape and wrinkle-resistance you've always wanted. Plus the protection of London Fog's own water-repellent formula. On that you can rely."

Maxell Video Tape (1983). Illustration of Bogart holding a videotape. "With Maxell videotape, even after 300 plays you can still say . . . 'Play it again Sam.' It's the videotape you'll appreciate more and more . . .'as time goes by.'"

Pam Am Airline (1971). Publicity photo of Bogart in white dinner jacket and cigarette. The three-line headline reads: "Only Pam Am flies nonstop to Casablanca. Play it again, Sam. Only Pam Am flies nonstop to Casablanca."

Sara Lee Layer Cake (1996). Black-and-white photo from *Casablanca* of Rick turning to his piano player, saying, "How could I forget her, Sam? She stuck me with the Pepperidge Farm. And she took off with the Sara Lee."

Sony Color Trinitron Television (1976). A full-page newspaper ad, with a photo of Bogart impersonator Jerry Lacy in white dinner jacket, standing behind a huge TV set. Headline: "Play it again, Sony."

And, if that's not enough, through the magic of computer compositing—which combines classic film footage with newly photographed images—Bogart, Fred Astaire, Marilyn Monroe, and other legendary stars can now appear in dazzling new television commercials.

Chapter 13

Bogart on Radio and Television

Radio

The Lux Radio Theatre, to Los Angeles, was the class act of the airwaves. The movie studios felt that having one of its movies presented, or a star booked on the show gave them great prestige. Moreover, an appearance would ensure a better take at the box office.

The show presented sixty-minute adaptations of popular movies, often with the original cast members. The debut of *The Lux Radio Theatre* was on October 14, 1934, on NBC, with Miriam Hopkins and John Boles in *Seventh Heaven*. (The show moved to CBS in 1935.) The last entry was on June 7, 1955, with Walter Pidgeon in *Edward, My Son*.

(*The Lux Video Theatre* [CBS-NBC 1950–57] presented thirty-minute adaptations of plays and stories. The show expanded to sixty minutes in its fifth season, with adaptations of theatrical films when it moved to NBC.)

Humphrey Bogart appeared five times on *The Lux Radio Theatre*.

Bullets or Ballots (April 17, 1939) 60 minutes.

Edward G. Robinson and Humphrey Bogart repeat their parts from the 1936 Warner Bros. gangster yarn. Mary Astor and Otto Kruger assume the parts originally played by Joan Blondell and Barton MacLane.

Moontide (April 30, 1945) 60 minutes.

Humphrey Bogart and Virginia Bruce play the tough seaman and the suicidal young girl, characters portrayed in the 1942 Twentieth Century–Fox romantic drama by French import Jean Gabin and Ida Lupino.

To Have and Have Not (October 14, 1946) 60 minutes.

Humphrey Bogart and Lauren Bacall repeat their original roles from the 1944 Warner Bros. action-adventure, which was their first costarring screen venture.

The Treasure of the Sierra Madre (April 18, 1949) 60 minutes.

Humphrey Bogart and Walter Huston are "Dobbs" and "Howard" again, while Frank Lovejoy inherits Tim Holt's role of "Curtin," the younger prospector in this adaptation of the 1948 Warner Bros. classic in World War I Africa.

The African Queen (December 15, 1952) 60 minutes.

Bogart reprises his Oscar-winning role from the 1951 United Artists offering as the gin-soaked Charlie Allnut, while Greer Garson takes on Rose, the "psalm-singing old maid"—unlikely lovers, and unlikely heroes who sink a German gunboat.

OTHER RADIO APPEARANCES

The CBS Shakespeare Theater (CBS, August 1937) 60 minutes.

One-hour adaptations without commercials, done live before a studio audience.

Humphrey Bogart appears as Henry Percy in *Henry IV, Part One*, joining seasoned performers Walter Huston and Brian Aherne.

The Edgar Bergen and Charlie McCarthy Show (NBC) 30 minutes.

Humphrey Bogart is heard on this show on January 29, 1939, February 5, 1939, April 30, 1939, and September 12, 1943. Bogart trades barbs with Charlie McCarthy, the wisecracking dummy controlled by ventriloquist Edgar Bergen (who had won an Academy Award in 1937 for creating Charlie).

Bogart's other radio guest spots during the late 1930s include *The Rudy Vallee Show* (NBC, January 7, 1938); *The Bing Crosby Show/Bing Crosby's Kraft Music Hall* (NBC, May 19, 1938, January 26, 1939, and February 2, 1939); *The Kate Smith Show* (CBS, February 23, 1939); and *Community Chest* (syndicated, May 10 and May 18, 1939).

The Campbell Playhouse (CBS) 60 minutes.

From December 9, 1938, to March 31, 1940, this dramatic anthology series was an extension of Orson Welles's *Mercury Theater on the Air* after Campbell's Soup became a sponsor. It replaced *The Aldrich Family* for the summer.

From November 29, 1940, through June 13, 1941, after Orson Welles dropped out, the series featured stars such as Humphrey Bogart, Mary Astor, and Jeanette MacDonald in rarely-heard radio adaptations.

The Screen Guild Players (CBS, January 26, 1941) 30 minutes.

A series that presented adaptations of popular movies. Humphrey Bogart and Herbert Marshall do *If You Could Only Cook*, taken from the popular 1935 feature which headlined Herbert Marshall, Jean Arthur, and Leo Carrillo.

Shirley Temple Variety Show (CBS, December 26, 1941) 30 minutes.

Little Miss Temple stars in four variety specials for radio in 1941. Bogart is a guest star on one of the shows. Twenty years later, *Shirley Temple Theatre*, a children's show, airs for a season Sundays on NBC.

The March of Dimes Show (January 25, 1941) 60 minutes.

Eddie Cantor is host, with guest stars Fanny Brice, Humphrey Bogart, Fibber McGee and Molly, James Cagney, and Rudy Vallee.

The Gulf Screen Guild Theatre (CBS, November 2, 1941) 30 minutes.

Edward G. Robinson and Humphrey Bogart perform in a radio version of *The Amazing Dr. Clitterhouse*, reprising their roles from the 1938 Warner Bros. movie.

The Humphrey Bogart Show, aka **Humphrey Bogart Presents** (1941) 30 minutes.

Little is known of this radio program, which lasted for only one night, with a story called "Dead Man."

> Humphrey Bogart has four features released in 1940 and three in 1941, including the star-making *High Sierra* and *The Maltese Falcon*. He shows up on a number of radio shows to promote them. These included *The Kraft Music Hall/Bing Crosby Show* (NBC, January 4, 1940, March 21, 1940, May 22, 1941, October 31, 1941, and November 27, 1941). Also: *The Eddie Cantor Show* (NBC, March 5, 1941), and *Al Pearce and His Gang* (CBS, October 31, 1941).

The Jack Benny Lucky Strike Show (CBS, February 1, 1942) 30 minutes.

Bogart's first appearance on this popular comedy show starring tightwad funnyman Benny and his cast of regulars: Mary Livingston, Phil Harris, Don Wilson, Dennis Day, Eddie Anderson, et al.

Screen Director's Playhouse (NBC, April 26, 1943) 30 minutes.

Bogie is mystery man Rick Blaine in a radio adaptation of Warner Bros.' *Casablanca* (1942), which had opened around the country in January of 1943.

Romance (CBS, 1943–57) 30 minutes.

An anthology show of romance, high adventure, and touching little dramas, it changed formats and schedules many times over the seasons. From July 4, 1944, through August 27, 1946, the series features major film personalities in adaptations of popular movies. Stars such as Bogart, Shirley Temple, and Errol Flynn appear.

The Gulf Screen Guild Theatre (CBS, April 17, 1944) 30 minutes.

Humphrey Bogart and Ida Lupino do *High Sierra*, reprising their roles from the 1941 Warner Bros. film.

The Democratic National Committee Program (presented on all four networks, November 6, 1944) 60 minutes.

A documentary for American president Franklin D. Roosevelt that is basically a sixty-minute commercial. It is broadcast the night before his reelection to a fourth term. Judy Garland and Humphrey Bogart are among the Hollywood notables on the show.

Suspense (CBS, March 8, 1945) 30 minutes.

A radio adaptation of novelist James M. Cain's hard-boiled thriller *Love's Lovely Counterfeit* (1942), with Humphrey Bogart and Lurene Tuttle.

Command Performance (Armed Forces Radio Service) From 30 minutes to two-hour specials.

Called "the best wartime program" (*Time* magazine), it isn't heard in America—it is sent by direct short-wave transmission to the troops overseas. All services and talent are donated for the war efforts.

- April 29, 1945: master of ceremonies, Herbert Marshall.
  Guests: Janet Blair, Lauren Bacall, Humphrey Bogart, Eddie
  Arnold, Jimmy Durante, and Sons of the Pioneers.

Film star Herbert Marshall gives comedian Jimmy Durante pointers in wooing women like Lauren Bacall. Bogart shows up and fights with Durante over the sexy lady, who walks out on both of them.

- August 30, 1945: master of ceremonies, Frank Sinatra.
  Guests: Humphrey Bogart, Lauren Bacall, and Victor Borge.

Bogart hires crooner Sinatra as a bodyguard for Bacall, who swoons over the singer. Bogart and Sinatra brawl.

Academy Award (CBS, July 3, 1946) 30 minutes.

An anthology show of movie adaptations, often using the original stars. The mini-version of Warner Bros.' 1941 film, *The Maltese Falcon*, features Bogart, Mary Astor, and Sydney Greenstreet.

The Jack Benny Show (NBC, January 5, 1947) 30 minutes.

Guests: Humphrey Bogart, Lauren Bacall.

In the episode skit, Benny wants to act in *To Have and Have Not* opposite Bacall. Bogart is on hand to show Jack how it's done—first with Bacall, then with Jack's girlfriend [in real life, his wife] Mary Livingston.

Hollywood Fights Back (ABC, October 26, 1947) 30 minutes.
Hollywood Fights Back (ABC, November 2, 1947) 30 minutes.

Two broadcasts featuring prominent film stars, including Humphrey Bogart and Lauren Bacall, who protest the heavy-handed tactics of the congressional House Un-American Activities Committee which was then accusing certain Hollywood personalities of subversive activities and Communist sympathies.

The Prudential Family Hour of Stars (CBS, 1948–50) 60 minutes.

This show began life in 1941 as *The Prudential Family Hour*, offering thirty minutes of concert music, both operatic and popular. *The Prudential Family Hour of Stars* began on October 3, 1948, with six Hollywood luminaries billed as the Prudential "family": Gregory Peck, Bette Davis, Ginger Rogers, Humphrey Bogart, Robert Taylor, and Barbara Stanwyck.

Great Short Stories (Syndicated, August 17, 1949) 30 minutes.

Bogart stars in an adaptation of "Dead Man," which had been done first by Bogie on his own radio show, *The Humphrey Bogart Show*, in 1941.

Other Bogart radio appearances during the 1940s include *Rudy Vallee Sealtest Village Store* (NBC, February 19, 1942); *The Burns and Allen Show* (CBS, December 12, 1944); *The Milton Berle Show* (CBS, January 30, 1945); *The Ginny Simms Show* (CBS, March 22, 1946); *The Jack Benny Show* (NBC, January 5, 1947); *The Fred Allen Show* (NBC, November 30, 1947); *Louella Parsons* (ABC, February 1, 1948); and *Duffy's Tavern* (NBC, March 17, 1948).

Bold Venture (syndicated, 1951–52) 30 minutes.

Writers, Morton Fine and David Friedkin; music, composed and conducted by David Rose. Production company, Ziv Productions.

Cast: Humphrey Bogart (*Slate Shannon*), Lauren Bacall (*Sailor Duval*), Jester Hairston (*King Moses*).

In early spring 1951, the Bogarts costar in a weekly half-hour adventure radio series that is a spin-off of the characters and setting of their 1944 movie hit, *To Have and Have Not*. "Slate Shannon" owns a hotel in the Caribbean that's a crossroads for all sorts of adventurers and unsavory characters who would be right at home in *Casablanca*. King Moses is a "Sam"-type character, a black calypso singer who comments on the action in his songs.

Because radio is more closely censored than movies at the time, Bogart's character is changed to Bacall's guardian, rather than her lover—but that doesn't stop the clever exchanges, the wry humor, the sly innuendos. And she seems more than able to take care of herself.

Seventy-eight episodes are produced, which begin airing nationally in early spring 1951, on 423 stations across the country.

Audiotape collections of *Bold Venture* broadcasts are commercially available.

(Note: A syndicated television version of *Bold Venture* would be produced in 1959, with Dane Clark and Joan Marshall in the leading roles. This half-hour show would last for thirty-nine weeks).

The Screen Guild Theatre (NBC, May 18, 1950) 30 minutes.
A radio adaptation of Warner Bros.' 1941 film *The Maltese Falcon*, with Bogart as Sam Spade and Lauren Bacall as Brigid O'Shaughnessy (played by Mary Astor in the original movie).

Stars in the Air (CBS, May 3, 1952), 30 minutes.
An anthology series, an extension of *The Screen Guild Theatre*. Humphrey Bogart appears in a dramatization of Twentieth Century–Fox's 1945 film of the FBI versus Nazi spies, *The House on 92nd Street*, which had featured, originally, William Eythe, Lloyd Nolan, and Signe Hasso.

Theatre Guild on the Air (NBC, February 10, 1952) 60 minutes.
Humphrey Bogart and Lauren Bacall are heard in an adaptation of Herman Wouk's *The Traitor*, about a scientist who gives atomic-bomb secrets to the Russians, then regrets it. The 1949 play, starring Lee Tracy, Walter Hampden, and Wesley Addy received critical acclaim but flopped on Broadway.

The Bing Crosby Chesterfield Show (CBS, February 13, 1952), 30 minutes.
Bogart sings the "Bold Fisherman" chantey from United Artists' *The African Queen* (1951), and then Bing Crosby and Lauren Bacall join in to harmonize with Bogie.

The Bing Crosby Chesterfield Show (CBS, March 12, 1952) 30 minutes.

Lauren Bacall begs Crosby to dissuade Bogie from becoming a crooner—he's singing "Bold Fisherman" again! The three then do a comic adaptation of a scene from *The African Queen*.

Television

Humphrey Bogart made only two acting appearances on television:

The Jack Benny Program (CBS, October 25, 1953) Black-and-white, 30 minutes.

Bogart's television debut. He joins host Jack Benny and regulars Don Wilson and Bob Crosby in "Baby Face," a comedy sketch satirizing TV police series and Bogart's own past film characterizations.

There is a clip from this show included in the documentary *Bogart: The Man and His Movies* (1961), to prove again just how good Bogart could be at comedy.

The Petrified Forest on *Producers' Showcase* (NBC, May 30, 1955) Color, 90 minutes.

Director, Delbert Mann; producer, Fred Coe; writer, Tad Mosel.

Bogart portrays gangster Duke Mantee for the third time (after the original 1935 Broadway production and the 1936 Warner Bros. movie). Wife Lauren Bacall appears as the waitress Gaby, with Henry Fonda as the disillusioned poet Alan Squier. Others in the cast are Jack Klugman, Jack Warden, and Richard Jaeckel.

One of the most-heralded telecasts of the 1950s, the kinescope was thought lost and the production was not seen again until 1987, when The Museum of Broadcasting presented it in New York City.

Variety of June 1, 1955, suggests that the play appears less profound than when first presented, and wonders if the casting is at fault. "While there's no denying Fonda's capacities as one of the stage and screen's more gifted performers, neither in physical appearance, voice timber nor emotional conviction did he measure up to the ideal Alan Squier. His espousals of love and more ephemeral qualities of living were often tepid and none too convincing.

"Similarly in the case of Miss Bacall, her suavity and sophisticated demeanor leaves little illusion of the poetic dreamer buried in the Arizona desert. Both her voice and visual effect mitigated against the believability of the character.

"Bogart, of course, remains Bogart, but somewhere in the adaptation the part of killer Mantee shrinks to undemanding and unrewarding opportunities."

The New York Times also found fault: "The limitations of the TV camera . . . [detract] somewhat from the mounting tension embodied in Mantee's figure." The production came across as Fonda's show.

OTHER TELEVISION APPEARANCES

Person to Person (CBS-TV, September 3, 1954) Black-and-white, 30 minutes.

Host, Edward R. Murrow.

Murrow, based in New York, interviews Bogie and Bacall, via remote, in their Holmby Hills, California, residence. "The Bogart sequence moved fast, deftly and amusingly. It was a good switch on tough-guy Bogie to see him relaxed at home with wife and two charming kids, although he stayed in character with his down-to-earth, terse but friendly rejoinders. Actor was himself, natural, while Miss Bacall, a little stagy, hammed it up a bit. The Bogarts, a literate, witty, engaging couple indulged in entertaining chitchat about themselves, films and theatre, with some amusing criss-crosses of conflicting opinions on acting and living" (Variety, September 8, 1954).

Note: The Bogart-Bacall interview is included in the videotape Person to Person, Volume One, which also features Murrow's interviews with Marilyn Monroe, Louis Armstrong, Bing Crosby, Eddie Fisher and Debbie Reynolds, and Ella Fitzgerald.

The Ed Sullivan Show (CBS, July 1, 1956) Black-and-white, 60 minutes.

Host, Ed Sullivan.

Guests: Mary Astor, Lauren Bacall, Humphrey Bogart, Jose Ferrer, Sydney Greenstreet, Katharine Hepburn, John Huston, Walter Huston, Burl Ives, Peter Lorre, Billy Pearson, Gregory Peck, Vincent Price, Edward G. Robinson, Claire Trevor, and Orson Welles.

This program is supposedly a tribute to director John Huston on the release of Warner Bros.' *Moby Dick* (1956), but *Variety* dismisses it as just "one long commercial" for the sea drama.

Part IV

The Legacy

Chapter 14

The Movie *About* Humphrey Bogart

Kevin O'Connor starred as Humphrey Bogart in the made-for-TV movie *Bogie*, which aired on the CBS network on March 4, 1980. The tele-feature, adapted from the 1975 biography by columnist friend Joe Hyams, focused on the actor from the early 1930s until his death, from struggling actor to movie star.

John J. O'Connor, TV critic for the *New York Times*, liked the per-formances of O'Connor, Ann Wedgeworth as Mayo Methot, and Kathryn Harrold as Lauren Bacall, but had major reservations about the movie itself: "Except for sporadic moments, the biography refuses to come to life. Part of the problem is that Mr. Bogart's personal life wasn't terribly inter-esting. His true legacy, his films, are shunted to the sidelines . . . and reduced to titles popping up on the screen to remind the viewer that this character was really important.

"Without the films, Mr. Bogart is portrayed as a heavy-drinking loner, much more fragile and educated than the tough-guy he was usually playing on-screen. His relationship with Mayo was stormy, destructive, ultimately tedious. It takes Miss Bacall, his nineteen-year-old costar in *To Have and Have Not*, to discover that 'underneath that cynical front, you're a gentle, sensitive man'.

"What's left is a pair of friends climbing in and out of a yacht to facilitate various crisis scenes, and a good deal of name-dropping ('Spence just called—he and Katie want to come over for cocktails'). Bogie—and Mr. O'Connor—deserved better."

Lauren Bacall reportedly said she had no desire to see the made-for-TV movie.

There are interesting behind-the-scenes credits: The screenplay for *Bogie* is by Daniel Taradash, who co-wrote the screenplay for the Bogart film *Knock On Any Door* (1949). The director is Vincent Sherman, who co-wrote two Bogart entries—*Crime School* (1938) and *King of the Underworld* (1939)—and directed two others—*The Return of Dr. X* (1939) and *All Through the Night* (1939).

Bogie (A Charles Fries Production, CBS-TV, 1980) Color, 100 minutes.

Director, Vincent Sherman; executive producers, Charles Fries, Malcolm Stuart; producer, Philip Barry; teleplay, Daniel Taradash (from the Joe Hyams biography *Bogart and Bacall: A Love Story* [1975]).

Cast: Kevin O'Connor (*Humphrey Bogart*); Kathryn Harrold (*Lauren Bacall*); Ann Wedgeworth (*Mayo Methot*); Alfred Ryder (*Mike Romanoff*); Carol Vogel (*Mary Phillips*); Richard Dysart (*Jack L. Warner*); Anne Bellamy (*Louella Parsons*); Herb Braham (*Peter Lorre*); Ross Elliott (*Howard Hawks*); Arthur Franz (*Dr. Bogart*); Stephen Keep (*Leslie Howard*).

Chapter 15

The Bogart Documentaries

Note: All films are black-and-white unless noted.

Bogart: The Man and His Movies (A Film Shows Inc. Production, 1961) 70 minutes.

Producers, Paul Harris and Sandy Oliveri; writer, Paul Harris; distributed by Goodtime Home Video.

A compilation told mainly with movie trailers and other advertising materials. Includes footage from the 1944 *Report from the Front* short subject, in which Bogart appeals for donations to the Red Cross; the very funny 1954 Jack Benny TV show on which Bogie plugs *Beat the Devil* [1954]; an excerpt from the 1955 TV production of *The Petrified Forest*, costarring Lauren Bacall and Henry Fonda; and an excerpt from the 1954 *Person to Person* TV interview with Edward R. Murrow.

Hollywood and the Stars: "The Man Called Bogart" (NBC-TV, September 30, 1963) 30 minutes.

David L. Wolper Productions; writer/producer, Al Ramrus; executive producer, Jack Haley Jr.

Narrator, Joseph Cotten.

A straightforward and concise story of Bogart's life and career. It includes a wonderful montage of movie scenes of Bogie getting shot, and then a series of clips showing him dying.

Movie historian Anthony Slide (*Films on Film History*) calls *Hollywood and the Stars* "possibly the best television series ever produced on the history of the film industry." This thirty-minute NBC series aired from September 30, 1963 to September 28, 1964, and then was seen in syndication throughout the 1960s.

Other stars profiled in the TV series include Bette Davis, Natalie Wood, Paul Newman, Kim Novak, Al Jolson, Bing Crosby, and Rita Hayworth.

Note: This documentary was also released as **Portrait: Humphrey Bogart, the Story of the Ultimate Hollywood Legend** (Ciné Productions, Inc., 1991), distributed by Worldwide Entertainment Marketing.

Bogart (ABC-TV, April 22, 1967) 60 minutes.

Producer-director-writer, Marshall Flaum; executive producer, Sherman Grinberg.

Narrator, Charlton Heston.

Clips from Bogart's films, interspersed with interviews: John Huston, who directed him in six films; actress Joan Blondell, who talks about the early days in Hollywood; actress Ida Lupino, his costar in *High Sierra* (1941); costar George Raft, who turned down all the good parts so that Bogart could become a star; *Casablanca* (1942) costar Ingrid Bergman, who says, "I kissed him, but I don't know him at all"; Joseph L. Mankiewicz, who directed Bogart in one of his last projects, *The Barefoot Contessa* (1954); Stanley Kramer, director of *The Caine Mutiny* (1954), in which Bogart created one of his most memorable characters, the paranoid Captain Queeg; and "Prince" Michael Romanoff, owner of Bogart's favorite restaurant.

The trade paper *Variety* liked the TV show, calling it "a fascinating exercise in nostalgia," but found Bogey's fourth wife/widow Lauren Bacall conspicuous in her absence.

The Humphrey Bogart Legend (HBO-cable, 1979) 25 minutes.

Narrator, Richard Basehart.

A brief and concise overview of Bogart's life and career. It includes interviews with producer-director Stanley Kramer, who worked with

Bogart on *The Caine Mutiny*; and journalist friend Joe Hyams who published two books on the actor: *Bogie* and *Bogart and Bacall: A Love Story*.

Great Performances: "Bacall on Bogart" (PBS-TV, March 11, 1988) Color and black-and-white, 90 minutes.

Executive producer, Jac Venza; producers, David Heeley, Joan Kramer; director, David Heeley; writer, John L. Miller. A co-production of WNET–New York and Turner Entertainment Co.

Host-Narrator, Lauren Bacall.

This excellent documentary features a scene from the 1936 film *The Petrified Forest* and then, for comparison, the same sequence from the 1955 TV version. Also, comparative scenes from the three different Warner Bros. versions of *The Maltese Falcon*: starring Ricardo Cortez (1931); Warren William (1936, called *Satan Met a Lady*); and then the 1941 Bogart classic.

There are never-before-seen color home movies of Bogart on his beloved yacht *Santana,* on the set of *The African Queen* (1951), and on the set of *Beat the Devil* (1954).

Co-workers and friends share reminiscences, including actresses Ingrid Bergman and Katharine Hepburn; directors John Huston, Richard Brooks, and Peter Bogdanovich; commentator Alistair Cooke; and writers Julius J. Epstein and Budd Schulberg.

Bogart and Bacall are shown in a 1956 costume test for *Melville Goodwin, U.S.A.*, all that exists of a film project later recast due to Bogart's untimely death.

You Must Remember This: "A Tribute to Casablanca" (Turner Entertainment, 1998) Color and black-and-white, 36 minutes.

Producer-director, Scott Benson; writers, Benson, Rick Dasher, Tom Edwards, Doug George, and Edward Hastings.

Narrator, Lauren Bacall.

This short but important documentary was included on 1992's Fiftieth Anniversary Edition video and laserdisc release of *Casablanca*. It's also on the 1999 Special Edition video and DVD. The script is clichéd and familiar ("movie magic" is said three times), but the special lineup of guests provides ample compensation.

The on-screen commentators include TV personality Pia Lindstrom, who is the daughter of actress Ingrid Bergman; film historians Rudy

Behlmer and Ronald Haver; actor Dan Seymour ("Abdul the doorman" at Rick's Café Americain); composer Henry Mancini, who discusses the Max Steiner score for the film; Lee Katz, the movie's first assistant director; Francis Scheid, the head sound man; and screenwriters Julius J. Epstein and Howard Koch. Koch explains the appeal of the film classic: "It was a picture the world audiences needed. What it said was that there were values worth making sacrifices for. And it says it in a very entertaining way."

Of greatest interest are the remembrances of Irene Lee Diamond and Murray Burnett, telling their stories on-camera for the first time. Irene Lee was the West Coast story editor for Warner Bros. who discovered the unproduced play *Everybody Comes to Rick's* in 1941 and recommended it to production head Hal B. Wallis—who changed the title to *Casablanca*. Murray Burnett (with friend Joan Alison) wrote the play *Everybody Comes to Rick's*, much of which was retained for the movie. For instance, Burnett wrote the sequence in *Casablanca* when the Nazis, led by Major Strasser (Conrad Veidt), and the French, headed by Victor Laszlo (Paul Henreid) try to outsing each other with their respective national anthems. "I cried when I wrote it," says Burnett. "It was that powerful to me, and it was that powerful in the film."

This documentary also features brief scenes from the two failed attempts to turn *Casablanca* into a weekly television series: in 1955–56, on ABC, with Charles McGraw; and in 1982, on CBS, with David Soul. There's also a clip of a Warner Bros. cartoon with Bugs Bunny as Rick Blaine.

A&E Biography: "Humphrey Bogart: Behind the Legend" (A&E-cable, 1994) Color and black-and-white, 60 minutes.

Producer, Cress Darwin; director, N. Brice Shipley; writer, Bob Waldman.

Narrator, Larry Robinson.

Features Bogart friend and biographer Joe Hyams, and film reviewers Jeffrey Lyons and Michael Medved.

Bogart: The Untold Story (TNT-cable, January 5, 1997) Color and black-and-white, 60 minutes.

Producer-director, Chris Hunt. Iambic Productions.

Host-narrator, Stephen Bogart.

One of the best Bogart documentaries, but with little "untold" information. It features new interviews with biographer Joe Hyams; movie historian Robert Sklar; movie critic Ty Burr; Bogart's business manager Jess Morgan; actress friend Gloria Stuart, who remembers Bogart and third wife Mayo Methot battling on their wedding day in 1938; plus clips from earlier interviews with director John Huston and fourth wife Lauren Bacall. Actress Rose Hobart, who costarred with Bogart on Broadway in 1932, remembers, "He really loathed being an actor. He thought it was sissy—it was not something you did if you were a man."

Humphrey Bogart's son Stephen filed suit against the Turner network, charging that they had falsely promoted this documentary as being based on his own 1995 book of recollections (*Bogart: In Search of My Father*)—thus making it impossible for him to sell documentary rights to it.

Becoming Attractions: The Trailers of Humphrey Bogart (Turner Classic Movies-cable, 1997) 45 minutes.

Executive producer-director, Tony Barbon; producers, Dena Krupinsky, Charlie Coates; writers, Coates, Dena Krupinsky, and Robert Osborne.

Host, Robert Osborne.

A cursory look at how Warner Bros. shaped and marketed Bogart's screen career, as seen in the coming attractions for his movies.

Beginning with *The Petrified Forest* (1936), Bogey was advertised as "the toughest star." Even trailers for non-gangster movies such as *The Return of Dr. X* (1939) sold him as a gangster. Heroic virtues were added to the tough-guy image for *The Maltese Falcon* (1941) and *All Through the Night* (1942). Trailers playing off the success of *Falcon* were prepared for *Across the Pacific* (1942) and *Casablanca* (1942). The publicized love affair between Bogart and costar Lauren Bacall was exploited in the previews of coming attractions for *To Have and Have Not* (1944) and *Dark Passage* (1947).

"The trailers revised and reinvented Bogart," says host Robert Osborne.

Chapter 16

The Bogart Discography

Radio Programs on Audiotape

Academy Award Theatre (CBS, June 3, 1946) 30 minutes.
   The Maltese Falcon with Humphrey Bogart, Mary Astor, and Sydney Greenstreet.

The Bing Crosby Show (CBS, March 12, 1952) 30 minutes.
   Humphrey Bogart and Lauren Bacall are guest stars.

Bold Venture (Ziv Syndication, 1951), 30 minutes.
   Segments include "The Chinese Art Treasure Murders," "Framed for Murder," "Oil Field Strike," "Shannon's Place," "The Tabbard of Pizzaro," and "The Twelve Year Pact."

Great Short Stories (August 17, 1949) 30 minutes.
   The story "Dead Man."

Gulf Screen Guild Theatre (CBS, November 2, 1941) 30 minutes.
   "The Amazing Dr. Clitterhouse," with Edward G. Robinson and Humphrey Bogart.

The Humphrey Bogart Show (1941) 30 minutes.
The story "Dead Man."

The Lady Esther Screen Guild Players (CBS, April 17, 1944) 30 minutes.
"High Sierra" with Ida Lupino and Humphrey Bogart.

Lux Radio Theatre of the Air (CBS) 30 minutes.
April 30, 1945: "Moontide," with Humphrey Bogart and Virginia Bruce.
October 14, 1946: "To Have and Have Not," with Humphrey Bogart and Lauren Bacall.
April 18, 1949: "The Treasure of the Sierra Madre," with Humphrey Bogart and Walter Huston.
December 15, 1952: "The African Queen," with Humphrey Bogart and Greer Garson.

The Screen Guild Players (CBS) 30 minutes.
January 26, 1941: "If She Could Only Cook," with Humphrey Bogart and Herbert Marshall.
April 17, 1944: "High Sierra," with Humphrey Bogart and Ida Lupino.

Shirley Temple Time (1941) 30 minutes.
Of her four specials for radio, three are available: Lionel Barrymore, Humphrey Bogart, and Robert Young each costar in a segment.

Stars in the Air (May 3, 1952) 30 minutes.
"The House on 92nd Street," with Humphrey Bogart.

Suspense (CBS, March 8, 1945) 30 minutes.
"Love's Lovely Counterfeit," with Humphrey Bogart and Lurene Tuttle.

Radio Specials on Audiotape

The March of Dimes Show (January 25, 1941) 60 minutes.
Host, Eddie Cantor. With Humphrey Bogart, Fanny Brice, James Cagney, Fibber McGee and Molly, and Rudy Vallee.

Radio Programs on LP Records

The African Queen (Mark 56 668)

Casablanca (Radiola 1099)

Command Performance (Memorabilia 734)

Henry IV, Part Two (5-Murray Hill 898667)

Love's Lovely Counterfeit (Radiola 1061)

Love's Lovely Counterfeit / The Maltese Falcon (Command Performance 1)

The Maltese Falcon (4-Murray Hill 937239)

Moontide (Sandpiper 7)

The Star of Sheba / The Blue Moon (Command Performance 4)

To Have and Have Not (Mark 56 695) (Radiola 1007)

The Treasure of the Sierra Madre (Mark 56 610)

Compilation Record Albums

Academy Award Winners on the Air (Sandy Hook 2062; also Star-Tone 215)
    With Humphrey Bogart, Shirley Booth, James Cagney, Joan Crawford, Bing Crosby, Clark Gable, Celeste Holm, Bob Hope, Walter Huston, Fredric March, Paul Muni, Katina Paxinou, Ginger Rogers, and Jane Wyman.

Calling All Stars (Star-Tone 203)
    "Previously unreleased performances" including Bogart singing "Bold Fisherman" from *The African Queen*. Also, Charles Laughton and Elsa Lancaster duet on "Baby, It's Cold Outside," Orson Welles performs "You Made Me Love You," and Walter Huston sings "Let's Say Hello to the Ladies."

255

Casablanca: Classic Film Scores for Humphrey Bogart (RCA Red Seal, ARL1-0422; also RCA Gold Seal, AGL1-3782; RCA CD 0422-2-RG)

Performed by Charles Gerhardt and The National Philharmonic Orchestra, this 1974 offering includes excerpts from the soundtracks of *Casablanca*, *Passage to Marseille*, *The Treasure of the Sierra Madre*, *The Big Sleep*, *The Caine Mutiny*, *To Have and Have Not*, *The Two Mrs. Carrolls*, *Sabrina*, *The Left Hand of God*, *Sahara*, *Virginia City*, and *Key Largo*.

Fifty Years of Film (Warner Bros. Records, #3XX-2737)

This three-record set, released in 1973, commemorates Warner Bros.' fiftieth anniversary. Bogart is heard in scenes from *The Petrified Forest*, *The Maltese Falcon*, *High Sierra*, *Casablanca*, *To Have and Have Not* (with Lauren Bacall), *The Big Sleep* (with Bacall), *Key Largo* (with Bacall), and *The Treasure of the Sierra Madre*.

The Golden Days of Radio (2-Mark 56 713)

Narrator, Frank Breese. With Amos 'n' Andy, Edgar Bergen and Charlie McCarthy, Humphrey Bogart, Major Bowes, George Burns and Gracie Allen, Norman Corwin, John Dehner, Howard Duff, W. C. Fields, Greer Garson, Alan Ladd, Bert Lahr, Arthur Lake, Lum 'n' Abner, Fibber McGee and Molly, Louella Parsons, Will Rogers, Rudy Vallee, Orson Welles, and Ed Wynn.

The Hollywood Collection; Hollywood's 20 Greatest Hits (Déjà Vu, 2054)

This 1986 collection includes Gene Kelly's "Singin' in the Rain," Judy Garland dreaming of "Over the Rainbow," Marilyn Monroe doing "Diamonds Are a Girl's Best Friend," and Paul Robeson singing "Ol' Man River" . . . but also Laurel and Hardy harmonize with "Trail of the Lonesome Pine," Rita Hayworth does "Zip," and Humphrey Bogart sings "I've Got My Love to Keep Me Warm."

Hollywood's Heroes on the Air (4-Murray Hill 93723)

With Mary Astor, Ed Begley, Humphrey Bogart, William Conrad, Hans Conreid, Rosemary DeCamp, Errol Flynn, Clark Gable, John Garfield, Sydney Greenstreet, Charles Laughton, Dick Powell, Tyrone Power, Edgar G. Robinson, Ann Sothern, and Jane Wyman.

Hollywood's Immortals Perform Shakespeare (5-Murray Hill 898667)

With Tallulah Bankhead, Humphrey Bogart, Cedric Hardwicke, Leslie Howard, Walter Huston, Claude Rains, Edward G. Robinson, Rosalind Russell, and Orson Welles.

A *Salute to Bogie*—music from the classic Humphrey Bogart films, performed by The MGM Singing Strings. (MGM Records SE-4359)

Featuring, Side One: "Hong Kong Blues" from *To Have and Have Not*; "In a Shanty in Old Shanty Town" and "My Melancholy Baby" from *The Roaring Twenties*; "I Can't Believe that You're in Love with Me" from *The Caine Mutiny*; "Bless Them All" from *Chain Lightning*; "Am I Blue?" from *To Have and Have Not*.

Side Two: "It Had to Be You" from *The Roaring Twenties*; "The Gaucho Serenade" from *It All Came True*; "Love Isn't Born, It's Made" from *Thank Your Lucky Stars*; "All Through the Night" from *All Through the Night*; "Moanin' Low" from *Key Largo*; and "As Time Goes By" plus Bogart voice track from *Casablanca*.

Chapter 17

The Ultimate Bogart Trivia Quiz

Part Three

51. True or false: *Casablanca* (Warner Bros., 1942) was the first film in which Bogart wore a trench coat.

52. Trick question: Bogey played screen characters named "Red," "Turkey," "Duke," "Whip," "Chips," et al. Who was "Pard"?

53. Who was "Lulubelle"?

54. Can you name the first and last movies Bogart made for Warner Bros.?

55. Bogie nicknamed third wife Mayo Methot (1904–1951) "Sluggy" because "she slugs me so often." Their home was called "Sluggy Hollow." He bought a boat and nicknamed it "Sluggy." And, he also had a _____ which he nicknamed "Sluggy."

56. Here's a dumb question: In which picture does Bogart have the name of a lawman . . . but is a very bad guy?

57. Which popular Bogart costar made his first movie at the age of sixty?

58. What do you know about waspish Webb Parmalee Hollenbeck, who was a longtime friend of Bogie's, and might have become an opera singer instead of a dancer and stage/film actor?

59. What director guided Bogart through the most feature films?

60. Paul Henreid (1908–1992) plays the Resistance hero Victor Laszlo in Warner Bros.' *Casablanca* . . . but wasn't Laszlo the real name of one of the film's stars?

61. In a well-known teaming, John Huston (1906–1987) directed, and his father Walter Huston (1884–1950) starred in *The Treasure of the Sierra Madre* (Warner Bros., 1948). But do you know the *other* father-son combo in the film?

62. *Casablanca* was truly cosmopolitan in its diverse cast. Can you match the actor to his country of origin? (Note that a single country may be used more than once.)

1. Ingrid Bergman	*a.* Austria
2. Michael Curtiz	*b.* England
3. Marcel Dalio	*c.* France
4. Sydney Greenstreet	*d.* Germany
5. Paul Henreid	*e.* Hungary
6. Leonid Kinskey	*f.* Russia
7. Madeleine LeBeau	*g.* Sweden
8. Peter Lorre	
9. Claude Rains	
10. S. Z. Sakall	
11. Conrad Veidt	

63. How many Bogart films can you think of that have nautical settings or scenes?

64. In one year, Bogart made two feature films, in each of which he plays one of three escaped convicts who invade a household. What's the year, what are the movies?

65. In *The Treasure of the Sierra Madre* (Warner Bros., 1948) Bogart is unforgettable as Fred C. Dobbs, the prospector who goes crazy from greed and paranoia. How does Dobbs die?

66. What was the one thing Humphrey Bogart shared with show-business luminaries Charles Laughton, Noël Coward, James Cagney, and Alfred Hitchcock?

67. *The Gent from Frisco* was once suggested as a title for which Bogart detective thriller?

68. Bogart appeared in the first screen version of a particular story . . . and then, four years later, starred in its remake. Name the two titles.

69. Long before Robert Altman's classic 1970 film M*A*S*H and the long-running TV series (1972–83) based on the movie, *M.A.S.H. 66* was the original title for which Bogart picture?

70. True or false: Bogie's daughter Leslie is named after Bogart's *High Sierra* (Warner Bros., 1941) costar, Joan Leslie.

71. Who is Bogart's son Stephen named after?

72. Who was "the cast"?

73. Roscoe "Fatty" Arbuckle (1887–1933) is best known as the rotund silent screen star whose career was ruined by a sex scandal. Okay—in which project did Humphrey Bogart appear with Arbuckle?

74. "I killed a guy for looking at me like that!" Bogart warns someone, in one of his best-remembered feature films. Who's looking at him that way?

75. What is the one item that movie stars George Brent, Ray Milland, Dick Powell, and Bogart had in common?

Answers on page 270

Chapter 18

Bogart on the Internet

Please note: URLs for Internet Web sites frequently change.

Elizabeth's Humphrey Bogart Page:
www.reelclassics.com

Learning to Love *Casablanca*:
www.andypants.com/users/sta/casa.asp

The Maltese Falcon Home Page:
www.geocities.com/TheTropics/1772/

Rick's Café Americain:
www.//rickscafe.simplenet.com/

Schultez.com's Tribute to Humphrey Bogart:
www/schultez.com/bogie.html

Tribute to Humphrey Bogart:
www.macconsult.com/bogart

Welcome to the *Santana*:
www.geocities.com/Hollywood/Boulevard/2038/

Appendix 1

Answers to Quizzes

Answers—Trivia Quiz, Part One

1. Always tied.

2. *The Return of Dr. X* (Warner Bros., 1939).

3. They all played the prison escapee who takes over a suburban household, in *The Desperate Hours*. Paul Newman created the part in the original 1955 Broadway Production; Bogart starred in the first screen adaptation (Paramount, 1955); and Mickey Rourke headed the jazzed-up 1990 remake from MGM.

4. Wife number one, actress Helen Menken. In 1927, Helen was appearing on Broadway in the French drama *The Captive*, portraying a lesbian. At the same time, Mae West was starring in a play called *Sex*. In response to charges of "indecency," the police raided *Sex*, plus *The Captive*, plus a comedy called *The Virgin Man*; everyone was booked and then released on bail.

5. *Kid Galahad* (Warner Bros., 1937) or *It All Came True* (Warner Bros., 1940).

6. *The African Queen* (United Artists, 1951)—his sixty-fifth movie.

7. Director Howard Hawks.

8. *It All Came True* (Warner Bros., 1940).

9. Actor Robert Sacchi, who bears a strong resemblance to Bogart. He appeared as Bogart in the touring company of Woody Allen's 1969 Broadway hit *Play It Again, Sam*. In 1974, Sacchi toured in his own one-man show, *Bogey's Back*. Then in 1980, he starred in the movie *The Man with Bogart's Face* (Twentieth Century–Fox) which was later changed to *Sam Marlowe, Private Eye*.

10. It was designed in 1917 for wear by soldiers in the battlefield trenches of World War I.

11. The first Oscar-qualifying rule is that a film must have been seen in Los Angeles in the preceding year. *Casablanca* (Warner Bros.) opened in New York on Thanksgiving Day of 1942, but was not shown in Los Angeles until January 23, 1943; officially, therefore, it's a 1943 release.

12. *To Have and Have Not* (Warner Bros., 1944).

13. *Casablanca* (Warner Bros., 1942).

14. *The Maltese Falcon* (Warner Bros., 1941).

15. Aviator—Bogart was a fighter pilot, flying instructor, commercial pilot, or test pilot in *Body and Soul* (Fox, 1931), *Love Affair* (Columbia, 1932), *China Clipper* (Warner Bros., 1936), *Tokyo Joe* (Columbia, 1949), *Chain Lightning* (Warner Bros., 1950), and *The Left Hand of God* (Twentieth Century–Fox, 1955).

16. Just one: Humphrey Bogart.

17. Of his last ten movies, five were in color—the only color feature films he made; these are *The African Queen* (United Artists, 1951), *The Caine Mutiny* (Columbia, 1954), *The Barefoot Contessa* (United Artists, 1954), *We're No Angels* (Paramount, 1955), and *The Left Hand of God* (Twentieth Century–Fox, 1955).

Note: There was one more color film in which Bogart had a part, this time a cameo role, in *The Love Lottery* (1954), starring David Niven.

18. *Sabrina* (Paramount, 1995); a miscast Bogart starred in the earlier, 1954 version from the same studio.

19. His father was a doctor, his mother a very successful commercial illustrator.

20. Philip Francis Queeg.

21. The title role of the tough army general in *Melville Goodwin, U.S.A.*, from the 1951 novel by John P. Marquand. Bogart and Bacall shot wardrobe tests in January 1956, but Bogie's illness precluded further work. Kirk Douglas and Susan Hayward eventually starred in the Warner Bros. project, released as *Top Secret Affair* (1957).

22. Bogart is gangster-on the-run "Duke" Mantee in *The Petrified Forest* (Warner Bros., 1936), and three-time loser "Duke" Berne in *The Big Shot* (Warner Bros., 1942).

23. Santana Productions, named after Bogart's prized yacht.

24. James Cagney, in *Angels with Dirty Faces* (Warner Bros., 1938).

25. In the thriller *Dark Passage* (Warner Bros., 1947), Bogart plays a killer who escapes from prison and undergoes plastic surgery to alter his facial appearance. We do not see the man's face until the bandages come off, halfway through the movie, revealing Humphrey Bogart. But earlier there are two different newspaper stories shown on-camera, telling the public of the killer at large, and the photo is not of Bogie, but of a heavier-set actor . . . with a mustache. The doctor performing the face-lift emphasizes that in his new incarnation he will be clean-shaven.

Answers—Trivia Quiz, Part Two

26. The answer is (b)—be more considerate, pass that joint around. ·

27. Bogart is a father in *Black Legion* (Warner Bros., 1936), *The Great O'Malley* (Warner Bros., 1937), *Passage to Marseille* (Warner Bros., 1944), *The Two Mrs. Carrolls* (Warner Bros., 1947), and *Tokyo Joe* (Columbia, 1949).

28. At the end of *To Have and Have Not* (Warner Bros., 1944), Harry Morgan (Bogart) heads for Devil's Island to rescue a Resistance leader.

29. *Chain Lightning* (Warner Bros., 1950).

30. *Knock on Any Door* (Columbia, 1949).

31. A gold whistle, inscribed with her famous line from *To Have and Have Not*: "If you want anything, just whistle."

32. *Marked Woman* (Warner Bros., 1937), played by Eduardo Ciannelli; and *Key Largo* (Warner Bros., 1948), played by Edward G. Robinson.

33. *Three on a Match* (Warner Bros., 1932).

34. Bette Davis (1908–1989) appeared in six features, as did Ann Sheridan (1915–1967). (See chapter 11: The Warner Bros. Cast of Characters, *Other Costars*, for details.) Bogart, Davis, and Sheridan also made cameo appearances as themselves in the all-star film *Thank Your Lucky Stars* (Warner Bros., 1943).

    Ann Sheridan is said to have made a brief appearance in *Treasure of the Sierra Madre* (Warner Bros., 1948), but no one's been able to pick her out of the crowd in the final-release print. When and if she is positively identified, Ann will become *the* "actress in the most Bogart films." Until then, it's a Davis-Sheridan tie.

35. Lauren Bacall, of course, with four movies: *To Have and Have Not* (Warner Bros., 1944), *The Big Sleep* (Warner Bros., 1946), *Dark Passage* (Warner Bros., 1947), and *Key Largo* (Warner Bros., 1948). Also, Bogart and Bacall appear as themselves in a cameo in *Two Guys from Milwaukee* (Warner Bros., 1946).

36. Because one would have had to have taken second billing, and neither was willing. Fredric March was not too proud to take second billing to Bogie, however.

37. For the part of Rick's pianist in *Casablanca* (Warner Bros., 1942), the part was ultimately played by Dooley Wilson (1894–1953), another African-American talent.

38. *The Petrified Forest* (Warner Bros., 1936).

39. *Bold Venture*.

40. Jerry Lacy portrayed Bogart, trench coat and all, in Woody Allen's Broadway comedy *Play It Again, Sam* (1969), and then repeated the impersonation in Paramount's 1972 movie version. Robert Sacchi played Bogie in the touring production of Woody's play.

41. His father left it to him.

42. *The Return of Dr. X* (Warner Bros., 1939), in which Bogie is a killer who returns from the dead and lives on the blood of others. (They should have waited for Karloff or Lugosi!)

43. The first, in 1926, with wife Helen Menken, whose parents were deaf-mutes.

44. He wrote a song called "As Time Goes By."

45. (a) Ida Lupino in *They Drive by Night* (Warner Bros., 1940).
    (b) Mary Astor in *The Maltese Falcon* (Warner Bros., 1941).
    (c) Lizabeth Scott in *Dead Reckoning* (Columbia, 1947).
    (d) Agnes Moorehead in *Dark Passage* (Warner Bros., 1947).

46. Paul Lukas, a sentimental favorite, won for his comeback in *Watch on the Rhine* (1943), re-creating a role he had played on Broadway.

47. *Virginia City* (Warner Bros., 1940), as a half-breed bandit leader; and in *Passage to Marseille* (Warner Bros., 1944), as a French journalist.

48. *Dead Reckoning* (Columbia, 1947).

49. Lash LaRue.

50. Ida Lupino, Bogart's costar in *High Sierra* (Warner Bros., 1941).

Answers—Trivia Quiz, Part Three

51. False. He wore one a year earlier, in *Across the Pacific* (Warner Bros., 1942).

52. The little dog in *High Sierra* (Warner Bros., 1941), whose barking gives away gangster Roy Earle's (Bogart) hiding place to the police.

53. The Army tank in *Sahara* (Columbia, 1943).

54. First: *Big City Blues* (Warner Bros., 1932); last: *The Enforcer* (Warner Bros., 1951).

55. A Scottish terrier.

56. In *The Return of Dr. X* (Warner Bros., 1939), he's a vampire named Marshall Quesne.

57. Sydney Greenstreet (1879–1954), in *The Maltese Falcon* (Warner Bros., 1941).

58. That's the ungodly real name of actor Clifton Webb (1893–1966).

59. Lloyd Bacon (1890–1955), with seven Warner Bros. film entries: *Marked Woman* (1937), *San Quentin* (1937), *Racket Busters* (1938), *The Oklahoma Kid* (1939), *Invisible Stripes* (1939), *Brother Orchid* (1940), and *Action in the North Atlantic* (1943).

60. Laszlo Lowenstein is the real name of actor Peter Lorre (1904–1964), who plays Ugarte, the black marketeer who kills to get the valuable Letters of Transit.

61. Actor Tim Holt (1919–1973), who costars as Curtin; and the actor's father, cowboy star Jack Holt (1888–1951), who

appears briefly alongside Walter Huston in the sequence at the fleabag hotel.

62. *Casablanca* stars and countries: 1-g; 2-e; 3-c; 4-b; 5-a; 6-f; 7-c; 8-d; 9-b; 10-e; 11-d

63. *All Through the Night* (Warner Bros., 1942); *Across the Pacific* (Warner Bros., 1942); *Action in the North Atlantic* (Warner Bros., 1943); *Passage to Marseille* (Warner Bros., 1944); *To Have and Have Not* (Warner Bros., 1944); *Key Largo* (Warner Bros., 1948); *The African Queen* (United Artists, 1951); *The Caine Mutiny* (Columbia, 1954). . . . And he takes Audrey Hepburn sailing in *Sabrina* (Paramount, 1954).

64. 1955: *We're No Angels* (Paramount) and *The Desperate Hours* (Paramount).

65. This is a trick question. The last time you see Dobbs is when he's on the ground at the water hole and the three Mexican bandits come up behind him. According to the film's producer, Henry Blanke, the bandits chop off his head with a machete, off-screen—a scene that was deleted before the film was released.

66. They were all born the same year, 1899.

67. *The Maltese Falcon* (Warner Bros., 1941).

68. *Kid Galahad* (Warner Bros., 1937), set in the boxing world; and *The Wagons Roll at Night* (Warner Bros., 1941), a carnival story.

69. *Battle Circus* (MGM, 1953).

70. False. She's named after Bogie's actor friend, Leslie Howard (1893–1943).

71. The character "Steve," played by Bogart in *To Have and Have Not* (Warner Bros., 1944).

72. A cover name for Lauren Bacall. At the time Bogart met her, he was still married to his suspicious drunken wife Mayo Methot. When Bogie first began seeing Bacall after work, he would tell Mayo, "I'm having drinks with the cast."

73. They appeared together in the 1927 Broadway comedy *Baby Mine*, which Arbuckle hoped would take the public's mind off the three murder trials from which he had emerged innocent—but which had driven him from Hollywood.

74. Marjorie Main, in *Dead End* (United Artists, 1937), playing the Bogart character's *mother!*

75. At one time or another, each had owned the racing yacht *Santana*.

Appendix 2

The Annotated, Opinionated Bibliography of Humphrey Bogart

The Bogart Biographies

Barbour, Alan G. *Humphrey Bogart*. New York: Pyramid, 1973.
> One of the first titles in the paperback Pyramid Illustrated History of the Movies series. A brief overview with photos, filmography.

Benchley, Nathaniel. *Humphrey Bogart*. Boston, MA: Little, Brown, 1975.
> A biography by a good friend of Bogie's, the writer son of humorist Robert Benchley. A number of unfamiliar photos and many new stories.

Cooke, Alistair. *Six Men*. New York: Knopf, 1977.
> Biographical essays and analyses of comic actor Charles Chaplin, King Edward VIII of England, editor-writer H. L. Mencken, political figure Adlai Stevenson, philosopher Bertrand Russell, and Humphrey Bogart.

Duchovnay, Gerald. *Humphrey Bogart: A Bio-Bibliography*. Greenwood Press, Westport, CT: 1999.
> A detailed examination of Bogart's place in American popular culture, with scholarly articles and essays, previously published interviews, bibliographical checklist of Bogart sources, plus documented lists of his work in theater, film, radio, and television.

Eyles, Allen. *Bogart*. Garden City, NY: Doubleday, 1975.
A brief biography, a title in The Movie Makers series.

Frank, Alan. *Humphrey Bogart*. London: Hamlyn, and New York: Optimum, 1982.
A title in the Screen Greats series. A promotional/sale book, eighty pages. Filmography. Many photos, including more color shots of Bogart than in any other book: ten full-page photos plus eight color-poster reproductions.

Gehman, Richard. *Bogart*. Greenwich, CT: Gold Medal Books, paperback, 1965.
A brief overview.

Goodman, Ezra. *The Fifty-Year Decline and Fall of Hollywood*. New York: Simon and Schuster, 1961.
Goodman was a publicist for Warner Bros., a Hollywood columnist, movie critic, and Hollywood correspondent for *Time* magazine. This important book is a survey of Hollywood in decline, with chapters on producer-director D. W. Griffith, sex goddess Marilyn Monroe, "the kept press," and vivid portraits of Bogart, director Frank Capra, Columbia Pictures mogul Harry Cohn, actress Greta Garbo, movie producer Samuel Goldwyn, director John Huston, actress Kim Novak, and studio head Jack L. Warner.

_____. *Bogey: The Good-Bad Guy*. New York: Lyle Stuart, 1965.
Basically an oral biography—a breezy, quick-read portrait of Bogart, based on actual interviews with the man himself, plus Lauren Bacall, and a number of friends and co-workers. Many of the familiar stories and quotes by Bogie were recorded here first.

Hanna, David. *Bogart*. New York: Leisure Books, 1976.
A brief but valuable paperback portrait by a longtime film reporter who was the press representative for *The Barefoot Contessa* (1954), and observed Bogart firsthand.

Hyams, Joe. *Bogart and Bacall: A Love Story*. New York: David McKay, 1975.
An account by the writer-columnist. He also interviewed nearly a hundred friends and relatives. With a number of photos published for the first time. Lauren Bacall was very angry about this book.

"Can't he make a living doing anything else?" she demanded. "On the first book I thought he was still a friend. Now he's doing an update. How can you do an update on a man who's been dead for seventeen years?"

_____. *Bogie*. New York: New American Library, 1966.
More of a tribute from a friend than a full biography. Lauren Bacall wrote an introduction, but was later angered when the book became the basis for a 1980 television movie starring Kevin O'Connor as Bogart and Kathryn Harrold as Lauren Bacall. Clifford McCarty reviews this book at length in *Films in Review*, (February 1967). He notes that Hyams deliberately did not read earlier biographies of Bogart, and "wishes [he] had been less fearful of sullying the purity of his ignorance." There is no table of contents or index.

Kobal, John. *People Will Talk*. New York: Knopf, 1985.
Kobal, a leading photo archivist, interviews forty-one film notables who discuss working with Bogart. They include photographer George Hurrell; director Howard Hawks, who told Bacall how to lower her voice; actress Ida Lupino, who knew Bogart would be sensational in *High Sierra* (1941); and writer-director Vincent Sherman.

Mellen, Joan. "Humphrey Bogart: Moral Tough Guy," in *Close-Ups*, edited by Danny Peary. New York: Workman, 1978.
A collection of star profiles.

Meyers, Jeffrey. *Bogart: A Life in Hollywood*. Boston/New York: Houghton Mifflin, 1997.
The best Bogart biography: concise, insightful, and opinionated. Meyers finds the origins of the Bogart persona in the novels of writer Ernest Hemingway (1899–1961): "Bogart embodied Hemingway's hardened hero, torn between ironic fatalism and despairing courage, who seeks authenticity and adheres to a strict code of honor." Meyers sums up Bogart: "Bogart had not sold out or compromised his professional principles and had reached the end of an immensely distinguished career with his personal and artistic integrity miraculously intact."

Peary, Danny. *Cult Movie Stars*. New York: Simon and Schuster/Fireside, 1991.

Brief profiles of Bogart and 749 others. "He was the cinema's greatest tough-guy, but . . . his tough-guys always had chinks in their armor."

Pettigrew, Terence. *Bogart: A Definitive Study of His Film Career*. London/ New York: Proteus, 1977, revised 1981.

An excellent overview of Bogart's life and career, with many photos. Strongly critical of his many inferior films.

Ruddy, Jonah, and Jonathan Hill. *The Bogey Man, Portrait of a Legend*. London: Souvenir Press, 1965. Published in the United States as *Bogey: The Man, the Actor, the Legend*. New York: Tower paperback, 1965.

Self-described as the first full-length portrait of Bogart, begun shortly after the subject became ill, in 1956. Ruddy was a popular Hollywood correspondent to British papers; Hill was said to be the pseudonym of "a distinguished writer with a twenty-five-year association with the film industry." Be that as it may, the writing style is that of fan magazines and press releases.

Sklar, Robert. *City Boys: Cagney, Bogart, Garfield*. NJ: Princeton University Press, 1992.

Biographical studies of the three Warner Bros. star performers, within the framework of their performances as "city boys": the gangsters, reporters, detectives who provided models for urban males. Photos, notes, sources.

Smith, Wilburn. *Screen Greats no. 3: Humphrey Bogart*. Illustrated magazine. New York: Barren Screen Greats, 1971.

Sperber, A. M. and Eric Lax. *Bogart*. New York: William Morrow, 1997.

An exhaustive Bogart biography; a collaboration between Ann M. Sperber, who spent seven years researching Bogart's life and career, and Eric Lax, who spent two years completing the work after Sperber's death in 1994.

The book is 576 pages long, because the authors are not just concerned with telling us about Bogart: Whenever a major figure like directors John Huston and Howard Hawks or agent Charles Feldman enters the scene, we're given mini-biographies of them, as well. The book is also filled with scholarly notes, bibliography, credits for Bogart's stage and film work, and rare photos from the Warner Bros. archives. What the book is missing is any sense of passion or fascination for the subject or his movies. This is supplied by the Jeffrey Meyers biography which came out the same year. It has less detail but more excitement.

Wise, James E. and Anne Collier Rehill. *Stars in Blue: Movie Actors in America's Sea Services*. Annapolis: Naval Institute Press, 1997.
Just what the title says: Brief accounts of over fifty celebrities in the sea services. The writer questions the unlikely attack from a U-boat (two weeks after the armistice was signed) that supposedly damaged Bogie's upper lip. We do get Bogart's service performance ratings: In proficiency he's 3.0 on a scale of 1.0 to 4.0, and superior (4.0) in sobriety and obedience.

Bogart Remembered by Family, Friends, Co-workers, and a Few Enemies

Astor, Mary. *A Life on Film*. New York: Delacorte, 1971.
Astor costarred with Humphrey Bogart in *The Maltese Falcon* and *Across the Pacific*. She won the Academy Award for Best Supporting Actress in 1941 for that year's *The Great Lie*.

_____. *Mary Astor: My Story*. Garden City, NY: Doubleday, 1959.
An honest and revealing autobiography of the actress (1906–1987), originally written for her psychologist/priest.

Bacall, Lauren. *Lauren Bacall: By Myself*. New York: Knopf, 1980. A 506-page best-selling autobiography: a detailed account of a full life—as an acting hopeful, New York fashion model, overnight movie sensation, wife and then widow of Humphrey Bogart, infatuations with other men, marriage to Jason Robards from 1961 to 1969, a second career in the theater. Much of this material has found its way into the Bogart books.

_____. *Now*. New York: Knopf, 1994.
Bacall now tells us what she's learned about life and love, friendship, career, new beginnings.

Base, Ron. *"If the Other Guy Isn't Jack Nicholson, I've Got the Part,"* Hollywood Tales of Big Breaks, Bad Luck, and Box-Office Magic. Chicago, IL: Contemporary Books, 1994.

Base details the fascinating George Raft-Bogart history, and says Raft, who grew up with gangsters, never understood the difference between acting and real life.

Bergman, Ingrid, and Alan Burgess. *Ingrid Bergman: My Story.* New York: Delacorte, 1980.

A lengthy autobiography of the actress (1915–1982), with two pages on *Casablanca*. With the script being written daily, Ingrid did not know how to play her scenes because no one knew how the film was to end: "I didn't dare to look at Humphrey Bogart with love because then I had to look at Paul Henreid with something that was not love." She continues, "They were a wonderful group of actors, but because of the difficulties of the script we'd all been a bit on edge and I'd hardly got to know Humphrey Bogart at all. Oh, I'd kissed him, but I didn't know him."

Bishop, Jim. *The Mark Hellinger Story: A Biography of Broadway.* New York: Appleton-Century-Crofts, 1952.

A biography of the notable writer-producer (1903–1947) who died while forming a production company with Humphrey Bogart.

Bogart, Stephen Humphrey. *Bogart: In Search of My Father.* Foreword by Lauren Bacall. New York: Dutton, 1995.

"Combining the drama of Bogart's life with that of a son whose path of reconciliation first had to move through a very difficult time" (from the dust jacket). The author was eight years old when his father died, in 1957, and he felt the hurt for a long time. In interviewing many of the people in his dad's life, Stephen does not seem to realize that they've already told their familiar stories to numerous other writers doing books on Bogart.

There's a wonderful selection of family photos: Stephen couldn't be anyone but the son of Humphrey Bogart; Leslie (b. 1952) couldn't be anyone but the daughter of Lauren Bacall.

Brooks, Louise. *Lulu in Hollywood.* New York: Knopf, 1982.

An insightful and valuable collection of reminiscences and profiles by this cult film star (1906–1985), of people she knew or worked with.

She says Bogart was supremely confident of his attractiveness to women, that "it was security in sex that preserved Humphrey's ego until his eventual success after he had endured the bitterest humiliation, ridicule and failure."

Cagney, James. *Cagney by Cagney*. New York: Doubleday, 1976.

The autobiography of the actor. Although they appeared together in three Warner Bros. features, Cagney (1899–1996) has little to say about Humphrey Bogart in his recollections. He does include Bogie in his criticism of the Warner Bros. casting policy: "Albeit he [Bogart] was a tremendous personality, the studio didn't do anything about him until fortuitous circumstances put him opposite Ingrid Bergman in *Casablanca* [1942], and away went Bogie. Sheer accident. The studio had no thought of using him to the fullest, indeed of using *anyone* to the fullest bent of their talent. The policy toward talent was simplistic: just throw them in, then throw them out. Talent was not nurtured, it was simply consumed."

Cardiff, Jack. *Magic Hour*. London/Boston: Faber and Faber, 1996.

One of the great cinematographers, mainly associated with the films of British director Michael Powell and producer Emeric Pressburger, Cardiff (b. 1914) won an Academy Award for *Black Narcissus* (1947). He worked with Bogart on two United Artists films, *The African Queen* (1951) and *The Barefoot Contessa* (1954).

There is a get-together party for *The African Queen*: "Bogart silently stared at me with his somber eyes—like a gangster appraising someone before drawing his gun. Then he spoke in the gritty snarl of a tough-guy in a trench-coat. 'Listen, Jack—you see my face. It's got a lot of lines and wrinkles on it. I've been cultivating them for years, and I like them. They are me—so don't try and light them out and make me look like a goddamn fag.'

"I peered at the famous face and shook my head sadly: 'Bogey, I've had many a tough job trying to light out lines on actors' faces, but this time your face has got me beat. There's too much debauchery there, I can't do anything about it, so you'll be all right.'

"His eyes lit up, and that wolf grin appeared as he made a derisory gesture toward my glass of beer. 'OK, Cardiff. Put away that sissy drink, and let's have a real one.'"

Carmichael, Hoagy. *Stardust Road*. New York: Rinehart, 1946.

Carmichael, Hoagy, with Stephen Longstreet. *Sometimes I Wonder: The Story of Hoagy Carmichael*. New York: Farrar Straus, 1965.
Two memoirs of the songwriter (1899–1981) who made his first screen appearance in *To Have and Have Not* (1944).

Deutsch, Armand. *Me and Bogie and Other Friends and Acquaintances from a Life in Hollywood and Beyond*. New York: Putnam's, 1991.
The producer's breezy recollections, including accounts of the times Bogart would provoke him to anger, then back off before Deutsch (b. 1913) could hit him.

Donati, William. *Ida Lupino: A Biography*. Lexington, KY: The University Press of Kentucky, 1996.
Lupino (1914–1995) and Bogart appeared together at Warner Bros. in *They Drive by Night* (1940), and costarred in *High Sierra* (1941), a major success for each of them. When Bogey asked for the male lead in *Out of the Fog* (1941), opposite Lupino, she reportedly refused to work with him. (The role went to John Garfield.) Lupino later denied the story, saying it was Warner Bros.' way of controlling its demanding stars. The Sperber-Lax biography (cited above) suggests that Warner Bros. concocted the slight as a way of keeping Bogart off the film. The author of this biography, Donati, does not ask Ida Lupino about the incident. He quotes her as saying of Bogart, "He was the most loyal, wonderful guy in the world."

Geist, Kenneth. *Pictures Will Talk: The Life and Films of Joseph L. Mankiewicz*. New York: Scribner's, 1978.
Mankiewicz (1909–1993) directed *The Barefoot Contessa* (1954), one of Bogart's final movies. Geist quotes Marius Goring, one of the film's featured players, as saying that Mankiewicz was "impatient and intolerant" of Bogart, "did his best to provoke him," and "was much happier working with Ava Gardner." Goring's view may be biased because of his distaste for Bogart's obscene conversation ("there's nothing more boring than a man who uses 'fucking' in every sentence"), excessive drinking, and dependence on schtick, such as his noted cheek tremor to indicate suppressed anger, which led Goring to refer to him privately as "Humphrey Bogus."

Bogart's wracking cough, caused by his constantly smoking unfiltered Chesterfields, presented another problem, and actor Edmund O'Brien recalls that "many takes were printed simply for the lines Mankiewicz could get between the coughs." Mankiewicz admits "Bogie wanted you to be afraid of him a little. He made perfectly sure that you knew he was going to be an unpredictable man. . . . I caught on to that, and I played my own little game of keeping him off balance by never giving him his opportunity. You forestall it by kidding him out of it."

Greenberger, Howard. *Bogey's Baby, A Biography*. New York: St. Martin's Press, 1978.

A detailed biography.

Henreid, Paul, with Julius Fast. *Ladies' Man*. New York: St. Martin's Press, 1984.

An exciting life presented unexcitingly. Henreid (1908–1992) had costarred with Bogart in *Casablanca* (1942), and actively protested the HUAC hearings alongside Bogart. He says he was stunned when the older actor recanted. "I felt Bogart's statement was a form of betrayal, and it was also the end of our friendship—and the end of Bogart's other friendships."

Hepburn, Katharine. *The Making of the African Queen: Or How I Went to Africa with Bogart, Bacall and Huston and Almost Lost My Mind*. New York: Knopf, 1987.

Katie (b. 1907) writes of Lauren Bacall: "She and Bogie seemed to have the most enormous opinion of each other's charms, and when they fought it was with the utter confidence of two cats locked deliciously in the same cage." Then, remembering Bogart: "What an odd man. So—how shall I put it—so pure. Like a little kid. Dear Bogie. I'll never forget that close-up of him after he kisses Rosie [the Hepburn character], then goes around in back of the tank and considers what has happened. His expression—the wonder of it all—life."

Huston, John. *Humphrey Bogart Memorial Address*. Los Angeles, CA: Seiler Press, 1957.

A tribute written and read by John Huston at the memorial service on January 18, 1957. Privately printed.

_____. *An Open Book*. New York: Knopf, 1980.

The autobiography of the writer-director (1906–1987) associated with some of Bogart's most memorable work: *High Sierra* (1941), *The Maltese Falcon* (1941), *The African Queen* (1951), etc. A straightforward, "And then I directed . . ." approach with little insight or color. He has surprisingly little to say about his relationship with Bogart.

Kanin, Garson. *Together Again! The Stories of the Great Hollywood Teams*. Garden City, NY: Doubleday, 1981.

From Greta Garbo and John Gilbert, Jeanette MacDonald and Nelson Eddy, Humphrey Bogart and Lauren Bacall, Fred Astaire and Ginger Rogers, to Woody Allen and Diane Keaton.

Kelley, Kitty. *His Way: The Unauthorized Biography of Frank Sinatra*. New York: Bantam Books, 1986.

A 576-page biography which Sinatra (1915–1998) unsuccessfully tried to stop with legal action. Kelley discusses Sinatra's friendship with Bogart, and then with Lauren Bacall after she became a widow in 1957. Sinatra wanted to inherit Bogart's tough/cool manner, *and* his Rat Pack. However, he turned what had been a private group of friends into a public spectacle, an anything-for-a-laugh act for Las Vegas.

Madsen, Axel. *William Wyler, The Authorized Biography*. New York: Crowell, 1973.

Bogart played the killer "Baby Face" Martin in Wyler's *Dead End* (1937). It was such a rewarding experience for him that, eighteen years later, he called director Wyler (1902–1981) and asked for the lead in *The Desperate Hours* (1955), about a family held hostage by escaped convicts. The original story called for the convicts to be young—Paul Newman starred in the original 1955 Broadway production. Wyler had been thinking of James Dean or Marlon Brando for the leading role, but Bogart was able to convince Wyler that the age of the convicts was not important.

Negulesco, Jean. *Things I Did . . . and Things I Think I Did*. New York: Linden Press/Simon and Schuster, 1984.

Autobiography of the Romanian-born artist (1900–1993) who became a film director, a book of breezy recollections of Paris and Hollywood, illustrated with many of his own sketches. He socialized with the Bogarts, and spent a weekend on the *Santana*.

Niven, David. *Bring on the Empty Horses*. New York: Putnam's, 1975.

_____. *The Moon's a Balloon*. New York: Putnam's, 1972.
Two breezy, lightweight memories of movies and friends and parties. Niven (1909–1983) was one of Bogart's West Coast sailing buddies.

Nolan, William F. *John Huston: King Rebel*. Los Angeles: Sherbourne Press, 1965.
A sketchy but worthwhile study of the director. Includes valuable bibliographical details on Huston's own published writings.

O'Brien, Pat. *The Wind at My Back*. An autobiography. New York: Doubleday, 1964.
A long and colorful career in theater, film, and television. There's much on the workings of Warner Bros., but Bogart is mentioned only in passing by O'Brien (1899–1983).

Parish, James Robert. *Hollywood's Great Love Teams*. New Rochelle, NY: Arlington House, 1974.
Twenty-eight popular pairs, including Bogart and Bacall, with biographical data, photos, filmography.

Parish, James Robert, and Whitney, Steven. *The George Raft File: The Unauthorized Biography*. New York: Drake, 1974.
The most detailed Raft biography. Includes full particulars on all his films, plus his radio and television appearances.

Plimpton, George. *Truman Capote: In Which Various Friends, Enemies, Acquaintances and Detractors Recall His Turbulent Career*. New York: Doubleday, 1997.
Includes five pages on the haphazard filming of *Beat the Devil* (1954), including John Huston's story of Bogart and Capote arm-wrestling.
Capote (1924–1984) kept friends up-to-date with chatty letters: "The last few weeks have been filled with peculiar adventures, all involving John Huston and Humphrey Bogart, who've nearly killed me with their dissipations . . . half drunk all day and dead-drunk all night, and once, believe it or not, I came to around six in the morning to find King Farouk doing the hula-hula in the middle of Bogart's bedroom."

Pratley, Gerald. *The Cinema of John Huston.* New York/London: A. S. Barnes/Tantivy Press, 1977.
An odd autobiography: Huston discusses his life and work, as distilled from fourteen hours of tape-recordings.

Quirk, Lawrence, J. *Fasten Your Seat Belts—the Passionate Life of Bette Davis.* New York: William Morrow, 1990.
Bogart was in her debut film, *Bad Sister* (1937); Davis (1908–1989) disliked him from the start.

_____. *Lauren Bacall: Her Films and Career.* Secaucus, NJ: Citadel Press, 1986.
An illustrated biography aimed at her fans.

Robinson, Edward G. *All My Yesterdays,* an autobiography, with Leonard Spigelgass. New York: Hawthorne, 1973.
Robinson (1893–1973) appeared with Bogart in five movies for Warner Bros.

Royce, Brenda Scott. *Lauren Bacall: A Bio-Bibliography.* Westport, CT: Greenwood Press, 1992.
Contains a brief biography; chronology; filmography, appearances on television, radio, stage; discography; awards; annotated bibliography.

Sakall, S. Z. *The Story of Cuddles: My Life under Franz Joseph, Adolf Hitler and the Warner Brothers.* Translated by Paul Tabori. London: Cassell, 1954.
The popular rotund character actor (1884–1955) appeared, memorably, with Humphrey Bogart at Warner Bros. in *Casablanca* (1942). He also was featured in three other Warner Bros. films in which Bogey made cameo appearances: *Thank Your Lucky Stars* (1943), *Two Guys from Milwaukee* (1946), and *Never Say Goodbye* (1946).

Sennett, Ted. *Masters of Menace: Greenstreet and Lorre.* New York: Dutton, 1979.
Dual biography of Sydney Greenstreet (1879–1954) and Peter Lorre (1904–1964), who appeared with Humphrey Bogart at Warner Bros. in *The Maltese Falcon* (1941), *Casablanca* (1942), and *Passage to Marseille* (1944).

Sherman, Vincent. *Studio Affairs: My Life as a Film Director.* Lexington, KY: The University of Kentucky Press, 1996.

Writer-director Vincent Sherman (b. 1906) worked with Bogart at Warner Bros. on *Crime School* (1938), *King of the Underworld* (1939), *The Return of Dr. X* (1939), and *All Through the Night* (1942).

"Bogey came from the theater, and all of us who came from the theater were dedicated, hard workers. A lot of parts we didn't like, but whatever we were assigned to do we tried to make them better and do the best we could. So, he was a very disciplined actor, hard working, and a wonderful guy to work with."

Stine, Whitney. *"I'd Love to Kiss You . . .": Conversations with Bette Davis.* New York: Pocket Books, 1990.

Stine, Whitney, with a running commentary by Bette Davis. *Mother Goddam: The Story of the Career of Bette Davis.* New York: Hawthorn Books, 1974. Davis and Humphrey Bogart shared billing in six movies. Their most notable moment together is in Warner Bros.' *Dark Victory* (1939), when the horse trainer (Bogart) confesses to the heiress (Davis) that he's always been attracted to her. Davis remembers: "Bogart, at the time of *Dark Victory* had not hit the great career he finally had. I thought his performance in this was just perfect. We had some very difficult scenes to play together. I thanked God for the help his performance gave me in playing mine."

Swindell, Larry. *Spencer Tracy, a biography.* New York: World Publishing, 1969.
The bond that held Bogart and Tracy (1900–1967) together as friends was the jealous pride in their profession. Bogie knew he was good and was proud of it, but he knew Tracy was better: "Spence is the best we have, because you don't see the mechanism at work. He covers up, never overacts, gives the impression he isn't acting at all. I try to do it, and I succeed, but not the way Spence does. He has direct contact with an audience he never sees."

Thompson, Verita, with Donald Shepherd. *Bogie and Me: A Love Story.* New York: St. Martin's Press, 1982.
Verita Thompson was Bogart's mistress (and, more important, did an excellent job with his toupee) from 1942, when he was married to Mayo Methot, until his death in 1957, when he was married to Lauren Bacall. She was written into his film contracts, and worked on all but

four of his last eighteen movies. By the time he had his second child, in 1952, she had given up hopes of ever marrying him. She tells him, "We're one of those two ships-passing-in-the-night basket cases—a couple of lousy navigators." Verita wrote her book to avoid becoming "a sleazy footnote" to Bogart's life. The Sperber-Lax biography questions the existence of her relationship with Bogart.

Viertel, Peter. *Dangerous Friends: At Large with Huston and Hemingway in the Fifties*. New York: Doubleday, 1992.
Viertel, who was there, recounts the details of the location filming in Africa of *The African Queen* (1951).

Wallis, Hal, with Charles Higham. *Starmaker: The Autobiography of Hal Wallis*. Foreword by Katharine Hepburn. New York: Macmillan, 1980.
Wallis (1899–1986) was a major force behind the success of Warner Bros. As production executive, he supervised Warners' A Productions—twenty of them a year!—mainly from the late 1920s to the mid-1940s.
Wallis and Higham cover a forty-five-year career in 240 pages, whizzing along on roller skates. Wallis disagrees that Bogart off-screen was a different man—he was a full-time tough-guy. Wallis himself wrote the alternate last lines for *Casablanca* (1942): "Louis, I might have known you'd mix your patriotism with a little larceny." And: "Louis, I think this is the beginning of a beautiful friendship."

Walsh, Raoul. *Each Man in His Time*. New York: Farrar, Straus and Giroux, 1974.
Autobiography of the revered director (1887–1980), who worked with Bogart on five motion pictures, notably *High Sierra* (1941).

Warren, Doug, with James Cagney. *James Cagney: The Authorized Biography*. New York: St. Martin's Press, 1983.
Cagney and Bogart had a lot in common, but had no use for each other. One might wonder if it had to do with Cagney growing up on the rough tenement streets of New York City, and Bogart being raised in wealth on the upper West Side.

Weld, John. *September Song*, An Intimate Biography of Walter Huston. Lanham, MD: Scarecrow Press, 1998.
Walter Huston (1884–1950) appears in an unbilled part in *The Maltese Falcon* (1941), as the captain of the tramp steamer who

stumbles into Sam Spade's office carrying a bundle wrapped in newspaper, and dies.

Walter Huston also appeared in Warner Bros.' *The Treasure of the Sierra Madre* (1948) without his dentures, at his son's request, to enhance the character. John Huston wrote in his autobiography that his father's performance was the finest in all of his films. *Theatre Arts* magazine called it the finest performance ever given on the American screen. The Academy voted Walter Huston Best Supporting Actor of 1948.

Zolotow, Maurice. *Billy Wilder in Hollywood.* New York: Putnam's, 1977.
Wilder (b. 1906) directed Bogart in *Sabrina* (1954), which Bogart considered one of his worst filmmaking experiences. Zolotow discusses the Bogart-Wilder conflict at length.

Yablonsky, Lewis. *George Raft.* New York: McGraw-Hill, 1974.
A biography written with the cooperation of the subject, plus interviews with many important people in Raft's life and career. Photos. Brief filmography, bibliography.

Youngkin, Stephen D., James Bigwood, and Raymond G. Cabana Jr. *The Films of Peter Lorre.* Secaucus, NJ: Citadel Press, 1982.

Bogart at Warner Bros.

Behlmer, Rudy. *Inside Warner Bros.* (1935–1951). New York: Viking Press, 1985.
The battles, the brainstorms, and the bickering, from the files of Hollywood's greatest studio.

Meyer, William R. *Warner Brothers Directors: The Hard-Boiled, the Comic, and the Weepers.* New Rochelle, NY: Arlington House, 1978.
Brief career profiles of nineteen directors, with photos and a filmography.

Roffman, Peter, and Jim Purdy. *The Hollywood Social Problem Film: Madness, Despair, and Politics from the Depression to the Fifties.* Bloomington, IN: Indiana University Press, 1981.
Special attention is given to Warner Bros., which made more social dramas reflecting the period than any other studio.

Silke, James R. *Here's Looking at You, Kid*: Fifty Years of Fighting, Working and Dreaming at Warner Bros. Boston, MA: Little, Brown, 1976.
A profusely illustrated history of the studio that resembled "a rough neighborhood." The emphasis is on colorful, gossipy, anecdotal stories.

Warner, Jack, with Dean Jennings. *My First Hundred Years in Hollywood*, an autobiography. New York: Random House, 1965.

The Hollywood Inquisition

Bernstein, Walter. *Inside Out: A Memoir of the Blacklist*. New York: Knopf, 1996.

Ceplair, Larry, and Steven Englund. *The Inquisition in Hollywood: Politics in the Film Community, 1930–1960*. Garden City, NY: Anchor Press/Doubleday, 1980.

Dunne, Philip. *Take Two: A Life in Movies and Politics*. New York: McGraw-Hill, 1980. Updated edition, New York: Limelight Paperback, 1992.
Dunne (1908–1992), prominent writer-director, was one of the main political activists behind the Hollywood resistance to the House Un-American Activities Committee. He helped plan the trip to Washington, D.C., in October 1947, in which Bogart was the most prominent member. He brushes aside the actor's recantation: "Bogart understandably gave way to ferocious pressures and apologized for his actions."

Goodman, Walter. *The Committee: The Extraordinary Career of the House Committee on Un-American Activities*. New York: Farrar, Straus & Giroux, 1968.
This is considered the definitive account.

Kanfer, Stefan. *A Journal of the Plague Years*. New York: Atheneum, 1973.
A highly readable history by an ex-*Time* magazine writer.

The Bogart Movies

Note: See separate entry for *Casablanca* (1942).

Behlmer, Rudy. *Hollywood's Hollywood: The Movies About the Movies.* Secaucus, NJ: Citadel Press, 1975.
   A profusely illustrated history. Bogart was a movie producer in *Stand-In* (1937), a screenwriter in *In a Lonely Place* (1951), and a director in *The Barefoot Contessa* (1954).

Fuchs, Wolfgang. *Humphrey Bogart, Cult-Star: A Documentation.* Berlin: TACO, 1987. English-language edition.
   A pictorial survey.

Hanson, Patricia King, executive editor. *The American Film Institute Catalog of Motion Pictures Produced in the United States. Feature Films, 1931–1940.* Two volumes. Berkeley, CA: University of California Press, 1993.

Kobal, John. *John Kobal Presents the Top 100 Movies.* New York: New American Library, 1988.
   Casablanca (1942) is number nine, *The Maltese Falcon* (1941) number thirty-eight; *The African Queen* (1951) number eighty-five.

McCarty, Clifford. *Bogey, the Films of Humphrey Bogart.* Secaucus, NJ: Citadel Press, 1965.
   The title was later changed to *The Complete Films of Humphrey Bogart.* A pictorial survey of every film made by Humphrey Bogart. Cast, credits, synopsis, and brief overview are given for each movie, with at least two or three photos for each entry, and more for the important productions. A brief biographical sketch is included. There is little in the way of critical evaluation.

Medved, Harry, with Randy Dreyfuss. *The Fifty Worst Films of All Time (and how they got that way).* New York: Popular Library, 1978.
   Grouped in with *Godzilla vs. the Smog Monster (1972)* and *Santa Claus Conquers the Martians* (1964), is *Swing Your Lady* (1938), a hillbilly musical starring Humphrey Bogart.

Michael, Paul. *Humphrey Bogart: the Man and His Films.* Indianapolis: Bobbs-Merrill, 1965.
   A pictorial survey, with cast and credits and a lengthy synopsis for each film. Similar to the McCarthy book above, but with a better selection of photos.

Parish, James Robert. *Prison Pictures from Hollywood*: Plots, Critiques, Casts and Credits for 293 Theatrical and Made-for-Television Releases. Jefferson, NC: McFarland, 1991.

Sinclair, Andrew. *Spiegel, The Man Behind the Pictures*. Boston: Little, Brown, 1987.
Biography of the Austrian-born producer (1903–1985) of *The African Queen* (1951), *On the Waterfront* (1954), *The Bridge on the River Kwai* (1957), and *Lawrence of Arabia* (1962). Spiegel had major problems dealing with Huston on *The African Queen*—the director wanted the hero and heroine to be killed at the end. It will be "just another wonderful financial failure," Spiegel told screenwriter Peter Viertel, who repeated the line in his novel *White Hunter, Black Heart* (1953).

Viertel, Peter. *White Hunter, Black Heart*. Garden City, NY: Doubleday, 1953.
An acclaimed roman à clef on the filming of *The African Queen* (1951), Viertel's best-selling novel recounts the drama and tragedy of filming the Africa adventure *The Trader*. "Phillip Duncan" (Bogart) and "Kay Gibson" (Katharine Hepburn) make only brief appearances. Duncan is "a nice, insecure man, given to aggressiveness when not entirely sober, a not uncommon Hollywood trait." The story is of director "John Wilson" (John Huston) a man who "had abandoned himself to his appetites."

White Hunter, Black Heart was filmed in 1990, starring Clint Eastwood (who also directed) as the macho film director obsessed with killing an elephant. Richard Vanstone played the Bogart-inspired character, and Marisa Berenson was Katharine Hepburn.

Published Screenplays

The African Queen, in *Agee on Film, Volume II: Five Film Scripts*, by James Agee. New York: McDowell, Obolensky, 1960.
Introduction by John Huston. Contains the scripts of *Noa-Noa* (never filmed), *The African Queen* (1951), *The Night of the Hunter* (1955), *The Bride Comes to Yellow Sky* (1952), and *The Blue Hotel* (never filmed).

The Big Sleep, in *Film Scripts One*. New York: Century-Appleton-Crofts, 1971.

Casablanca. In *Casablanca: Script and Legend*, by Howard Koch. Woodstock, NY: The Overlook Press, 1973.

Casablanca: The Illustrated Screenplay, told in 1,400 frame enlargements plus dialogue from the film. New York: Darien House/Avon, 1974.

Dark Victory. Edited by Bernard F. Dick. Madison, WI: University of Wisconsin Press, 1981.
A volume in the Wisconsin/Warner Bros. screenplay series.

High Sierra. Edited by Douglas Gomery. Madison, WI: University of Wisconsin Press, 1979.
A volume in the Wisconsin/Warner Bros. screenplay series.

The Maltese Falcon. Edited by Richard Anobile. New York: Avon Books, 1974.
The film in 1,400 frame enlargements.

To Have and Have Not. Edited by Bruce Kawin. Madison, WI: University of Wisconsin Press, 1980.
A volume in the Wisconsin/Warner Bros. screenplay series.

The Treasure of the Sierra Madre. Edited by James Naremore. Madison, WI: University of Wisconsin Press, 1982.
A volume in the Wisconsin/Warner Bros. screenplay series.

The Casablanca *Books and Articles*

Behlmer, Rudy. *America's Favorite Movies: Behind the Scenes*. New York: Frederick Ungar, 1982. Republished in 1990 by Samuel French as *Behind the Scenes: The Making of America's Favorite Movies*.

Eco, Umberto. "*Casablanca*: Cult Movies and Intertextual Collage," in *Travels in Hyperreality*. New York: Harcourt Brace, 1986. (Included in Koch: *Casablanca: Script and Legend*.)

Francisco, Charles. *You Must Remember This . . . The Filming of Casablanca.* Englewood Cliffs, NJ: Prentice-Hall, 1980.

Harmetz, Aljean. *Round Up the Usual Suspects: The Making of Casablanca*—Bogart, Bergman, and World War II. New York: Hyperion, 1992.
The definitive account, by the ex-*New York Times* reporter who also wrote *The Making of The Wizard of Oz.*

Haver, Ron. "Finally the Truth about *Casablanca,*" in *American Film* magazine, June 1976.

Koch, Howard. *As Time Goes By*, Memoirs of a Writer. New York: Harcourt Brace Jovanovich, 1979.
Koch wrote the radio script for Orson Welles's *War of the Worlds* broadcast in 1938, and spent twenty years writing scripts (sharing an Oscar for *Casablanca*), before being blacklisted and sent into exile. On *Casablanca*: "Conceived in sin and born in travail, it survived its precarious origin by some fortuitous combination of circumstances to become the hardiest of Hollywood perennials, as tough and durable as its antihero, Humphrey Bogart."

Koch, Howard, editor. *Casablanca: Script and Legend.* Woodstock, NY: The Overlook Press, 1973. 50th Anniversary Edition, 1992.
The complete screenplay by Julius J. and Philip G. Epstein and Howard Koch. Commentary and analysis by Charles Champlin, Richard Corliss, Roger Ebert, Umberto Eco, Aljean Harmetz, and J. Hoberman. Original reviews by Howard Barnes and Bosley Crowther of the *New York Times*.

Miller, Frank. *Casablanca: As Time Goes By*. Fiftieth Anniversary Commemorative Edition. Atlanta, GA: Turner Publishing, 1992.

Osborne, Richard E. *The Casablanca Companion: The Movie Classic and Its Place in History.* Indianapolis, IN: Riebel Roque Publishing, 1998.
The author describes the political situation of the period, detailing the delicate relations between the Germans and Vichy France, and the sides taken by different countries. He ties incidents in the screenplay to the actual historical events.

Peary, Danny. *Cult Movies: The Classics, the Sleepers, the Weird and the Wonderful*. New York: Delacorte, 1981.

"*Casablanca* is that rare *lucky* film where everything came together, clicked, and there was perfection."

Rosenzweig, Sidney. *Casablanca and Other Major Films of Michael Curtiz*. Studies in Cinema 14. Ann Arbor, MI: UMI Research Press, 1982.

Schickel, Richard. "Some Nights in Casablanca," In *Favorite Movies: Critics' Choice*. Edited by Philip Nobile. New York: Macmillan, 1973.

Siegel, Jeff. *The Casablanca Companion: the Movie and More*. Dallas, TX: Taylor Publishing, 1992.

A behind-the-scenes account of the filming; biographies, photos, trivia quizzes, who wrote what, etc. The author is adamant that Bogart was not born on Christmas Day.

vanGelder, Peter. *That's Hollywood: A Behind-the-Scenes Look at Sixty of the Greatest Films Ever Made*. New York: HarperCollins, 1990.

The Casablanca Novels

Leopold, Christopher. *Casablack, A Novel*. New York: Doubleday, 1979.

Intended as a sequel to the 1942 classic: Steve Wagner, who looks like Bogart but is much seedier, less certain and more scared, tells what really happened.

Walsh, Michael. *As Time Goes By, A Novel of* Casablanca. New York: Warner, 1998.

A widely publicized stunt. The author explains the challenge: "My solution [is] to present the lives of the characters before and after the action of the movie, placing Rick Blaine, Ilsa Lund, Victor Laszlo, and the others in a larger historical context. . . . Imagine the film elongated at either end to reveal the epic, wide-screen version, of which the events depicted [in the movie] are but the middle of the story."

Taking off from the skimpy details in the screenplay, Walsh deduces that Rick Blaine was a Jewish gangster from East Harlem named Yitzik Baline.

Bogart in the Theater

Bonner, Edwin J. *The Encyclopedia of the American Theatre 1900–1975*. San Diego/New York: A. S. Barnes, 1980.

Leonard, William Torbert. *Theatre: Stage to Screen to Television*. Two volumes. Metuchen, NJ: Scarecrow Press, 1981.
    Documenting the history and credits of plays that have also been made into movies or TV productions, from the beginnings up to 1979.

Marill, Alvin H. *More Theatre: Stage to Screen to Television*. Two volumes. Metuchen, NJ: Scarecrow Press, 1993.
    Updating the Leonard base volumes, with productions between 1980 and 1992, plus additions and corrections.

New York Times Theatre Reviews, The: 1920–1996. New York: The *New York Times* and Arno Press, 1971.

Bogart in Fiction and Poetry

Baxt, George. *The Humphrey Bogart Murder Case*. New York: St. Martin's Press, 1995.
    One of a popular series of lightweight murder mysteries featuring real-life Hollywood personalities who get involved in murder mysteries.

Bergman, Andrew. *Hollywood and Levine*. New York: Holt, Rinehart and Winston, 1975.
    Jack LeVine, "A private dick with the wise and forgiving heart of a Talmudic sage" investigates the death of a screenwriter, in 1940s Hollywood. Real characters appear, including Humphrey Bogart and Richard Nixon.

Block, Lawrence. *The Burglar Who Thought He Was Bogart*. New York: Dutton, 1995.
    One of a series of novels featuring Bernie Rhodenbarr, full-time book dealer, part-time burglar, and fan of Bogart. Bernie meets a woman "who seemed to believe that the Bogart on-screen persona would tell you all you needed to know to cope with life. And who was I to say her nay?" Famous lines from Bogart's films are sprinkled over the pages as freely as New Year's Eve confetti.

Bogart, Stephen Humphrey. *Play It Again*. New York: Forge/Tom Doherty, 1995.

A mystery novel featuring private eye R.J. Brooks, the son of a legendary couple much like Humphrey Bogart and Lauren Bacall. Bogie himself makes an appearance.

———. *The Remake, A Mystery Novel*. New York: Forge/Tom Doherty, 1997.

Private eye R. J. Brooks returns, because Hollywood plans to make a sequel to his parents' greatest movie, *As Time Goes By*. When some of the yahoos involved are murdered, R. J. becomes a suspect.

Brooks, Richard. *The Producer*. New York: Simon and Schuster, 1951.

A novel by the director/screenwriter.

"[Bogart] loves to needle. He needled me into writing *The Producer* and finishing it. There is a character, Steve Taggart, an actor, in the novel who is very much Bogart. I asked Bogey if I should use the character. 'Is it an honest character?' Bogey asked. 'I think it is,' I said. 'Wanna read it?' 'If you say it's honest, I don't care. You have a clearance,' Bogey said. Actually, it wasn't too complimentary a character. But Bogey went around after the novel appeared saying to people: 'That's me.'"

Fenady, Andrew J. *The Man with Bogart's Face*. Chicago, IL: Contemporary Books, 1977. Avon paperback, with photos from the film, 1979.

A man has plastic surgery to look like Humphrey Bogart. He changes his name to Sam Marlow, private investigator, and promptly gets involved with a case that looks suspiciously like *The Maltese Falcon*. A popular success, this book was filmed, unsuccessfully, in 1980, starring Bogart look-alike Robert Sacchi. The title was later changed to *Sam Marlowe, Private Eye*, but that didn't help, either. Victor Buono is a very good Fat Man.

———. *The Secret of Sam Marlow*. Chicago, IL: Contemporary Books, 1980.

The further adventures of the man with Bogart's face.

Kennedy, Adam. *Just Like Humphrey Bogart*. New York: Viking Press, 1978.

In this mystery novel, an American expatriate in Paris looks a lot like

Humphrey Bogart, which gets him acting jobs in foreign films . . . and gets him into big trouble.

Roosevelt, Elliott. *Murder at Hobcaw Barony*. New York: St. Martin's Press, 1986.
One of a series of murder mysteries featuring the author's mother— one of the century's great women, Eleanor Roosevelt (1884–1962), wife of President Franklin Delano Roosevelt, and a great fan of the movies. In this outing, Eleanor Roosevelt solves a murder mystery on a lavish South Carolina estate. She's a houseguest there, along with stage legend Tallulah Bankhead, movie star Joan Crawford, movie mogul Darryl F. Zanuck, and Humphrey Bogart.

Stanley, John, with Kenn Davis. *Bogart '48*. New York: Dell, 1980.
A 430-page paperback original. A novel of Hollywood in 1948, with witch hunts, booze and drugs and sex, and a plot to blow up the Academy Awards. Humphrey Bogart and Peter Lorre are characters, as is Norma Jean Baker (i.e., Marilyn Monroe).

Thomson, David. *Suspects*. New York: Knopf, 1985.
An entertaining collection of imagined life stories of movies characters, from Marlene Dietrich in *Morocco* (1930), to Kathleen Turner in *Body Heat* (1981), and Bogart in *Casablanca* (1942).

Wagner, John, and Alan Grant, art by Robin Smith. *The Bogie Man: The Manhattan Project*. London: Tundra Publishing, 1992.
A "graphic novel," a cinematic story told in comic-book form— basically a comic book for grown-ups. "Bogie" is actually Francis Forbes Clunie, an escaped mental patient who thinks he's Bogart: "His thoughts follow no logical pattern. He can switch from one scenario into another without even knowing it. Every Bogart film, every pulp detective novel, they're all jumbled together in Francis Clunie's mind." Clunie stumbles into murder mysteries like Mr. Magoo or Inspector Clouseau.

_____. *The Bogie Man*. Two adventures: *Farewell, My Looney* (1989) and *Chinatoon* (1993.) New York: Paradox Press, 1998.
The Bogie Man was produced as a BBC-TV film starring chubby actor Robbie Coltrane, familiar to American audiences from the popular *Cracker* television series.

Other References

Dunning, John. *On the Air: The Encyclopedia of Old-Time Radio.* New York/Oxford: Oxford University Press, 1998.

Goldberg, Lee. *Unsold Television Pilots, 1955 through 1988.* Jefferson, NC: McFarland. 1990.

Nowlan, Robert A., and Gwendolyn Wright Nowlan. *Cinema Sequels and Remakes, 1903–1987.* Jefferson, NC: McFarland, 1989.

Pitts, Michael R. *Radio Soundtracks: A Reference Guide.* Second edition. Metuchen, NJ: Scarecrow Press, 1986.

Index

Numbers in *italics* refer to pages with photos.

About the Author

Ernest W. Cunningham is the author of *The Ultimate Marilyn* and *The Ultimate Barbra*, the first two titles in a pop-culture series from Renaissance Books.

His background is in entertainment advertising, notably as a copywriter for the New York City agency Diener-Hauser-Bates, as well as for two major TV networks which will remain nameless.

He is now a dealer in movie memorabilia, mainly on Internet auctions. He also does freelance copywriting, editing, proofreading, and researching.